Sounding Art

Eight Literary Excursions through Electronic Music

KATHARINE NORMAN

ASHGATE

Published by
Ashgate Publishing Limited
Gower House
Croft Road
Aldershot
Hants GU11 3HR
England

Ashgate Publishing Company
Suite 420
101 Cherry Street
Burlington
VT 05401-4405
USA

Ashgate website: http://www.ashgate.com

British Library Cataloguing in Publication Data
Norman, Katharine.
    Sounding art : eight literary excursions through electronic music
    1. Electronic music – Analysis, appreciation
    I. Title
    786.7′4

Library of Congress Cataloging-in-Publication Data
Norman, Katharine.
    Sounding art : eight literary excursions through electronic music / Katharine Norman.
        p. cm.
    Includes bibliographical references (p.), discography (p.), and index.
    ISBN 0-7546-0426-8 (alk. paper)
        1. Electronic music—History and criticism. I. Title.

ML1380.N67 2003
786.7—dc21

2003049624

ISBN 0 7546 0426 8

Typeset by LaserScript Ltd, Mitcham, Surrey.
Printed and bound in Great Britain by MPG Books Ltd, Bodmin, Cornwall.

Contents

List of figures

Acknowledgements

It seems to me that acknowledgements often end by thanking the long-suffering spouse or partner. But this is a slightly unconventional book, and I would like to thank Jonathan, my husband, first and foremost. Without his encouragement and belief that this book was a good idea, I would never have started to write in the first place (so you have him to blame as well).

But, of course, there are a huge number of others to thank wholeheartedly. Financial and professional support for research and writing was enabled by grants from the Arts and Humanities Research Board, the University of London Central Research Fund and sabbatical leave from Goldsmiths College, University of London. Among those in the UK who supported my various applications I would like especially to thank Peter Manning and Roger Wibberley. A term as a visiting fellow at Princeton University allowed me to renew my love affair with the Firestone Library. I am grateful to all who helped make that possible, especially to Scott Burnham, Marilyn Ham, Paul Lansky and Paula Matthews.

My gratitude also to Scott and Paul for taking a peek at bits of the book-in-progress, expressing enthusiasm and suggestions, and for generally making me feel it was worth a try. The same goes for Daniel Biro, Li-Chuan Chong, Andrew Deakin, John Lely, Alan Shockley, Ian Stonehouse and others who I apologize for forgetting. Grateful thanks to Eric Clarke, Jonty Harrison, and to the many online acquaintances I made, who generously provided me with information and places to look for more.

In addition, I would like to thank Ashgate for taking on this book, in particular the Director of Humanities, Rachel Lynch, who supported my development of an experimental text even though this was far from what she (or I) had initially been expecting. And my enormous gratitude to Linda Cayford, who arrived later as a friendly and professional editorial guiding light, and took great pains to help me clarify my intent. Thanks also to Jean-François Denis for kindly correcting my typing of French texts on Xenakis.

Many of the musicians whose works feature in this book also took the trouble to communicate at length, and were frequently inspiring – my especial thanks to Sean Booth, Luigi Ceccarelli, Terre Thaemlitz and Barry Truax. But my enormous thanks to *all* the people whose work I discuss, for making such fascinating music in the first place. I would like to thank in particular the two composers who I interviewed at length: Francis Dhomont for listening behind my stumbling French, and Hildegard Westerkamp for talking through a walk in the rain. Both have become firm friends, despite these indignities, and both have supported me far more than I can say. Thanks also to all those friends who helped to keep me together – in particular to James Pritchett and Frances White for curry and gardens, and more.

Writing this book was an experience that has enabled me to clarify my thinking about both music and my own position as a composer in the world. I am indebted to that experience for helping me initiate a big leap during the last chapter, from an academic life in the UK to a more precarious freelance existence on an island near Vancouver.

Katharine Norman

Introduction

This book is a deliberate provocation, and a call to 'stretch your ears', as Charles Ives, that great experimental listener, once wrote.

Electronica, microsound, lowercasesound, electroacoustic music, computer music, IDM, analogue music, post-digital music, glitch, acousmatic, noise, sonic art ... The approaches to making questing music with the assistance of technology are now a multifarious explosion of different kinds of listening. The use of technology itself can no longer define a genre. And for that I am very glad, since people – *listening* – make music happen.

The time has long gone when 'electronic music' could be relegated to a two-page afterthought at the back of a music history book. And the time has more recently gone when any all-encompassing 'history of electronic music' could be adequately covered by one book, or that anyone would want to try. And this particular book is not a history of anything: it is an invitation to listen differently to music as sounding art. By which I mean music as an art that can 'sound out' – and sometimes change – the way in which we listen to both our inner and outer worlds. My focus is on sounding the depths of these worlds through electronic music. But although I talk about a great many pieces of music, none is intended to stand for certain repertoires or genres, or anything other than themselves. And this book is an unashamedly personal response, to both my own listening and the outer reaches that drive my interest in sound, as both composer and writer. Most of the works I talk about are for 'sound alone', composed for the space between your ears – only a few are intended solely for the concert hall. Although I think there is a broad range of approaches among the works I talk about, I make no attempt at any kind of systematic survey. There are many other books written, and to be written, on the different and glorious varieties of approach in 'electronic music'. And even those two words are a problematic restriction, employed here as a useful short-cut. In this book electronic music is part of a wider brief, just as being a composer is, I believe, part of a wider responsibility than just dealing with sound.

The chapters are paired by approach or subject matter, and the whole sequence traverses its own unorthodox arc towards a kind of disintegration. Each chapter reflects its subject in the way that it is written and structured, and each tackles various linked obsessions. But that is by no means to be taken as any kind of progression, and the chapters can be read as stand-alone extended essays. Feel free to go in any direction.

To help you along your way, here is a brief description of each chapter's territory. The Contents page also provides some keywords for those in search of named composers or specific areas of discussion. I would also advise a visit to the Bibliography for sources and more conventional reference texts. Web page references are also cited throughout the book. Because web pages often move or disappear, I will also maintain a list of those references at soundingart.novamara.com and endeavour to keep it up-to-date. Above all, please do take time to listen: the enclosed CD of examples is an essential and vital element of this book. Throughout the book the play symbol ⏵ indicates the points where listening to the relevant audio example is integral to following the text. I am immensely grateful to all the composers who so willingly agreed to both share their work and allow me to write about it.

Chapter 1 is, on the face of it, an exploration of small and tactile sounds, taking Xenakis' *Concret PH* as an inspirational starting point for a variety of small histories. This is interwoven with stories about the early history of sound technology. As my writing tries to illustrate, history can be viewed as a mass of small but significant moments, often conflicting, but coalescing over time to say something larger through retrospective listening.

Chapter 2 is an emblem book. One subject under discussion is metaphors of flight in works for instrument and tape and, in one case, a work for film and music. But there is also a rather quirky analysis of perspective in a painting by Leonardo da Vinci, and a celebration of Gaston Bachelard's philosophical writing on poetic metaphors for ascent.

Chapter 3 concerns listening, in particular to the sounds of the real world recontextualized as recording, and in music. As listeners we all map out our personal response to the world (whatever world we may be traversing at the time). This chapter is also about cartography.

Chapter 4 is an interview with composer and researcher Hildegard Westerkamp, in particular a discussion of her work, *Talking Rain*. It is also a walk in the woods and a reverie on different kinds of listening.

Chapter 5 is about radio, radio voices and compositions that subvert the voice of authority in one way or another. The writing also has its own programme, whose segments are linked by a mystery female voice. This chapter is a call to listen differently to 'other' voices that still, too often, find it easiest to broadcast outside the mainstream of electronic music.

Chapter 6 is a multilayered endeavour that analyses a listening response to Francis Dhomont's *Sous le regard d'un soleil noir* alongside an interview with the composer. Dhomont's work concerns the experience of schizophrenia, and my writing tries to mirror that concern with its own psychological confusion, to a point where reality, language, speech and the inner world just won't translate.

Chapters 7 and 8 are tied together in a mutually confused way. Chapter 7 is about noise as an immersive music, and the structure and tone of the chapter is its own illustration. Chapter 8 is about plunder, appropriation and cover versions, and what these might intend. This chapter doubles as the 'endnotes' for Chapter 7 (as befits a chapter about appropriation, it was originally intended for some other purpose). I think the only way to explain these chapters more fully is to suggest that you read them.

Perhaps you will find at least some of what I've written inspiring, engaging, boring, different, aggravating, fascinating, pretentious, imaginative, foolish, creative or even just mighty strange. Like all of us concerned with electronic music as a sounding art, I hereby share my listening, and I look forward to yours.

Katharine Norman
Pender Island, June 2003

Part 1

Sounding ... spaces

Chapter 1

Concrete tales and touching times

Here is a small collection of related and unrelated fragments – some brief stories about technology and sound, some small sounds as aesthetic objectives, and several short walks around the Philips Pavilion.

The early history of technology and sound is a mass of interesting presences, discrepancies and confusions. There were dreams of money, and there was the crackle of creative interference in the air. Reading back through the evidence, it sometimes seems as if the late nineteenth and early twentieth centuries bred a bunch of particularly irascible and avaricious pioneers, who fought it out over prestige and cash in equal proportions.[1] Those early years of invention and growth were a mass of small, aggressive ventures, rising in a constant buzz of connected and disconnected possibilities. As invention after invention was demonstrated (and patent after patent was filed) one thing often led, by tangents, to another. The end result was sometimes a surprise; for instance, technology developed with the deaf in mind evolved into the telephone. Suddenly the world was becoming a place where it might be possible to stay in touch with everything at once, and pick up the phone, hear the film, play the record, tune in the radio.

There's less money in the small world of experimental music, but the early history of electronic music in the 1950s and 1960s was certainly pioneering in terms of putting technology to diverse creative ends, and this glorious appropriation has continued into software and instrument design.[2] There are several excellent books that collate the evidence of the early practitioners and, of course, several of these are still around to tell, and continue telling, the tale.[3] And an electronic music is developing in which not only sonic, but aesthetic, objectives are driven through the 'aid of electrical instruments',[4] to quote the prescient voice of John Cage. Not all of these objectives were foreseen in exactly the form they are coming to take, and not all come down to the useful appropriation of different bits of equipment. Cage was careful to avoid the words 'electrical *musical* instruments', and indeed distanced his credo from a concern with inventing new interfaces for playing old music. He was entranced by the possibility of 'a music' that would be imbued with what technology can or might express in composing with organized sound. As a precision tool, technology can be instrumental in expressing the presence and depth of structures inside sound, and also inside listening – as a creative engagement with touch, memory and experience. Yet, in some respects, much electronic music composition is conservative, and essentially continues to mine an existing seam of abstract music expressionism, albeit with shiny new tools that can orchestrate a wider palette and really get 'inside' those sounds.

As an extension of human ability and presence, it is certainly true that technology enables the minutiae of sound to become present to our ears. Perhaps this has contributed by reversal to another approach – a small left-shift to a position where sound becomes an expression of equivocal encounters with technology's pervasive presence and control. And if technology is aiding the coalescence of several small aesthetic shifts, it might be of instrumental assistance in creating 'a music' that is new rather than merely producing new kinds of instruments for the music that we have. Some have called this a post-digital music. But why are we always following one thing with another? All our histories are filtered through the cultural practice and knowledge – the 'technology' – of the time. Sometimes a straightforward relation of what happened reveals less than the gaps between what was envisaged, what actually came to pass, and how and why accounts differ. It's worth listening between.

Here are various small accounts that jolt back and forth, and land up against each other in various configurations. I hope they might coalesce over time to make a kind of sense to you. So there are chronicles of some small, but telling, moments in the early histories of sound technology; there are journals on some small objects and touching presences in electronic music, and on some music where the enormity of small spaces and times is laid bare by a telling click. Between all these tales are reports surrounding a very small piece of music that – unlike the space it occupied – remains as a mass of influential embers. To finish up, there are a few touching anecdotes.

In what follows, most is concrete, much is remembered, and some has just a touch of make-believe. You can read it either way, since this history doesn't necessarily proceed from A to B.

SOME SMALL PRESENCES

Chronicle:
1857 – a trace of smoke

Imagine – the rustle of silk dresses settling down and a few murmurs of anticipation. They crowd around him, straining their necks to see. There is a smell of cigars. A log spits in the grate. Silence falls.

Then he bends over the machine, turns the handle, and speaks into the cone. The displaced air reaches a stretched membrane, which vibrates in response. The fluctuating movement of this membrane drives in turn the travel of a small stub of bristle; it scrapes back and

forth across the rotating cylinder of smoke-blackened
paper. And, as it moves, the bristle's erratic journey
rubs a wavering path through the clouded surface.
At present, it is a kind of magic.

In 1857 Léon Scott de Martinville invented the
phonautograph, an early mechanical means of
preserving a visual record of a sound. Sadly, this
delicate analogy could not be reversed to recreate the
sound itself. The only thing audible after the fact
would be gratifying gasps of admiration from your
dinner-party guests.

So the first recordings of sound were small histories
of absence, scratched through smoke. And – at the
same time – they were a reminder that someone had
been there. It would be only a matter of time before
the telephone started ringing.

Hello? Can you hear me?
Hello? Is there anybody there?
Hello? What does it sound like at your end?

In a rather gory development, the Ear Phonautograph
of 1874, Alexander Graham Bell and Clarence Blake
took the human–technology interface a step further;
their detailed explanation of exactly how to dissect
and attach a human ear to the apparatus makes rather
gruesome reading. And yet it also draws attention to
the fact that the phonautograph's invention was
motivated by a desire to understand more about
human perception; by modelling the mechanics of
human physiology and observing the results we would
know ourselves more clearly. In mimicking the ear the
emphasis was on hearing, not on the production of
sound. No matter that there was nothing left to hear,
there was – once – and the silent evidence remained.
A visual record of what was heard offered at least
some reasonably objective data from which to pursue
a common ground between individual subjectivities.
It's for this reason perhaps that Bell and others
envisaged the phonautograph as having exciting
potential for enabling the deaf to speak. And he
couldn't resist writing home:

If we can find the definite shape due to each sound –
what an assistance in teaching the deaf & dumb!!
(Alexander Graham Bell)[5]

There were hopes for visual vocabularies for sound,
aids for the deaf, libraries shelved with faded images
that would speak silently to those for whom sound
was an inaudible mystery. But nothing really came of
it; the crossing between aural and visual image was an
irreversible gulf. Then, the possibility of re-hearing a
recorded sound could only be envisaged. Now, a
visual rendition of a sound on screen is a mere
mnemonic for what's coming through the headphones.

REPORT: CROWDS ATTEND SPECTACLE

⏵ CD[1] *Concret PH*, by Iannis Xenakis (excerpt)

Deux minutes d'intervalle, et huit minutes de spectacle. Pre-
mière décision: le contenant sera une sorte d'estomac, avec une
entrée et une sortie différentes pour cinq cent personnes.
Deuxième décision: le public étant debout et regardant devant
lui, disposer de deux parois concaves presque verticales, qui
permettent aux spectateurs de voir au-dessus de la tête des
voisins.
(Le Corbusier, 1958, p. 24)

[A two-minute interval, and eight minutes for the show. First
decision: that it would be contained in a sort of 'stomach' with
a different exit and entrance, for five hundred people. Second
decision: the public would be standing and looking ahead,
arranged between two concave partitions, allowing the spectators to see over the heads of their neighbours.]

This is what the architect Le Corbusier had in mind for the Philips
Pavilion, in which Varèse's monumental — some might say slightly
ponderous — *Poème Electronique* was first performed at the Brussels
World Fair in 1958, as part of an elaborate audio-visual spectacle that
was repeated several times a day for the duration of the event. The
pavilion was commissioned by the Philips Company — specifically L.C.
Kalff, the artistic director for the project and an executive at the
Eindhoven branch of Philips. Varèse was offered the services of
Philips' studio in Eindhoven to create his work. Le Corbusier put
together the visual component, which involved complex lighting and

slides of strange and marvellous images, and of ordinary images made larger than life; some of these were reproduced in a commemorative book overseen by Le Corbusier, which was also entitled *Poème Electronique*, along with essays, documentary photographs and reflections by those involved. These images are diverse: children, babies, reproductions of paintings, a Madonna, a bull's head and bullfighter, exotic tribal masks, a group of miners in helmets, surgeons at work, an array of toy tanks, clouds, birds — everything you could think of, crowded together in a fragmented reminiscence of all that life holds (though, for the most part, images outside the experience of more ordinary lives, with an emphasis on the exotic). And, in the same book there are photographs of the spectators who passed through this secular pantheon — a crowd of assorted people in 1950s overcoats and haircuts, packed together shoulder to shoulder. Naturally, the visual and aural spectacle that filled the empty space of the pavilion emanated from Philips light bulbs, sound equipment and other bits and pieces, although these were largely hidden from view. Technology became invisible and amazing. People stood in the darkness, open-mouthed.[6]

The Philips Company executives were none too keen on Le Corbusier's choice of composer. They had originally been considering Benjamin Britten, a composer with more general appeal. At one point they almost gave up on Varèse completely and commissioned a French composer, Tommasi, to write a piece of conventional *son et lumière*. Le Corbusier fulminated until Varèse was reinstated. In the end, the pavilion was a huge success, with over two million people passing through to stand and stare, and listen. The partnership of Varèse and Le Corbusier would go down in history as a defining moment in the collaboration of architecture and sound.

> *You ask me why my name is not mentioned.*
> *1. Because Philips approached Le Corbusier, architect of world-renown, and not me.*
> *2. Because I am an employee of Le Corbusier and have no firm:*
> *'Xenakis — Architect'*
> *3. Because Le Corbusier is a miser, an egotist, an opportunist who is capable of trampling upon the corpses of his own friends.*
> (Letter from Xenakis to Scherchen, 25 June 1957. In Matossian, 1990, pp. 119—120)

Initially, it seems that Le Corbusier took all the public credit for the Philips Pavilion, despite the fact that his assistant, Xenakis, had been involved significantly in the design work. Xenakis protested vociferously in public and — so it appears — maliciously in private, claiming that he had played the major role in bringing the building to fruition. History in the making was reluctantly revised to include his involvement: in the book, *Poème Electronique*, Xenakis' name appears beside Le Corbusier as designer. Even so, the final list of credits is very small indeed, and there's no reason to turn the page unless you're looking for the information.

> *Le Poème Electronique. Le Corbusier: Pavillon Philips pour l'exposition universelle de Bruxelles 1958. Création du Poème*

Electronique. : Le Corbusier. Architecture: Le Corbusier et
Jean Xenakis. Scénario et images: Le Corbusier et Jean Petit.
Cinéaste: Philippe Agostini: Composition sonore: Edgard Varèse.
Interlude sonore: Jean Xenakis. Animateur et organisateur: L.C.
Kalff. Expert acoustique: W. Tak. Calcul (etc. ...)
(Unnumbered 'credits' page, Le Corbusier, 1958)

Since the Philips Pavilion was part concert hall, part exhibition
space, it was a practical necessity that the public should stay in it
for only a limited time. The throughput required encouraged an event
that was less an installation than a performance to a captive audience,
subsequently regurgitated back into the air, blinking, en route for
another attraction. Time became a rather mundane quality, and people
became a space-occupying mass. Le Corbusier's original idea for a
'stomach' seems strangely apposite.

> I think quite positively I remember that we entered the Philips/Corbusier/[Xenakis] building
> (Xenakis's name appeared nowhere, that I remember) with a group and that we waited inside
> for the beginning of the performance – I have images of bare concrete, suddenly disappearing
> in the flood of coloured light. ... I do believe therefore that the visit indeed was conceived as a
> performance, beginning, say, every 30 minutes. Another reason to think so is that the Fair
> proved successful far beyond expectation and that several pavilions had to organize timed
> visits, lest they be overcrowded.
> (Professor Nicolas Meeùs, email correspondence)

JOURNAL ENTRY: 18 AUGUST 2002

▶ **CD[2]** *Petit jardin*, **by Magali Babin (excerpt)**

Hello? Can you hear me?

Magali Babin's brief piece, *Petit jardin*, is a sonic exploration of largely metallic
objects, itself neither an improvisation, nor a recording of one. Babin is no longer
there because this piece exists only on CD. I press 'play' and the sounds of small
metallic objects fill my ears. We don't communicate directly but, yes, I immediately
recognize the kinds of things that might have produced those sounds. I feel that I
know them. Nearly all the sounds imply actions. Someone or something 'did' these
things.

   And I am listening – to music, since my definition is a broad one, and this is
evidently organized sound. The sounds are placed together in a manner that makes
for an interesting abstract tapestry. This placing took place at different times – there
was an improvisation, and then a mix in the studio. (There is nothing extraordinary
about this approach, although there are perhaps fewer pieces of experimental
electronic music that overtly reference a recording of a performance.) There are

easily distinguishable layers: the slowly reiterated striking of a low gong-like object; a higher-pitched and less regular clunking – perhaps made by hitting a smaller vessel, maybe a bowl; a spattering of small objects, metallic (I think), that is formed from much faster iterations, with some sense of a pulse. I'm a little less sure of how that last one was done.

So all this is all going on as I work backwards from the sound that's in front of my ears right now. Perhaps it's so obvious that it almost doesn't warrant discussion, although it may well be different for you – listening is imprecise unless it matters. I don't bother to envisage exactly what happened to make those sounds back then, when they were 'now'. But it's enough to know that the sounds I'm hearing are somehow of 'human' proportions; they are not amplified or enlarged beyond realism.

Hello? Is there anybody there?

Later on, things become much more clear-cut and the spotlight shifts from substance to presence, but now it is less a case of 'the striking of' a gong as 'there's somebody doing that'. Performance is an issue. Yes, there is somebody there; I can hear the trickling sounds of pebbles or shards of metal falling through her fingers on to a surface and in particular, towards the end of the piece, there's the sound of her slowly swirling a hand about in a container full of densely-packed grains – or perhaps rice, or tiny pebbles, or even sand. At least, that's how I heard it, the last time I listened. And I'm finding that 'swirling hand' sound especially satisfying and immediate, probably because it reminds me of that pleasurable sensation of plunging a hand deep into a sack of grain, or whatever, and scrunching around for the pure enjoyment of the physical sensation. I'm not sure I have any specific memory of a precise instance of doing that, but I certainly seem to remember how it feels. I'm muddling my tenses, back and forth.

Petit jardin's mix of past performance and present sound involves, and convolves, times. There are already two recorded present tenses – the time of improvisation and the time of putting these sounds together as composition in the studio. And at the time of mixing, making and reconstructing, other 'performers' apply another layer. They are duly credited in realizing the final composition – sound recordist, mixing engineer, the studio itself. And that's all before listening to the work on CD, at the time when it fills my sitting room with small metallic sounds. Despite all these temporal backs and forths, this piece continues to come across as a direct and personal exploration, where a single, performing human being's touch reaches out towards objects in search of sounds.

At some level in my listening I imagine what kind of movements she is making to produce those sounds. (There's nothing unusual in that; we've all played varieties of air guitar.) Then again, she's doing more than moving. I can hear her *listening*, because I can hear thinking behind the scenes, in the pace of events – the striking of the gong is a slow iteration, by somebody who waits (or has waited, once, at that time?) for the sound to die down before they hit again. If this piece were to be mimed by a performer employing fast, angular movements, I'd be unconvinced by the sync. And if someone had merely come on stage and clicked on 'compile and play' to produce those sounds, as sometimes happens, I'd be disappointed by this visual discrepancy. Imagining physical movement is part and parcel of listening to a record of 'a performance'. But there's nothing to see now, and I can't reconstruct exactly what might have happened, so I have to make a fiction of it. The onus is on me, and perhaps that changes my listening.

In summarizing their research into data gleaned from the body movement or 'sway' of a pianist, Eric Clarke and Jane Davidson come to the sensitive conclusion that '[i]n any musical tradition in which improvisation plays a significant role it is far more obvious that the dynamics of movement may strongly influence (even at times determine) the sonic outcome' (Clarke and Davidson, 1998, p. 89) And surely it works both ways; in an exploratory improvisation the 'dynamics of sound' might strongly influence the performer's subsequent decisions (or subconscious responses) of *movement* too. Performance becomes a dance between listening and touching. Imagine the recorded sounds as the only trace of a visual performance that is now absent. Humour me: here is a blank trail where the sound traces a bodily presence that is no longer here. An aid for the blind, perhaps.

As 'she' performs, there seems to be something in the way that wasn't part of her performance but is happening now: a spatter of small sounds places a kind of veil between presence and absence. She is in the mix behind these metallic sounds that don't themselves sound, quite, part of her time. They are slightly 'exotic' because they were very small, ordinary sounds, that are newly processed and mixed to become a foreground screen of significant objects. There are many tracks where the singer's voice is intentionally placed 'inside', rather than apart from, the mix. Björk's album *Homogenic*, for instance, has a tendency for dense mixes that frequently foreground technological presence. Her voice is processed just enough to dislocate a vocal performance. 'Hunter', track 1 of *Homogenic*, has a continual foreground layering of fast, incisive reiterations that have some similarity to *Petit jardin*'s high-pitched metallic sounds: neither are background patterning and both provide a shield in front of a central performer. But a voice tends to transmits a stronger human presence – and probably a visual image of Bjork or at least a mouth moving to produce those sounds – whereas *Petit jardin* doesn't have a voice, and the 'her' is an invisibly moving body that dissolves, disappears and occasionally reappears behind a gentle rain of tiny, half-familiar objects, realized in sound.

Hello? What does it sound like at your end?

Which reminds me – there's a tactile quality to these sounds. Listening even becomes a proxy for touching. When I listen to Babin's 'metallic sounds' my mind is reinhabited with sensory images of quite specific kinds, and these are memories derived from touch. Somewhere along the line between hearing and listening I stuck out a hand. Any baby would understand that this is a significant intuitive grasp; I am inwardly 'confirming' what I hear, through recollections of haptic investigation. Perhaps these recollections come from a long, long time ago, but these tactile imprints step up and 'capture' aural perception as if the imagined surface was there at my fingertips, right now.

This personal, empirical analysis of listening reaches much too far to come to conclusions, and these matters fluctuate back and forth according to each subject's individual experience. But, in general, it is safe to say that sounds release information that – trailing through our back catalogue of experiences – we use to make educated guesses; we trace a digit over our discoveries. Barry Truax's granulated soundscapes, Horacio Vaggione's pointillistic fabrics of instrumental samples, Kim Cascone's use of computer-generated 'dust' – the sonic clicks and pops of digital detritus; these are just a few composers whose differing approaches encourage tactile associations, in works where flurries of fragmented sound become metaphors for touch. But *Petit jardin* is an example of a performance of a specifically improvisatory kind, where there is an essential connection between listening and performance as related explorations. The piece is *about* the activity of feeling, touching and reaching towards the sonic presence of an object, and it transmits the experience of listening and interacting with the sounds that result from this activity. Although there is no human voice to be heard amongst these sounds, there are questions in the way the sounds are made: 'Is there anybody there?', 'Can you hear me?', 'What does it sound like at your end?' The trail works both ways: the sounds are present as the result of her investigations, and the trace of her touch is present in these sounds. She remains invisible.

Anecdotal evidence: THUMB

There is a small piece of prehistoric Cypriot pottery in the Metropolitan Museum, New York, labelled 'man or monkey eating fruit'. The seated figure has no facial features other than a crude nose and mouth (but, I grant you, definitely no breasts) and is three inches high at most. And he is definitely eating – holding something unidentifiable to his mouth, with both hands. While he enjoys his delicious hunk of fruit, he has crossed his legs at the ankle, looping one foot over the other in a childlike, awkward manner. Absorbed in his pleasurable activity, he is so wrapped up in the taste that he isn't aware of this little touch of bodily involvement. I guess that at this moment he isn't even aware of being human (or not). This small pottery anecdote must have been made in a very hurried moment of wonder because there's a life-sized thumbprint in the clay; and it's this touch that provides a concrete reminder of a past that was someone else's presence.

SOME SMALL DISCREPANCIES

Chronicle:
The space betweentimes

You know how it is with memory, it tends to forget the facts. So if you want to ensure the smallest gap between how it is and how it will be recollected, it's probably best to write it down at the time.

France – 30 April 1877

'... Dans tous les cas, le tracé en hélice sur un cylindre est très-préférable, et je m'occupe actuellement d'en trouver la réalisation pratique.' (Charles Cros)[7]

[... In any case, the spiral trace on a cylinder is much preferable, and I am currently occupied with finding a practical realisation of this.]

Imagine – he adds his signature, blots the ink and carefully reads through, repeating a few phrases out loud and nodding to himself in confirmation. His handwriting leaves a fluent trace across the page – rather untidy, the writing of someone whose ideas get ahead of him, out of his control. The letters and poems, and the short plays and dramatic interludes he pens for Parisian soirées have the same enthusiastic slant. He folds the paper, slides it into an envelope and seals it.

The other papers he has worked on recently had dwelt on that new luminous art, photography. But there is something in this alternative path away from visual things – it pleases his musical ear. He knows it would work, and just knowing that is almost enough, but not quite. His chair scrapes suddenly on the floor as he rises quickly, looking at the clock ... there is no time to lose.

On 30 April 1877 the inventor, poet and writer Charles Cros deposited a sealed envelope containing his paper on 'A procedure for recording and reproducing phenomenon perceived by the ear' at the Académie des Sciences in Paris. He did not have the wherewithal to realize his idea, but he was convinced that it would work. Although he took the precaution of filing this confidential document, it seems likely that he also enthused about his ideas with various professional colleagues and likely benefactors. In November 1877 an article based on his idea appeared in *La Semaine du Clergé*.

Charles Cros was aware of Edison's interest in the area and was anxious to make his own ideas public. On 3 December 1877 Cros asked that the papers he had lodged at the Académie be opened and published. This was done the very same day.

America – 12 August 1877

At about the same time, American inventor Thomas Edison and his well-funded team of researchers carried out the first practical experiment in recording and reproducing sound on 12 August 1877, although there is some dispute as to the actual date since Edison didn't file the patent until 12 December. Edison's method was an almost perfect realization of the method Cros had described in detail. Who knows . . .

It was just in the air
Perhaps, the same idea

Certainly Charles Cros spent much of his life trying to prove that he got there first. But, for him, recorded sound remained a silent certainty. For Edison, it was a rather different history.

'*Le brevet de M. Edison*, pour tout ce qui y est dit du phonographe, *est nul.*'[8]

Whether Edison first invented sound recording or not, he was still stuck for amplification and had to resort to banks of phonographs or one-person cinemas to make sound heard. (Perhaps understandably, the kineto-phone – a one-person sound cinema, complete with peephole and earpieces – was a short-lived solution.)

Technology moves on in fits and starts. One person may record the inaudible on paper, and another might subsequently write the same ideas in sound; but these events may or may not be connected. Perhaps there is no useful narrative, and it is as informative to make a patchwork indeterminacy from isolated stories, diaries and other short reports. (This has been done before, and will continue to be done.)

REPORT: A LARGE NUMBER OF SPEAKERS

Over time, memories can soften and opinions change:

> *It was the first time I had ever met a man with such spiritual force, such a constant questioning of things normally taken for granted . . . [He] opened my eyes to a new kind or architecture I had never thought of. This was a most important revelation, because quite suddenly, instead of boring myself with more calculations, I discovered points of common interest with music* (Xenakis on Le Corbusier, in Bois, 1967, p.5).

It is quite usual for architectural practices to operate under the name of one famous, founding father (mothers are less usual) who imbues the projects undertaken with his particular ethos or artistic 'stamp'. So it could be said, looking at it from a different angle, that the hyperparabolic curves of the Philips Pavilion were a Le Corbusier creation. Yet Xenakis had been exploring the same shapes and preoccupa-tions in recent musical works, in particular in the visual parabolas that indicate string glissandi in *Metastaseis*, completed in 1954. Accounts vary, one person influences another — and vice versa — and the sliding truth will always hang somewhere in the air between them. Books on architecture tend to sideline Xenakis' part in the Philips Pavilion, whereas books on music tend to focus on his essential role. Perhaps authorship is a relatively small thing.

The sound projection for *Poème Electronique* was an architectural feat in itself. Even in the simplest installation — the playing of sound and visual projections in an empty space — time needs to be choreographed a little, and the placing of loudspeakers becomes akin to directing the *corps de ballet*. Within the electronic work it's often essential to hear things at the 'right' time and place. With a perambulatory audience, time and space are constantly shifting dimensions, and the history of a sound can change on a moment-to-moment basis. The innovative design that Xenakis created involved the placing of some 350—425 speakers (apparently — although documented evidence conflicts) within the swooping, contoured construction that perhaps only a composer—architect collaboration could have success-fully realized.

> *Les cent cinquante haut-parleurs du pavillon étaient répartis en 'groupes' et en 'routes'. Les groupes étaient disposés au-dessus de l'entrée et de la sortie et dans les trois faîtes, tandis que les haut-parleurs pour les routes étaient disposés le long des arêtes. On avait en outre monté une route horizontale, et, derrière la barrière, tout en bas, se trouvaient vingt-cinq grands haut-parleurs pour la reproduction de la gamme des notes graves et de sons spéciaux. Tous ces haut-parleurs devant être mis en circuit à un moment précis par la signalisation, et leur montage ayant dû s'effectuer avant que la composition ne fût achevée, les câbles de chacun d'eux furent conduits individuel-lement vers la cabine de commande du pavillon; un tableau de contacts permettait alors d'effectuer les choix nécessaires. Les routes et les groupes de haut-parleurs avaient été répartis sur dix amplificateurs de 120 W ....*
> (No author given, but presumably Xenakis, in Le Corbusier, 1958, p. 203)

[The hundred and fifty loudspeakers of the pavilion were divided up into 'groups' and 'routes'. The groups were arranged above the entrance and exit, and in the three pinnacles, while the loudspeakers for the routes were arranged along the 'ribs'. There was also a horizontal route, and, behind the barrier, down below, there were twenty-five large loudspeakers for boosting the range, low notes and special sounds. All these loudspeakers had to be put into action at a precise moment by signals, and they had to be put up before the composition could be achieved, the cables had to be individually run to the pavilion's control room where a contact board let one effect the necessary changes. The routes and the groups of loudspeakers had been divided between ten amplifiers of 120 W ....]

However many loudspeakers were eventually hauled into place, there was quite a crowd of them, and their disposition was precise. The tracking of the sounds, and the simultaneous presentation of the images, were carefully planned. In particular, the images were 'themed' to give the spectacle distinct sections, which were mirrored in terms of lights and sound. The effect of this multilayered control was, paradoxically, intended to provide a sense of random activity in which the position of sounds and images would be unpredictable in both time and space. Yet, underneath this apparent chaos, everything was in order. There was only a small gap between the appearance and sound of disorder and carefully orchestrated space.

Xenakis in an interview, going through a folder of old scores and exercises, comments:

This is a rhythmic exercise based on the golden section.
*   I used to have a bad tape-recorder which left a little noise*
on the tape when you pressed the button. When I noticed that, I
exploited it: I measured the length of the tape and marked it at
certain points in pencil. I pressed the button of the machine at
every mark, and when I played it the noises followed one another
according to the golden section. In other words, I received an
exact aural picture of that proportion.
*   I had taken the idea from architecture.*
(Xenakis, in Varga, 1996, p.30)

The whole Fair was very much oriented toward technology: to give you an idea, it is there that for the first time I saw a TV set; also, visitors were offered the possibility to phone the United States, something that apparently was unaccessible to the layman until then. The American pavilion presented cinemascope on a 360° screen, etc. All this is what I went to see with brothers and friends.
(Professor Nicolas Meeùs, email correspondence)

JOURNAL ENTRY: 21 August 2002

It was just in the air

Ryoji Ikeda, *zero degrees*

      Click

             Noise

      Click

Noise

      Click

Individual grains with a duration of less than about 2ms ...

             Noise

      Click

(actually, there's also a silent gap)

Noise

    Click

       Noise

(between the noise and the click, each time)

    Click

Noise

    Click

... *sound like clicks.*
(Roads, 2001, p. 88)

      Noise

   Click

Noise

Zero degrees commences with a series of eight 'click-noise' pairs. The noise alternates between left and right speakers; the click is in the middle each time. There's a gap between the noise and the click. The click can be most obviously interpreted as a 16th note upbeat, with the noise as a one-beat downbeat followed by three-and-a-bit beats of silence. Subsequent events confirm this. It's simple. In fact, the inbuilt 'speaker test' on my laptop produces remarkably similar bursts of left-right white noise (but without the click, thank goodness). Perhaps that's where he got it.

There, I've made something of it. It's very clear, and after a couple of repetitions seems easy to anticipate. My listening runs enthusiastically ahead of itself, looping back and forth in time like bad handwriting; I've already made an educated guess at how the future will be. After that initial eight-measure preamble there will be more activity but, already, my mind has confidently grouped up the sonic troops and is determined to stay with a four on the floor. Yes, this is easy to understand (I'm tapping in time to one heck of an assumption).

But the click makes and breaks it. Or, rather, the relationship between the click, the noise and the space between them makes a riddle from the most minimal of ingredients. There's no time at all to waste. This click is too short a sound to have human connotations: it's too short a time to have thought about banging a gong. Unlike Babin's *Petit jardin* there is no human presence concealed inside Ryoji Ikeda's *zero degrees*. He is absent now. Nobody performs, hits a gong or trails a hand through implicitly substantial sounds. Instead, the sound is apparently laid bare and has no aural secrets.

As Curtis Roads describes it, a click is too short to hold on to as a pitch. A single, lonely click has nothing going on for it as a rhythm, either. And a click is over before there's time for listening to pick up much usable information on timbre. Because our listening gives no time to it, we have no time for its presence: a click is generally an interruption before we return to what we were trying to listen to. It is not part of the experience: it is too short to leave a mark on listening, so it takes up no space in memory. There needs to be something else to make sense of it – as in Ikeda's piece, where the click becomes a miniscule upbeat to another sound. My listening effects that grouping, and then, later on, events confirm it. But all these unconnected attempts at definition collect together after the fact, whereas at the time 'a click' is just there – horrendously present, and horribly alone. I use these adverbs advisedly: a click is an awful thing because it doesn't seem to have a sufficient existence. To identify with a click is to become brutally irradiated by sound. No time at all. Quick, get rid of it in favour of recordings of human presence! (And just at this moment my husband puts his head round the door to ask if my laptop has 'some terrible hard disk error'.) Perhaps it is comforting to articulate associations for sounds because then there are images – and then there can be words, and then we're talking to one another. But if I say that this sound reminds me of a plastic bottle's 'crack!' as it snaps back into shape, *you* might think that this is because the sound is loud, very short and not of my doing. But really I'm trying to describe the sudden presentness of time that this sound illuminated, and the fact that this realization made me flinch in response to the mundane but obliterating instant that had sliced across my time 'going on'. See? But these words are too much pretension: listen, sometimes *concrète* associations for sounds are inventions that prove to be limiting without amplification. Think about the sound and you have set yourself going on a chain of imagined possibilities that might lead you away from my particular fiction. No matter, we may still end up together at the double barline.

Perhaps, the same idea

A digital connection breeds discontinuities: one instantaneous state replaces another, and in that metaphor there's no smooth transition between these two points, however much we attend to the gap that's in-between.

> ... *I am warm or cold, I am merry or sad ... I look at what is around me or I think of something else.*
> ... *we are obliged, when the change has become so considerable as to force itself on our attention, to speak as if a new state were placed alongside the previous one. Of this new state we assume that it remains unvarying in its turn, and so on endlessly.*
> (Bergson, 1910, p. 3)

In Bergson's thinking, we carry within us not just our memories, but the whole of our past experience in our unconscious. He offers 'duration' as the *'past which gnaws into the future and which swells as it advances'* (ibid., p. 4). To his mind, this difficult weight lies beyond consciousness, and we are only aware of irruptions into our present when the past re-becomes present as recollection. On this premise we are our past, and the specious present is always in the process of becoming past. As fast as the phonoautograph's stub of bristles trails a record of what happened, the smoke pushes back in again to cover up the path. And when we envisage this very instant, setting it in relation to the past or future, we do this because we are 'obliged to' by our limitations. The click-noise pairs in *zero degrees* might be seen as a metaphor for such a pragmatic discontinuity. And yet there is a short, silent gap between these two sounds, and – at this instant – it is *this* that has reoccupied my mind. For it seems to me that the discontinuity may not be between two things – a click, then a noise – but between small ways of articulating duration. *Here* is a click, and, with the 'aid' of electrical instruments, digital signals and all that these can metaphorically represent, it is a 'now' – present, here, instant; *there* is a silent gap that has been measured out (with the aid of noise) as 'three-and-a-bit beats' of duration. My toes count the beats out as a way of keeping track, since I am obliged to try to find a way of explaining duration to myself.

Bergson's poetic grappling with time, space and 'duration' is replete with references to real-world metaphors and associations. He calls upon sound regularly, noting how the way we count the strokes of a bell, or mentally collect together pitches as melody, are examples of removing events from durational time into space. The sounds of a tolling bell fade one after another in duration, but the conceptual space their enumerated traces inhabit remains, different.

> *If the sounds are separated, they must leave empty intervals between them.*
> *If we count them, the intervals must remain though the sounds disappear:*
> *how could these intervals remain, if they were pure duration and not*
> *space? It is in space, therefore, that the operation takes place ... .*
> (Bergson, 1910, p. 73)

Essentially Bergson is trying to make sense of perception, and as Bertrand Russell muttered dismissively, what he essentially provides is 'an account of the difference between perception and recollection – both present facts' (Russell, 1946, p. 767). Bergson spends much time and space building poetic images to articulate how memory is our process of becoming, and it is difficult not to keep on quoting him indefinitely since these images provide a particularly familiar and helpful resonance for thinking about listening and sound. I'm sure he would have turned an ear to those eight 'click-noise' pairs (that's just an image I gave you to hang on to). We think words are strong, when really they are poor attempts at giving voice to our limitations. And yet these imperfect images can be gloriously evocative personal belongings. In the face of Bergson's notion of the ever-growing past, for example, my mind casts up images of sleeping whales, piling up in dormitories on the seabed of my experience.

What does this say about me? What do you envisage? What does this say about you? Perhaps we shall continue to share images indefinitely in a vague hope that we will make enough sense to one another across an existential plane; and sometimes such romantic gestures are images in sound. A click, then a vast amount of space, and then a noise that continues. Zero degrees – where nothing moves, except time.

Anecdotal evidence: FINGERS
In the grounds of a university where I recently spent some time there is a large bronze sculpture by Henry Moore called 'Oval with Points'. It is indeed a huge upright oval, which encompasses two outstretched points that reach across towards each other but don't – quite – touch.
I used to pass by this sculpture every day, and it would always lift my heart. Though it's green with oxidization now, I also knew it ten years previously when it was merely dulled and slightly tarnished (and I was more green). But across the divide it has remained constant in one respect: the bottom of the oval is rubbed shiny by the backsides of the numerous human beings who have been in touch over the years: lovers, chatting, seated astride it; toddlers who have been passed through it giggling and smiling; groups who have clustered around it for their photo opportunity. And it also seems that many people have tried to bring those two bronze points together – they gleam from touching efforts to heal the gap, over time.

SOME SMALL CONFUSIONS

Chronicle:
December 1923 – crossed lines and a failure of mass communication

It was not an auspicious beginning.

The history of early radio is rowdy with battles and arguments, lawsuits, claims and counterclaims, continuing well into the early twentieth century. Sound communication became a battle of egos and economical truths.

Crossed lines: 14 April 1912

On a bad day he felt like a circus freak, sitting in the window, twiddling the knobs back and forth to induce a crackle of static and occasional voice from the air. Office clerks passing through during their lunch hour or children with dirty knees would peer over his shoulder inquisitively.

But this was a good day. Suddenly he was the most important man on earth.

The young David Sarnoff was sitting in the window of Wanamaker's department store, where he had been hired to show off the new technology, when he inadvertently picked up the *Titanic*'s SOS broadcast. He was the only radio operator to stay on line after all the others had been ordered to stand down by the president himself. He remained at his post for three whole days and nights without rest, holding the fort.

On the other hand. ... In 1912, radio contact with the sinking *Titanic* was severely hampered by the cacophony of amateur radio activity which cluttered up the airwaves and prevented communication. This chaos contributed to the formulation of radio licensing regulations which would prevent such a disaster happening again. And it is very unlikely that Sarnoff's story was any more than a self-aggrandizing fabrication. However, he went on to become head of the Radio Corporation of America.

Failed communication: December 1923

In 1923 Edwin Armstrong married David Sarnoff's secretary and gave his bride a rather cumbersome wedding present.

Imagine – the radio was a ridiculous thing to bring with them, and of course she knew that it wasn't really for her at all. She was proud of his invention, but really! Edwin had dragged it down onto the beach and dusted it down with far more reverence than he'd paid to her. And now here they were, squinting into the sun while the photographer set up his apparatus and

*Edwin dictated technical information to a bemused
reporter, spelling out 'superheterodyne receiver' in
somewhat pompous tones. Her only reminder of their
honeymoon would be a photo of the two of them,
sitting awkwardly on the sand with that damned
apparatus interposed between them and the sea
crashing endlessly behind.*[9]

Edwin Armstrong's story is not a happy one. In 1954,
at the brink of bankruptcy as a result of lawsuits, and
anguished at his failure to retain the rights for his
inventions, he jumped from a window and died of his
injuries.[10] His wife – who had left him earlier – went
on to fight and win all the legal battles on his behalf.

*The radio was an ever-present reminder of their lack of
communication.*

Today, Edwin Armstrong is universally recognized as
the inventor of FM radio.

REPORT: SUBSTANTIAL SOUNDS

How did it come about that you wrote Concret PH **as a kind of
introduction to Varèse's** Poème Electronique**?**
I composed it at the request of Le Corbusier.
It lasts only a few minutes.
*Yes, it has a duration of two and a half minutes. It was an
introduction to the spectacle designed by Le Corbusier, which
lasted six minutes. Or, more precisely, it played the role of
prelude or interlude between spectacles.*
(Xenakis, in Varga, 1996, p. 30)

*... two minutes for entering and leaving. These two minutes of
music I have entrusted to Xenakis (so that he should have a part
in all this) and so that he can let loose the din of St.
Polycarpus on all the devils.*
*(Le Corbusier, in a letter to Varèse, quoted in Matossian, 1990,
p. 111)*

So the audience would have filtered through *Concret PH* as they arrived
and departed in this strange place, and its effervescent sonic clouds
would have fluttered around their ears in a random scintillation —
ephemeral, sparkling and soon to be erased from memory by the weighty
headline act. It may have happened like that; I have found no record of

exactly how it went. *Concret PH* is indeed under three minutes in length, possibly as a result of Le Corbusier's original intentions for it.

In music history books mention is often made of the 'PH' in *Concret PH*, and its reference to the hyperbolic paraboloids of the Philips Pavilion. It's satisfying to point out this not-so-subtle hint at Xenakis' involvement in the construction of the Philips Pavilion. But the association with concrete things is also worth digging into a little, as it may reveal a closer connection between sound and architecture. The pavilion was indeed constructed from concrete — a challenging task, since the curved shape of the walls necessitated curved materials. Xenakis oversaw the construction of pre-cast concrete slabs which were made from pouring concrete into appropriately shaped sand moulds, much as you might cast bronze for a sculpture. The slabs were numbered, shipped to the site and were then suspended from steel cables attached to the structural backbone of the building. In this way the mass of concrete slabs coalesced to form a 'skin' that was only five centimetres thick. At the time, this was deemed extraordinary and there were doubts as to whether such a elaborate process would make the transition from idea to reality. Although the French noun generally used for the substance — *béton* — differs, it seems likely that Xenakis might have made a concrete connection. *Concret PH*'s flurry of transposed and filtered sounds filled a building that was itself light and lifted up by technology; and both were made concrete by the coming together of many smaller components.

> *... if there is a crowd, I can no longer distinguish the individuals, because they are too numerous. On the contrary, what I can see are the aspects, the characteristics of the crowd.*
> (Xenakis, 1985, p. 33)

Another slab of '*concret*' is the overt association with '*musique concrète*', the expression coined by Pierre Schaeffer and thereafter gleefully solidified in the annals of music theory. Outwardly referring to the substantial nature of the material — recorded rather than synthetic sounds — Schaeffer's expression, and the surrounding thought that led him to employ it, has implications that reach far beneath the surface of the sound:

> *En réalité, la musique concrète, sitôt découverte, se trouve débordée non seulement par la pullulation du matériau mais par l'éclatement des formes.*
> Pierre Schaeffer, *l'Expérience Concrète en Musique* (in Schaeffer, 1952, p.125)

> [In reality, *musique concrète*, as soon as it was discovered, was found to be bubbling over not only with the proliferation of material but in the breaking open of forms.]

Xenakis had been associated with the GRM studio, where Schaeffer was based, since 1954, and *Concret PH* was the second piece he composed there. The piece is constructed from a one-second recording of crackling

charcoal embers. Although it was composed quite intuitively, using
relatively limited equipment, it has the same shifting complexities
that characterize much of Xenakis' instrumental music built by the more
rigorous application of stochastic principles.

The Philips Pavilion, though made of concrete, was a temporary
construction; it was ripped down on 30 January 1959, shortly after the
World Fair ended. But through the wonders of technology, and the
archival diligence of GRM and the Electronic Music Foundation, *Concret
PH* is now re-available on CD. *Poème Electronique* — the title of the
visual—aural collaboration between those two ageing giants, Le Corbusier and Varèse — makes a weighty allusion to a symbiosis of technology
and art. Perhaps *Concret PH* is a more snappy realization of the sparks
that touch between substance and idea, made concrete through technology. Reports differ.

> The Philips pavilion was an empty concrete structure, with the audience standing in the middle
> (or walking around). Lights and sounds came from invisible sources spread all over the place,
> moving around in an unpredictable way. We must have spent much of the time looking in the
> corners (if I may say so, no surface was flat), unsuccessfully trying to discover how it worked.
> . . .
> Unfortunately, I am afraid these recollections can hardly be accepted as decisive evidence for
> your research . . . . I hope that they can be of some help, though.
> (Professor Nicolas Meeùs, email correspondence)

JOURNAL ENTRY: 25 August 2002

Even if it was played in the central interior of the Philips Pavilion, *Concret PH* was
performed as an interlude. It was designed as something to come between events –
a temporary edifice in sound. Perhaps its mass of pinprick sounds barely disguised
the sounds of equipment being reset for the *Poème*, or the irreverent whispers of the
technicians, or the muted chatter of the public who were either entering in
excitement or leaving feeling slightly disorientated, bemused or entranced. I'm
trying to imagine how it must have felt to hear these crackling embers rise that first
time out of the more ponderous timbres of *Poème Electronique*.

Performed in a more conventional concert hall, the rapidly changing densities still
have an attractive allure, and through headphones the physical sensation of hearing a
multitude of short, high-frequency sounds is positively ticklish. Despite its brevity
Concret PH has no clear beginning or end and refuses to take on the usual 'concert
work' bargain with performed time. There are no metrical signposts. It just begins,
happens for a while, and then no longer happens. Perhaps this was because it was
designed to fill a bounded space rather than articulate a duration in which things
'went on'. I think the piece evades both 'world' and 'work' time quite successfully
because it has no sense of time at all: the events that do occur promise no particular
continuation. While listening to it, I feel that it will never end. Instead there is a

scintillation of fragmented sounds that perform fluctuating and unpredictable dances in the air. These sound masses shift constantly in terms of density, frequency, timbral content and spatial direction but do so in a manner that is apparently random – at least to my human ears. All my perceptual surfaces are bent out of shape by this purposeless sonic architecture, and I can hear no clues to any logic that might have been involved in deciding what went where.

> *When I need a great number of possibilities, I must manage to use*
> *characteristics of large numbers; which are, for example, density traits,*
> *traits of order or disorder, special distribution, sound-space distribution*
> *(such as pitch, time, order, disorder, etc. dimensions), and there we find*
> *potential tools to make certain choices. I am not saying that this applies to*
> *all choices . . . .*
> (Xenakis, 1985, p. 33)

The sound of spitting, popping charcoal embers is the sound of a process of decay. There's no going back to touch the source of that sound, because the source itself is insubstantial. The source is fire, and this is not a concrete substance but a voracious and random phenomenon, with a great many possibilities. There are allusions to heat, fire, burning and the symbology of creative, or destructive, fire; there is fire as illumination and as lightness, without tangible form. In a darkened concrete building where nothing could burn, these sounds might bring all kinds of associations to mind. The '*concrète*' part of *musique concrète* refers to the substantial nature of the real, physical objects that produced the sounds. But these sounds are out of time. Like the crackle of the radio, or the scratching of a bristle, they are irreversible traces of a vanished past – even more than usual, since the cracking of embers leads back to an activity that is about disappearance and decay. Yet *Concret PH*'s clouds of fizzing sound are made from pre-cast components: the original sounds are filtered and transposed and – paradoxically – have acquired more substance because the transpositions change the timbre and the filtering accentuates certain resonances and creates implications of size and substance. The lower-pitched sounds become longer, and 'bigger' in this context. They are hard and brittle, with a tactile appeal.[11] Whereas they were once the incidental sonic residue of fire, now they are also small, substantial objects in their own right – a crisp spatter of sparkling moments that fly back and forth to light a fantastic space.

Anecdotal evidence: TOES

Here is my touching John Cage anecdote (sometimes it seems that every listener has one): I once went to hear Cage read his *Lecture on Anarchy* in a converted synagogue in London. As I remember it, he sat on a rickety chair at a little desk and read random newspaper cuttings and quotations for over an hour. After about 20 minutes, Cage's voice began to be accompanied by a strange sound, which emanated from upstairs in the balcony. At first this enigmatic noise was composed of just a few intermittent squeaks, but gradually it built up into a continuous spatter of little creaks and cracking sounds, with the occasional muted thud. At times Cage was almost drowned out by all this sonic activity, which was actually made by people attempting to sneak out of the building unobserved – and certainly nobody downstairs could *see* them. Since they weren't in the habit of listening, in a Cagean sense, the departing audience members hadn't noticed the sonic effect as their politely tiptoeing feet touched the unforgiving floorboards. Because they couldn't be seen, they had thought that nobody would hear them; but it doesn't necessarily work both ways, of course. So, as they left, the audience stamped small aural imprints all over the performance. But John Cage didn't seem to mind one iota: he just continued reading out loud, smiling with his customary joy while his vanishing listeners danced a mass communication of unintended sounds. (I would like to say that this moment was transcendent but, personally, I was rather annoyed.)

Concrete: a mass, formed when particles coalesce
(it takes time).

Notes

1 The historical examples in this chapter are researched from a variety of sources. Rather than cite them individually here in the text, I here give a list of materials consulted:

Information on Cros, Sarnoff, Armstrong and the early days of radio includes research from various Internet sources:
http://memory.loc.gov/ammem/edhtml/edcyldr.html – 'The History of the Edison Cylinder Phono-graph'.
http://history.acusd.edu/gen/recording/cros.html – 'Charles Cros' (excerpts from Charles Cros's paper (in translation)).
http://web.mit.edu/invent/iow/deforest.html – page on Lee De Forest.
http://world.std.com/~jlr/doom/armstrng.htm – 'Edwin Howard Armstrong' (includes reproduction of photograph of Armstrong and his wife with radio).
http://www.150.si.edu/chap9/9horn.htm and http://www2.nlc-bnc.ca/gramophone/src/phonauto.htm – a photograph of a phonautograph.
http://www.pitt.edu/~jsterne/earphon.html – the ear phonoautograph.
http://www.localhistory.scit.wlv.ac.uk/Museum/Engineering/Electronics/history/earlytxrx.htm – 'Early Transmitters and Receivers' (a history of early radio).

In addition, the following texts were consulted Gelatt (1955); Godfrey and Leigh (1998); Koenigsberg (1969); Marco (1993); Millard (1995); Read and Welch (1959); Secor (1920); and the works of Charles Cros (1960, 1992). See Bibliography for full details.

2 For instance, the first graphical sound analysis program I ever used, in the late 1980s, was a legal hack by James Pritchett, Cage scholar and programmer *extraordinaire*. To make 'EdSnd', Pritchett took a sample sound program provided with the NeXT computer and enhanced it to make it more 'composer-friendly'. FFT spectral analysis was added by a medical researcher, who had come across the software at this stage and needed additional features. Pritchett then merged these changes. The practical end result of this back and forth between science and art made many grateful composers very happy.

3 I recommend Joel Chadabe's *Electric Sound* (1997), as an interesting (albeit rather US-centred) fusion of documentary, reminiscence and oral history by those involved in the early days of electronic music.

4 'I believe that the use of noise to make music will continue and increase until we reach a music produced through the aid of electrical instruments' (Cage, 1966, p. 3 – 'The Future of Music: Credo'). First delivered as a talk by John Cage, 1937, Seattle.

5 Letter from Alexander Graham Bell to Alexander Melville Bell, Eliza Symonds Bell, Carrie Bell and Charles J. Bell, 6 May 1874 (Alexander Graham Bell Family Papers at the Library of Congress. Online version at http://memory.loc.gov/ammem/bellhtml/bellhome.html).

6 The material concerning the Philips Pavilion is gleaned from a variety of historical sources, I also include, separately, personal reminiscences from Professor Nicolas Meeùs, to whom I am extremely grateful. See the Bibliography for full details of sources.

7 The final sentence of Cros's paper, 'Procédé d'enregistrement et de reproduction des phénomènes perçus par l'ouie' in Cros (1960).

8 This and the historical material is taken largely from Chapter 6 of Cros, *Inédits et Documents* (1992).

9 See http://world.std.com/~jlr/doom/armstrng.htm for a photo of Armstrong and his new bride, and a rather cumbersome gift.

10 Information on Armstrong is from web research and Godfrey and Leigh (1998).

11 Hildegard Westerkamp's *Kits Beach Soundwalk* incorporates her personal response to this same work, during which her words lead the listener through dreams, reflections and commentary relating to the sound of that piece, and what it means to her. In fact I first came across *Concret PH* through listening to her work.

Chapter 2

Several infinities (an emblem book)

The emblem book is a quirky kind of hypertext that reached its peak in Europe in the mid-seventeenth century.[1] Often, each emblem is composed of three elements: a motto or quotation, a visual symbol and some epigrammatic prose, usually of a religious nature, that proceeds to amplify the theme. This assemblage of poetic, visual and literary spaces invites personal reflection on the various analogies to be made between its separate components. As a form, it invites readings from several directions and offers the opportunity for each reader to reach their own individual conclusions. The various metaphors, symbols and digressions allow room for internal flight within the space of interpretation. There is freedom to travel back and forth.

Every metaphor has within it a potential for reversibility. The two poles of a metaphor can play the role of the real and the ideal alternately.
(Bachelard, 1988, p. 55)

In my appropriation of the emblem book I've made a few adjustments: there is only one visual reference throughout and only one secular author for the quotations. My writing, you may be glad to hear, is neither a religious tract nor an attempt to make a case for rectitude in electronic music. But I remain naively evangelical about the inherent 'magic' of electronic sound.[2] As a writer and composer, I am convinced that electronic sound as part of music can contribute uniquely to metaphors for immeasurable space, and that these metaphors can issue from images embedded in the medium, or more properly in the ways we listen to it. I believe that, through these images, our listening can be developed and deepened to provide metaphors of great strength and meaning.

So this emblem book is an essay on spatial metaphors: it is about metaphoric images for space that are inherent to electronic sound; it is about sonic metaphors for flight that have nothing to do with movement; it is about music as a metaphor for an other, infinite space and it is about some metaphoric associations between the space of electronic sound, acoustic sound and visual images. In a roundabout way, my writing is also an attempt to create a literary metaphor. Like the other texts in this book, this writing tries to be what it is about (I am speaking metaphorically of course). My aural emblems come from works by Ferrari, Harvey, Ceccarelli and Niblock.

But this is also an essay about a painting.

Figure 1 *Annunciation*, 1472–75 (oil on panel) (post-restoration) by Leonardo da Vinci (1452–1519), Galleria degli Uffizi, Florence, Italy / Bridgeman Art Library

EMBLEM: a broken wing

... if we want to study objects that truly produce *motion and that are truly the initial causes of movement, we may find it useful to replace a philosophy that deals with kinematic description with one that studies dynamic production.*
(Bachelard, 1988, pp. 255–56)

The angel in Leonardo da Vinci's painting, *Annunciation*, has got a terrible pair of wings. In fact this is hardly Leonardo's fault, since the wings have been tampered with. Somebody – in a fit of restorative embellishment, or perhaps as a mistaken 'improvement' – appears to have added extra length, colour and weight at a later stage. You can still just see the outline of the originals, which would have been quite perfect for flying; they were neatly tucked in, with the right kind of muscles and not too much extraneous decoration – great for buzzing around the heavens, and they wouldn't get tangled up in your robes (perhaps they still flex impatiently, underneath the paint). But even the original wings were a bit of an overrationalization, borrowed from Leonardo's observations of real birds. The winged figure seems grounded by the didactic symbolism of religious iconography. Paradoxically, the flowers that tickle the angel's feet are obviously painted from life.

So it appears that Leonardo[3] was content to opt for a familiar off-the-shelf metaphor for his narrative religious painting. Birds have wings, birds can fly, flying is what angels do, so angels must have wings. In this quick-fire chain of associations it is easy to forget why we decided that angels could fly in the first place.

Metaphors are often fleshed out by contemporary preoccupations, and their images shift and slide to accommodate this. In the 1600s the mind was seen as a theatre; in the 1970s it became a computer (and it has only recently begun to lose that metaphoric image, as we realize computers aren't quite that brainy).[4] Although the winged angel remains potent as an enduring icon, many mass media angels turned secular a while back, and they are more likely to be 'good' than specifically 'godly'. After all, since most mainstream movies are narrative films, hell-bent on our immersion in the cinematic diegesis, we need to be able to identify with a kind of reality. So the angels that alight in Berlin in Wim Wender's *Wings of Desire* are kind, compassionate and all-round nice guys, whereas the divine messenger from God that da Vinci depicts wasn't selected on personality (perfection was a given). The contemporary feature film angel is frequently wingless, though perhaps with a disconcerting tendency to disappear and appear at will since, nowadays, dematerialization claims that *frisson* of tentative possibility. In film, flight is 'real', frequently placing the viewer in the pilot's seat, *doing* flying – as in the beginning of *Wings of Desire*[5] where, gazing through the camera's prosthetic eye, we glide effortlessly from one place to another, swooping and dipping above and into the life of the city.[6]

But, as a defining principle, whether flying down from the heavens or appearing in a cloud of pixels from an alternative reality, an angel hails from another place and continues to contribute to a metaphor that is to do with a displacement from there to here and, by reversed implication, with our desire to go from here – to there.

Alien timbres, moving pictures

From at least Louis and Bebbe Barron's soundtrack for *The Forbidden Planet* onwards, electronic music – in particular synthetic timbre – has impersonated alien worlds in film. Those sounds are so strange that we just can't envisage where they come from. But now that the 'amazing', 'unreal' timbres of electronic synthesis have become familiar and acquired their own integrity, that particular connotation has waned somewhat. Contemporary sci-fi films are more likely to be bathed in opulent orchestral tonality (Luke Skywalker may be the new Siegfried, but too much chromaticism still makes us choke on our popcorn). Even so, a whole truckload of ambient 'space music' shows the extent to which electronically created timbre continues as an easy – some would say devalued – metaphor for otherworldly states.[7]

Analogue burbles or syrupy strings are just one side of the metaphorical coin. The phrase 'Cinema for the Ear' regularly crops up as a title for electronic music concerts and appears to cover several bases, in alluding to sitting in the dark, and to pre-recorded rather than 'live' and also to the dynamic movement of sonic 'images'. But this metaphor has shifted a bit. Increasingly, it is adopted to refer variously to an emphasis on aural, rather than visual, matters or to a distinction between 'audio art' and 'music' or even just to electronic music performed in a cinema rather than in a conventional auditorium. As the tagline for *Modulations*, a documentary on techno and its roots, it provided – along with nods to Pierre Henry and Stockhausen – some high art authenticity.[8] Another reason that, I think, the cinematic metaphor has become somewhat weakened is because the imaginative metaphors that we create from aural and visual experience are frequently incomparably different, and particularly so when it comes to specifically musical processes and sound. Perhaps 'cinema for the ear' is a confused metaphor in the first place, in that it sometimes seeks to be a term rather than an allusion. For this reason, I venture to suggest, it has become a little heavy and no longer flies. It is not a metaphor that springs directly from our listening to electronic sound. Instead, it can tend to treat that sound as a musical soundtrack for a silent (and invisible) narrative.

◉ CD[3] *Presque Rien avec Filles*, by Luc Ferrari (excerpt)

Luc Ferrari's *Presque Rien avec Filles*,[9] opens with an insistent, slow and low-pitched beat, over which there is a high-pitched sound reminiscent of flapping wings, and another, unidentifiable fast, tapping or 'whipping' sound – perhaps a rope or a ribbon, buffeted by the wind? – plus a bit of general 'outdoors' ambience (see how description fails). After a minute or so, background sounds of wind in the trees and birdsong become increasingly apparent. There is nothing to see. The sounds are not about seeing. This passage makes the open space of 'the outdoors' audible through allusions to wind and sky. The aural cues speak of movement in an unconstrained place. But several musical constraints enrich and enlarge these airy metaphors, and point to the fact that this place is different from the real world. The 'flapping wings' sound is only *reminiscent* of birds since now it is a looped rhythmic pattern that becomes an ostinato for the drumbeat. The difference between the low-pitched beat and high-pitched timbre of the other sounds places the wings, metaphorically, 'above' the listener. Because there is nothing explicit in this allusion to birds, the aural metaphor points away from real wings towards the movement of flight. We do not see birds (the abstraction of the sound removes even tenuous assumptions as to the shape, weight or nature of the body producing the sound), but we hear them move above us, in another place, where flying is possible.

An image of another place can provide a metaphor for flight.

An image of flight can provide a metaphor for another place.

EMBLEM: a moving ribbon

When we accept slight amazement, we prepare ourselves to imagine great amazement and, in the world of the imagination, it becomes normal for an elephant, which is an enormous animal, to come out of a snail shell. It would be exceptional, however, if we were to ask him to go back into it.
(Bachelard, 1994, p. 105)

Flight, as Leonardo might well have written, is difficult to describe. Perhaps this is because the essence of the achievement lies not in wings but in that amazing plunge from one state to another And that instant of transition is hard to capture. Leonardo had an earlier dream for his angel's flight. In Oxford there's a little preparatory sketch for the *Annunciation*, taken from his Notebooks – a study for an angel's sleeve. It is just an arm in a sleeve: the ability to fly is taken as read.[10]

And maybe you can see a hint of this understated assumption in the painting, if you look from a different perspective and concentrate on detail. Take another peek. Nothing moves – the trees are upright and motionless, the boats in the background are becalmed, and the Madonna sits frozen and (not surprisingly) aghast. There is evidently no activity, and the day is still. But yet, on the angel's sleeve, a ribbon flutters backwards in a gust of air: perhaps this angel is caught in the moment of moving from there to here. It would be quite normal, in such circumstances, to create a bit of a breeze.

In his philosophical consideration of air, dreams, and the dynamics of imagination, Bachelard remarks that '... in the dream world we do not fly because we have wings; rather, we think we have wings because we have flown.' (Bachelard, 1988, p. 27) In our dream, he avows, we instinctively lift ourselves off the ground without particular effort, by the slightest of impulses.[11] But, on waking, our attempts at expressing this dreamed ability, through words, images or other creative means, demand some kind of rationalization. We know that birds can fly, and so we appropriate their wings in our description. But, really, all it took was a little push from within, and it is not an expression of the *motion* of flight that matters, but the expression of the *ability*, that

Bachelard suggests we 'know' in dreams.[12] A metaphor for that ability involves images about what flight means to us: the amazing *difference* between being here and then, suddenly, being there. (And don't we intuitively sense this when we take a plane journey? It's that moment when the wheels stop rumbling on the tarmac and the plane is suddenly aloft that makes our heart skip a beat.) And a metaphor for this amazement may itself contribute to a larger metaphor for unfettered travel; once you're off the ground, the sky's the limit. But finding an image for the metaphor is the first task.

Electronic sound frequently employs metaphors of dynamic movement in a very direct manner – through timbre, pitch and, especially, spatial trajectory. Consideration of dynamic gestures, at both macro and micro levels, continues to prove particularly attractive to composers and theoreticians working from post-Schaefferian[13] principles that – it would appear – evade the more ingrained methodologies of note-based music. An upward glissando can be a fine means of indicating ascent, and can be enriched by learnt or symbolic sonic associations along the way, but there are limitations to this visual–aural transliteration. Even if a composer extends or amplifies a glissando's metaphorical 'reach' by making it travel around the auditorium, the sound still slides continuously up or down in pitch, and may or may not remind us of a police siren. Of course, sometimes that is exactly what you want. Yet I would like to delve about here for some other images from which to compose metaphors. We don't need to rely on borrowed wings. Pushing off the ground is a shift, not a slide – a sudden change of state without any continuity – and this is an awareness of difference. And it is also a great amazement, which may benefit from a bit of preparation.

⏵ CD[4] *Birds*, by Luigi Ceccarelli (excerpt)

Luigi Ceccarelli's *Birds* 'for bass clarinet and tape with clarinet and bird sounds', is an extrovert piece with a fast, regular tempo that might well encourage a listener to move about a bit. But, despite both this and its title, *Birds* initially seems far removed from any metaphors of bodily ascent. The timbres of bass clarinet and, later, of birds, are not changed significantly – a fact the composer makes a point of emphasizing in both title and programme notes – and the piece has a sectional structure that eschews transitions or other musical conventions for 'growth'. And to make things worse, a bass clarinet is a slightly elephantine beast that might appear a little low on the list of believable aerial beings. But *Birds* is, I think, a piece that cuts straight to the detail and goes beyond the surface of some of the more worn-out sonic metaphors for flight. Instead, there are stronger, more subtle allusions to the ability to take off and inhabit another space, and these allusions are built through an accumulation of 'differences'. These are layered to provide a patinated image that has depth and endurance. A gradual collecting of 'slight amazements' contributes towards an underlying drama in which we, listening, become attuned to appreciating change. Ultimately, it only requires the smallest, almost inaudible impulse for a bass clarinet to take flight.

Some slightly amazing differences

... between acoustic and electronic sound

Electronically produced sound and acoustically produced sound are different in terms of *where* the sound appears to come from. Surely this simple listening distinction precedes any theoretical deductions as to how we might comprehend apparent origins for *concrète* sound, or any complex analysis of directional cues? This ordinary, only slightly amazing difference is something we pick up very quickly indeed when the acoustic and electronic sounds coexist. It has more to do with our sensitivity to spatial position than any awareness of amplification. For this reason, sound reinforcement of acoustic sound is a delicate psychoacoustic art since we are easily discomfited when the visual source and its sound are unintentionally split apart.[14] On the other hand, the deliberate amplification of acoustic sound can separate performers and sound in an intentionally aggressive manner so that the sound 'hits' our ears as a force to be contended with, rather than as the distant result of activity from the mere mortals on the stage. Contemporary ensembles such as (in my recent experience) 'Icebreaker' or the 'Bang On a Can All Stars' frequently amplify their acoustic sound to an extremely high level, imitating rock band scenarios, but using acoustic instruments. The effect is a 'wall' of amplified sound that dissociates performers and sound. This is perhaps a politicized aesthetic of enlargement as inclusivity, where amplification is regarded as synonymous with appeal and energy.[15]

In *Birds*, Ceccarelli is conscious of wanting to maintain the spatial distinction between acoustic and electronic sound, even when using some necessary sound reinforcement in order to achieve an audible balance. The distinction between acoustic and electronically produced sound is also, as he recognizes, infiltrated by an obvious visual difference in performance:

> ... with regard to the live clarinet, it would also be possible to move it around, from an acoustic point of view, but in general it seems to me that, especially in a piece where there are sounds reproduced from a tape machine (therefore without a visual correspondence), it is more appropriate to maintain the spatial correspondence between the instrument's sound and its image.
> (Luigi Ceccarelli, email correspondence)[16]

... between performance and emanation

But when live acoustic and recorded electronic sound are combined, the difference between them contributes to another difference – that between a performer on stage producing sound directly, through visible, physical effort from a fixed point and a simultaneous effortless 'emanation' of sounds appearing 'invisibly' from speakers. The latter may be moved around a space at will, but the spatial dislocation between electronic sound and the antics of someone at a central mixing desk means that the live-ness of that 'will' is of no real concern to the average audience member.

... between performer and tape[17]

A work for instrument and tape invites us to listen to a live performer enacting 'living in another space', and sometimes that other space feels a great deal larger than the concert hall. Even the most active electronic tape part offers, I suggest, an image for another space, rather than being perceived as another, offstage performer – and this sonic metaphor is strengthened through the differences described above.

A soloist's position in relation to a pre-recorded tape is, I think, perceived somewhat differently from that of an ensemble and tape. As listeners, we tend to identify with the soloist's presence, and perhaps we try to put ourselves in their position, as they listen to the electronic world around them. We are denied this 'projection' in relation to an ensemble where perhaps more often the taped material comments on, or extends away from, the group's self-sufficient interactivity (as with the example to come, from Harvey's *Bhakti*). In fact there are relatively few pieces for small ensembles and tape although there are probably more involving the additional interactivity of live electronics. I am, of course, leaving aside the use of recorded electronic material as a support or 'backing' to a soloist or band, or as more straightforward descriptive theatrical sound design.

... between them and us

Perhaps also the space of the tape part can be perceived in this metaphoric way because we are ourselves not immersed in *its* spatial dimension. We remain apart: we listen *to* a piece that is itself a theatrical enactment of the difference between 'live performer in time' and 'recorded sound in space'. But if we rustle our programme inadvertently, the fluttering pages reverberate in the space of the auditorium, which is somewhere else again. Yet the tape part's 'fictional' universe is just a part of a totality that reaches our ears via the 'real' space that is an inescapable fact of perceiving sound. When the space conveyed by the tape part – a fictional, possibly infinite, world – physically *surrounds* our listening, then perhaps the space of the auditorium can become infused with its immensity. In this sense, then, real space is always a player that takes an acting role within a dramatic scenario, a possibility to which Ceccarelli is evidently sensitive:

> My long experience of working with sonorous space has convinced me even more that each space possesses its own particular sound and that each space substantially influences the music. This realization obliges me to think of how a certain ambience will 'sound' or how the music will be or 'live' within it ... .
> ... We perceive the sound through the space and therefore we sense the sound of the sounding space exclusively, and never directly perceive the 'pure' sound, that in reality can't exist in those terms.
> (Luigi Ceccarelli, email correspondence)[18]

... between live and recorded

In the repertoire of works for soloist and tape there are certainly many pieces that emulate a live cause-and-effect relationship between acoustic and electronic sound, but this is less common now that reliable and affordable technology enables the real thing. More often the 'tape part' is there to provide a universe for the live performer to inhabit. (When this is not the case, the metaphor is often being reversed for a reason, as in the Harvey example to come). The tape part's universe is temporally preordained, and I remain convinced that this contributes in some way to the persistence of 'instrument and tape' as a name for a *genre*; we are hanging on to the end of that metaphorically spooling ribbon of time, even though today it's more likely to be a CD, and no doubt tomorrow it will be some other means of delivery.

A universe needs to offer some attraction to prospective inhabitants. As is often the case, the tape part in *Birds* makes use of sounds sampled from the solo instrument. But, in *Birds*, the timbres do not serve to take over where the instrumentalist's abilities leave off. The taped clarinet sounds do not – as the composer takes pains to point out – lose their original character. Rather the *performative* behaviour of the bass clarinet has been extended upwards and downwards – in pitch, timbre and place of origin – through a kind of 'lamination' made from layers of pitch (essentially a single pitch at various octaves), timbre and spatial position. The bonding of tape and live performer is highly successful in that it is difficult to hear which is which, but it is also difficult to forget that there is a tape part 'going on' around a live player who appears to have stepped into a huge, expansive 'bass clarinet' space. We are set up to expect this tight relationship between soloist and tape, and for several minutes these expectations are fulfilled. This makes a sudden difference all the more noticeable.

... between up and down

A dynamically moving sound can certainly activate a space, just as a torch can suddenly illuminate the dimensions of a pitch-black cave. But *Birds* seems more concerned with an ongoing illumination of spaces created by 'static' minimalist textures. Perhaps it is not 'ascent' but the 'ability' to ascend that is being prepared for. A metaphor for suddenly being *able* to ascend requires images that strengthen the difference between being in the air and being on the ground.

The piece starts with a short passage of fast, breathy squeaks and rhythmic activity from both taped and live bass clarinet. There is very little pitched material in this passage. After 20 seconds or so, the prevailing loud, dense and much lower-pitched texture made from layered bass clarinet articulations commences suddenly. What was the role of that strange opening section, which started in the stratosphere but didn't explore any flighty connections with birds, and was brief and introductory? I would suggest that it triggered our awareness of the ground that followed. This difference between 'up' and 'down' prepares us for a subsequent difference between 'above' and 'below'. It does so through metaphoric images from pitch, timbre and also 'effort' (breathy squeaks as opposed to the subsequent earthy, full-throttle minimalist patterns).

At about 2 minutes 30 seconds (well into a piece of around nine minutes in duration) these patterns stop abruptly, in mid-flow. We hear birdsong. Although regular tempo is abandoned (or, rather, is ambiguous due to the naturalistic birdsong rhythms) the birdsong fragments are still layered in the same kind of temporal vein, so that when a rhythmic pattern starts up within the birdsong it is barely noticeable for a few seconds. Although it is clarinet-based (squeaks and 'breath' sounds, as in the opening seconds) there is initially some aural confusion between birdsong and bass clarinet sound, due to the similarity of timbres: they are, however, in both cases 'natural' and unmodified). At around 2 minutes 56 seconds the loud, layered, low bass clarinet patterns return suddenly and the live bass clarinet and tape re-embark as before.

... between slight and great amazement

The birdsong is the apotheosis of a metaphoric image that has been prepared for through several differences.

Birdsong is, of course, an immediately recognizable source, with immediate associations for everyone. It is, in real life, invisible and in space. We may occasionally look to try to find the singer, but more often than not we are content to be aware of this sound above us that emanates from an aerial place. So birdsong is at home emanating from speakers – in fact, it is one of few 'real-world' sounds that might appear completely and convincingly 'real' in this situation. But it is not a sound particularly associated with flight, since birds tend to stand still while performing their recitals. And this is not a cinematic image since birdsong is not an aural transliteration of a visual trajectory. If anything, birdsong is an image of an invisible space that is beyond our reach. Here, that space is derealized through use of a slight reverberation and the absence of any 'real-world' outside ambience. These birds enable the fruition of a metaphor for that moment of difference between being 'on the ground' and being 'in the air'. 'Up' and 'down' have already been established in terms of the clarinet's aural universe. Now – suddenly – there is no ground beneath the performer's feet, and the only sound is an unequivocal 'aboveness' that is *more* than the relative difference between high and low. The bass clarinet sounds re-emerge, in a breathy pattern that mingles ambiguously with the sound of birdsong. It is quite difficult to hear each as a separate entity (despite the fact that they are not processed electronically), but it is clearly evident that they occupy the same place. The bass clarinet is no longer on the ground. And it only took a slight impulse to achieve this moment of great amazement.

An image of another place can provide a metaphor for amazing ability.

An image of amazing ability can provide a metaphor for another place.

EMBLEM: a distant point

In order to hear things that belong to infinite space, we must reduce to silence all the noises on earth. ... All profound contemplation is necessarily and naturally a

hymn. The function of that hymn is to go beyond reality and to project a world of sound beyond the silent world.
(Bachelard, 1988, p. 49)

The vanishing point in Leonardo's *Annunciation* is somewhere beyond that brief patch of open sea that's just visible between the trees. This is the place where all lines of sight converge and disappear into oneness. Viewed alternatively, this is the point from which all lines emanate towards us, towards where the image is finally reassembled and becomes meaningful in our eyes. Either way, some important journeys are taking place.

Yet in a painting, the view keeps still (we're not at the pictures, you know). Leonardo's *Annunciation*, like the sun, 'does not move', but we do; our sight follows the dimensions of the space he represents and takes in the story. In a narrative painting such as this is, the vanishing point is often a way of throwing a spotlight on the dramatic 'high point' of the tale – it directs the viewer to the lovers' lips, the dagger in the hand, the Christ-child's face, or to the astonishment of an anointed virgin.

But Leonardo leads us into the sea, and then onwards to an invisible destination where the horizon melts and the distant hills are shrouded in haze and mystery. The objects in the distance are, of course, depicted as much smaller, but he also conveys distance through aerial perspective, painting the furthest objects as more blue and indistinct. This mimics how we see in real life, so we perceive his analogy and interpret accordingly. But the vanishing point itself is apparently beyond even the blurred horizon, at a place we cannot see at all. In this vision the angel and the virgin are just the beginning of the story.

Bachelard's call for us to hear the 'things that belong to infinite space' is all very well but, of course, he is not talking about sounded music, or even sound. He is working towards some kind of image for the internalized dynamic of a transcendent, poetic contemplation. Our experience of listening informs us that to hear the 'things' is to know their space, since all sounding objects signal information on both where they are and how near they are to our ears. But what are the 'things' that belong to infinite space? Though the things may be inconceivable, our experience of auditory perspective allows for some educated guesses, just as our experience of visual perspective in real life enables us to appreciate a Leonardo. So perhaps it is possible to have a go at imagining some audible qualities for a space with no walls, no barriers and no further obstruction. How can we aurally represent a thing, or a presence, in a space that is 'going on for ever'? You'll be needing a long reverberation time for that.

To go back to visual analogies: in real-world experience we cannot see forever. Even if blessed (or cursed) with superhuman eyesight, we'd eventually encounter an object in our visual path. Perhaps Leonardo's vanishing point gets around that barrier because it's possible to imagine that we could, had we the stamina, stand in front of the *Annunciation* forever; staring onwards into his representation of unobstructed infinity until – at the sound of the last trumpet – we encountered something worth waiting for. In the meantime, the visual representation would remain before our eyes (well, at least for the foreseeable future) to guide our imagination.

We allow ourselves a little reality. We make a deal with the two-dimensional representational perspective painting that, given sufficient encouragement, we will respond to the clues that indicate three-dimensional space *as if* this image *is* a three-dimensional space. The painting's illusion is assisted by the fact that all images enter the eye as two-dimensional images in any case. And although we will not generally regard the things or the space represented in a painting as 'actual', 'here' or 'real', we can be fairly easily fooled by optical tricks of various kinds.[19]

There is no direct sonic analogy to this infinite contemplation of Leonardo's invisible vanishing point. You can't stand in front of a sound that disappears endlessly into the distance because all sounds end eventually, or are in the process of ending. Certainly repetition or stasis, or any kind of apparent 'incessantness', can offer a kind of listening experience of transcendence, or of being in an infinite or boundless environment. But this is a metaphor for being *in* no-time, rather than of standing apart and appreciating infinity as an other, unknown and endless. Perhaps the representation of infinite space is difficult to convey metaphorically in sound because we are inclined *not* to hear sound as a representation of a place, but instead as evidence of an object's activity. It is quite easy to 'fool' the ear with a recording of a closing door, an exhaling sigh or a chorus of twittering birds. But these things do not represent the space itself. A huge amount of time is spent on discussing how various perceptual confusions and congruities that arise in listening might define an aesthetic for electronic music, especially that flavour of *musique concrète* that relies on a history of disembodied doors and sighs. But let me come at this from the perspective of a naive realist for a moment and suggest that, although all this is of extraordinary interest to our listening to transformed sounds, we don't perceive that much of a difference between the meaning of a recorded door sound and a live door sound if both are disembodied. (This is perhaps why the sound of a stool falling to the ground in Normandeau's multichannel acousmatic work, *Malina*, has everyone looking to see who fell off their chair and the sound of the invisible voices in a performance of Beckett's experimental radio play, *Cascando*, might be either a recording or a live performance, and we'll never know which unless the lights go up.) In addition, the space created by the sounds may be fictional – fooling the ear with added reverberation and spectral cues – but it is 'finite'. Because if we are to build an aesthetic governed by the movement of objects in space, we'll need to measure distance. Things can't go on for ever. And this, I think, is why electronic music of this 'referential' kind has a difficulty when it comes to finding strong sonic metaphors for the infinity that lies beyond things.

But strong sonic metaphors do exist elsewhere. So, I would like to take make a very detailed journey, into an aural space that extends to infinite dimensions.

⏵ CD[5] movement IX from *Bhakti*, by Jonathan Harvey

> Ultimate contraction of pitch, expansion of spirit. Three massive G's, mostly electronic, enlivened by internal manipulations of the spectrum. Each lasts a whole minute, and the last reverberates into space.

> 'The quarters of the sky live on the oceans that flow out of her in all directions. The whole universe exists through the undying syllable that flows from her.'
> 1.164 (Rig Veda)
> (Jonathan Harvey, liner note to *Bhakti*, movement IX)

Bhakti, a large-scale piece for 15 instrumentalists and quadraphonic tape, is about devotion as a way of approaching the presence of eternity. In the ninth movement of this work, Harvey's sonic metaphors for infinite space become explicit and unequivocal. And his metaphoric image is an illusion: it plays with the perceptual 'rules' we apply when interpreting a space through the sounds we hear within it. The three 'massive G's, mostly electronic' are made from a single accented G from ensemble, with an electronic 'G' that continues long after the initial instrumental attack.

Some rules that are made to be broken

... sounds begin and end

Our visual perception of a 'thing' continues until we choose to close our eyes, but sounds start and finish, and then are gone. By starting, a sound infers that it will end. But Harvey is trying to express the sound of travelling sound in a world with no beginning or end.[20] His 'massive G's' do not pass in and out of existence in this disconcerting way because they were always there – G is the pitch around which pitches gather at the very opening of the work. These Gs are never-ending. Certainly each of them articulates time (more on that later), but they are not a surprise. They have already started sounding in the previous movement, where the pitch emerged from a texture, and they will continue to inhabit the fabric of the movement that follows. Although we cannot close our ears, we can turn our attention towards and away from the presence of a pitch – and in music it's common practice to encourage that shift of perspective. So this appears quite normal. The Gs merely come forward and take centre stage for an infinite minute or three, before returning to being still.

... timbre indicates proximity and effort

There are two opposing rules here:

1   The closer a sound is to us, the more intense its spectrum, or timbre. As the sound moves further away, the higher frequencies within its timbre will appear to diminish. When sounds reverberate in space, the higher frequencies tend to fade out first.
2   For naturally produced sounds, a louder sound tends to have a brighter spectrum or 'colour' than its softer counterpart.

In practice, we prioritize. If a loud sound is produced at some distance from us, we will decide that it is louder, even though the volume, or energy, indicates otherwise.[21] So the trumpet shall sound, but a distant trumpet played loudly will be perceived as louder than a muted trumpet played up close, even if they both register exactly the same decibel level, since the distant but loud sound will have a brighter timbre. Changes of timbre within a note provide strong auditory cues for proximity; they tell us where we are in relation to a sound. Harvey's treatment of timbre sabotages that cue.

After an initial attack, each of the electronic Gs changes its timbre continuously, through an unpredictable swelling and contracting of its inner spectrum (as Harvey describes in his programme note). This might well make perceptual sense for a sustained orchestral texture lasting a minute or so, but various contributory factors lead us to think of this sound as belonging to a single 'being' or presence, *in addition* to that presence indicating a virtual 'space'. Each 'note' is indeed centred *around* a specific pitch, although the actual timbre encompasses a wider range. This 'single' note is not behaving in the same way as a sustained orchestral unison: the timbre is undergoing a continuous and unpredictable variation, shaped by a single 'envelope' in terms of both volume and spectral change. It sounds as if 'one thing' is making the dynamically evolving sound. That thing has human connotations because the timbre has vocal qualities (through the use of spectral characteristics peculiar to the human voice) and yet it cannot possibly be perceived as human, because the timbral evolution and the duration precludes this likelihood. And an inhuman, endlessly evolving breath that nevertheless has some human associations is difficult to envisage, because it is unknowable. And we don't know *where* it is either because, in terms of auditory perspective, it indicates a space that is all around us, in quadraphonic space, and yet one that cannot exist in the real, external world. If this were a drawing, perhaps we'd give it wings.

... the sound indicates the nature of the space

Normally, these cues for auditory perception fuse to provide an aural picture of the shape, size and the type of walls for a space.

The first two Gs each stop abruptly, after fading and swelling in unpredictable ways. Between each of these Gs there is a short 'outburst' from the tape, which at first seems so incongruous as to be even an 'error' perhaps. Between the first and second G there are three very short bursts of sound – one a snippet of the timbre just heard, the following two higher transpositions of the same kind of sound. Between the second and third G there is just a single burst of similar timbre. Are these perhaps the 'things' that create an impulse for some kind of decay? But the long electronic Gs extended from an instrumental ensemble 'attack' and then faded into the distance, whereas these bursts of sound appear to *follow* the Gs, since there is no outburst before the first G (although, on the other hand, there is no outburst after the last G either). These apparent interruptions have such presence that they appear almost to reach out and touch us: both loudness and intensity indicate proximity. And I think that, although these interjections indicate space, they have been taken out of time. They have been dissociated from the 'decay' of the long notes, and they have also been dissociated from 'before' and 'after' because they do not measure anything except a kind of 'now'.

In the external world that we know, these various aural cues are inseparable (and we know this too). But in this space, there is time. In fact, this frozen time is reinforced by another separation. Those bursts of sounds are indicated as cues for the conductor and players to 'adopt motionless positions as if just about to play'.[22] So the sudden aural activity from the invisible tape coincides with a drawing of attention to the sudden 'absence' of live performance in our real-time present. This absence is indicated visually, but the visual image is a metaphor for a lack of sound. There are two places. There is the place that is here. And there is the place that is there. After each outburst there is a silence of a few seconds (after the first G, seven seconds, after the next G, twelve seconds). This complete absence is an empty place where even the G no longer is. As the poised performers visually suggest, it is a space full of desire for the G's return.

... a reverberation will fade

When a sound reverberates in space it will eventually decay to nothing. It will fade out gradually. This may seem obvious, but that is precisely because this cue is so vital to our understanding of dimension.

The first two long Gs do fade; it takes a full minute, but eventually the sound drains away to nothing. The endpoint of the sound in both cases is in fact rather abrupt with an unexpectedly short reverberation (if it seemed too short, we must have been expecting something else). And each of these Gs is, of course, followed by a continuation of what came before, with the short bursts of sound in the interim. The last G stops abruptly too, but the reverberating, echoing repetition that follows tells us that this massive G – this 'thing' – is resounding in a vast place. However, the sound is decaying. If that massive G had continued as an 'ever present' drone, always at the same demanding level of intensity, we wouldn't be thinking about this other vast space, we'd simply feel ourselves to be *in* the space (a feeling on which my next example relies). But, then again, although the G fades, it doesn't go away. In fact the next movement begins with horn calls over and across the same immensity that we are hearing now, and in the spaces between this movement's instrumental antiphony the echoes of that G will continue to reverberate, for ever.

The electronic sound surges up and down in both dynamic and timbre, moving from quasi-orchestral to quasi-vocal timbre, without being identifiable as one or the other. In this sense, it is disconnected from the acoustic instrumental sound that issues from the stage. Yet it is also perceived as the decay that proceeds from an initial attack in which acoustic and electronic forces combined, as did the spaces that they inhabit.

While the 'undying syllable' of the Gs on the tape does not fade, the live ensemble does. A staggered falling away of live presence bids a careful farewell to worldly space. For the first G, the instrumental attack – covering a wide registral space – comes from clarinet, bass clarinet, horn, crotales, harp, piano and solo strings. The G is grounded by the middle and lower register being sustained for twenty seconds or so. In consequence, the electronic G appears to relate to the 'real world' of the live ensemble. For the second G, the clarinet and bass clarinet are absent. The first instruments to depart are breath-based ones, capable of holding a long, sustained note, and whose complex timbres perhaps relate most closely to the tape timbre. So the second tape part G has fewer earthly ties. By the last G, only crotales and harp remain, and even the lower octaves of the harp attack have gone. The last G has virtually no relationship to real space: the crotales and harp that colour the attack are very loud, but their presence is unearthly – these timbres are already venerable sonic metaphors for transcendence and are soon subsumed into an endless reverberation.

An image of another place can provide a metaphor for measureless dimension.

An image of measureless dimension can provide a metaphor for another place.[23]

EMBLEM: a gap in the wall

There will always be someone who will do away with all complications and oblige us to leave as soon as there is mention of space – whether figurative or not – or of the opposition of outside and inside. But if reduction is easy, exaggeration is all the more interesting, from the standpoint of phenomenology.
(Bachelard, 1994, p. 97)

Leonardo sets out his story with the assistance of some traditional devices. The angel has brought along white lilies – symbol of the Madonna's purity and grace, and also indicative of the Easter to come. And the Madonna is receiving the heavy news whilst seated in her own enclosed garden (it must be hers, she has the furniture): that garden is another poetic metaphor for virginity.[24] All in all, I'd say the angel has got the girl, apart from one thing that bothers me a little; there's a gap in that solid wall that divides background from foreground.

Mary, or rather the lilies that represent her, is poised in that gap between the enclosed garden and the real world that continues on the other side of the wall. In the garden, time has stopped, and the only movement is a vestige of eternal flight. But in the real world there are indications that time goes on regardless: ships travel from one harbour to another and a river flows away to meet the sea – these both have aspirations that may repeat indefinitely but are symbols of life, not of infinity. But whether this virgin ultimately has a choice or not, perhaps there's enough time for her to feel she could make a wise decision; she is caught in a moment of suspense in the gap between two spaces – between her desire and her destiny. Now, she just might look towards us and declare, 'You know, I'd rather not today, if it's all the same to you.' Because we are there *too*: in this large-as-life[25] painting the flowery lawn extends towards our feet and the foreshortened perspective implies our participation inside the narrative frame. We are merely out of shot for the moment.

That was a personal, slightly exaggerated, point of view (a metaphoric emblem for this book perhaps). Now, I want to turn the sound down low for quite a few moments, and pass the visual image under several expert pairs of eyes before considering how metaphors for this gap might be drawn out of a composed discrepancy between sonic and visual spaces.

Looking, and its analysis through perspective techniques, was a Renaissance cross-disciplinary obsession that painters grabbed with gleeful alacrity. At last, surround vision! (Well, almost.) Alberti's influential thesis on the subject of perspective in painting would have been Leonardo's well-thumbed guide, and no doubt Alberti's proclamation that the canvas was to be treated as 'an open window' was quoted *ad nauseam* by diligent young artists.[26] There is another *Annunciation* in the Louvre – for a while, also attributed to Leonardo. This one takes Alberti rather at his word: the edges of a fictional window appear at the corners of the painting, and we look through this window to observe a similar angel meeting a similar virgin. But Leonardo has a photographer's eye: he is looking for a more involved spectator.[27]

Stanley Cavell sets our reception of painting and photography (including film) in opposition, and suggests that the photograph maintains 'the presentness of the world by accepting our absence from it' while 'to maintain our presentness, painting accepts the recession of the world' (Cavell, 1979, p. 23). In observing the photograph we understand and *feel* it as an image of a 'present', but only because we are set apart from it, in an 'outside' present that is now. But the painting, in Cavell's view, doesn't deal with fixing that sense of presentness. We do not feel that the painting extends outwards beyond the frame as any kind of previous or transfixed reality. There is a present 'inside' the painting, but that present was never ours.

But wait a minute. When there's an opportunity to step through the frame onto the painted lawn, I would say we are going into a situation where our 'now' is flickering precariously. We are now perceived (by ourselves) as a presence in the image that we view. Our feet on the grass are implied and, although we are invisible to ourselves, we feel we might be seen. The rationalization for our invisibility involves some kind of belief that the image is directed from our eyes and is thus a representation of *our* 'looking'. The painting takes on our time, so when we see that gap in the wall, we feel that we came across it in the course of looking around. *We* move, just as we feel *we* move when the film camera pans a scenic view around us. It's almost real; it's just that our sense of reality is rather different and the space is a little strange.

Michael Kubovy is my last witness. His thesis on the psychology of Renaissance art considers 'the spectator's experience of his or her location in space with respect to the physical surface of the painting and with respect to the room in which the painting is viewed'. We do not always look at an image full on, and in taking a sideways glance we may catch a hidden detail from the corner of our eye.[28] Perhaps that's when that particular 'something' can look out across the gap and address us, personally. Barthes (1993, p. 49) talking about photographs, called that 'something' the 'punctum' – that point, perhaps a miniscule detail, that seems to leap out from the image and strike the viewer as unexpectedly poignant or moving (something as trivial as a wing, a ribbon or a spray of lilies). And in perceiving that personal, mysterious emblem, we are suddenly brought back to our *feeling* of time and space.

Kubovy contends that Renaissance painters 'deliberately induced a discrepancy between the spectator's *actual* point of view and the point of view from which the scene is *felt* to be viewed'. Certainly Leonardo's *Annunciation*, with its vanishing point technically 'too high' and to the right of the composition, and a foreshortened perspective that lands the viewer in the grass, does invite us to *feel* as if we are standing in the garden, perhaps nearest to the Madonna; and we are looking – significantly –

upwards and onwards to the distant sky. Of course, we're not *actually* looking from that position – we're probably in a rather crowded gallery surrounded by other sticky tourists – but I would like to take issue with Kubovy's rather flamboyant claim, that 'the result is a spiritual experience that cannot be obtained by any other means' (Kubovy, 1986, p. 16). This kind of spiritual experience may well employ discrepancy to build images for a metaphor of transport to another, transcendent space, but discrepancies of perspective can arise in other media as well. A discrepancy requires an opposition, and perhaps there is even more scope for composing discrepancy into a work when there are two types of media involved. If the opposition between these two media is exaggerated as part of the work, then there are bound to be sparks when the two are drawn together by an unexpected detail. And, even then, 'minding the gap' between one thing and another is a matter of personal choice. Perhaps it has less to do with the artist's conscious endeavours than with each audience member's responses.

ⓑ CD[6] *China*, by Phill Niblock (audio excerpt from audio-visual work)

Phill Niblock's *China* is a work in which nearly 45 minutes of documentary film is presented simultaneously with a musical work, separately titled *Winter Music*.[29] Everything in Niblock's work is somehow larger than life – the duration of the work, the nature of the music, the size of the images. In performance, Niblock's videos are often 'multichannel' with more than one film running simultaneously on large screens; and the music is *extremely* loud, produced through speakers set up around the space. Often the musical element is a combination of live performance and multitracked tape, with both recorded instrumental and sampled sounds. Sometimes there is no live component (as in this video version of a work). Performances differ: you may be able to walk around, or you may be seated in a concert or theatre space. Often, Niblock's live events go on for several hours, and always at the same intense level of visual and aural amplification.

In *China*, as is usual for Niblock's videos, the original footage is film of people performing ordinary, manual tasks – here, it is Chinese peasants in the fields, sawing trees, picking crops, making baskets, sorting fruit, catching fish, herding goats. The filmed images concentrate on the physical actions required by these tasks, frequently going into close-up to concentrate on the movement. The camera just 'watches', it never moves in any overtly planned trajectory, other than to shift to get a better view of what's going on. In opposition to the dramatizing urge of the movie-director, whose editing makes 'a contrast that is sharper than the contrast between successive events in real time' (Sontag, 1982, p. 360), Niblock seems intent on making no contrast at all. He is certainly not interested in constructing a distinct narrative from these ordinary observations of seemingly ordinary things. The editing is virtually non-existent, and Niblock generally presents lengths of footage in the order in which they were shot, with little intervention other than intermittent cuts. There are no fades, no superimposed images and there is no location sound. Yet the documentation of the physically taxing tasks is mesmerizing. It's almost as if the subjects' endurance and fortitude is being projected onto our endurance in watching these yards and yards of film.

The images may appear silent and wilfully 'undirected', but the sound is deafening. The music is a multitracked and, in performance, multispeaker drone that is spatially all-enveloping. It is built from recordings of long notes on flute, bass flute, string quartet and sampled synthetic sounds. A huge E natural, distributed over several octaves, completely saturates aural space and obliterates any sense of natural dimension – unlike Harvey's Gs, it implies no space at all. The sustained notes, continuing unabated for long periods, and the volume level appear to leave no room for any other aural component. Microtonal tunings between different overdubbed drones impose their own timescale and encourage us to turn inwards. These loud microtonal clusters create beats, or difference tones, with the result that the sound is not only almost unbearably loud but has artefacts that invade even inner listening space through an aural hallucination.[30] The overwhelming effect of the music is an obliteration of any possibility of listening to anything other than its presence: there are no gaps, and there is absolutely no escape.

Within each medium, there is an opposition between our normal (that is, learnt) expectations for the medium and what we get. A 45-minute, relentless, microtonally tuned drone that only descends by a tone in the last few minutes (by then, a momentous event) is not what we expect of a soundtrack. A long patchwork of documentary footage is not what we expect of a narrative film, yet neither does this film declare itself unequivocally as purely an ethnographical record. And the complete opposition *between* music and film strengthens this subversion of their conventional respective roles. There are no points of contact between music and image other than those of our own composition. The filmed images are not only of people whose lives are culturally remote to our experience (in the majority of cases), but they are individually remote to us too, obliviously performing everyday routine tasks and getting on with living their present. Like the photograph, they are a recorded image of a past 'present'. And, for us, it is a very distant present since we are completely engulfed in the huge presence of the music. Unlike a movie music soundtrack, where the non-diegetic 'mood music' draws us in to the emotional world of the film, here the music sets us apart behind a screen of sound. But even while the searingly loud music invades the senses, it is almost impossible to ignore the even louder silence on the film. Film and music do battle to occupy the forefront of perception.

As with much of Niblock's work, *China* is, I think, so entirely built on discrepancy that it is in an almost *continuous* state of being able to offer each of us a gap – a punctum, or a metaphorical moment of infinite awareness. When you notice a gap – when one space crashes against another – the bridging of those discrepancies will be an achievement that deafens all else. The moment will be different for everyone. Here's mine.

A glance across the auditorium

... close-up of a man weaving a basket. This cuts to a shot of a herd of goats walking along a lane, moving from left to right across the screen . There are no people. Two young male goat-herders come into view, walking left to right, a third man and then a

fourth come into partial and then complete view, as they all stroll across behind the goats. As they pass the camera the men look at it in a mildly curious way, but without stopping or slowing down. The last man to leave the shot turns his head slightly to keep his eye on the camera as he walks past. There is a brief shot of the empty lane, then a cut to a view from behind of them passing on down the road, walking behind the herd . . . .

Figure 2 Stills from the video *China*, c. 8:30, Phill Niblock. Reproduced by permission

When that man turns his head and gazes back at the camera, I feel as if he has noticed me watching him, and of course he has indirectly, via the recording presence of Niblock and his camera. The opposition of two spaces is heightened by this revelation of a sudden gap in the wall when, it *feels* to me, that he and I meet in a moment out of time. For me, and quite possibly only for me, this is a 'punctum' in this work: suddenly the wall interposed between myself and the image is made explicit. The camera's interposing 'frame' is revealed; the distance between my presentness and the presentness recorded in the work is heightened by the overwhelming presence, but only in *my* present, of sound. (I feel as if the music is suddenly more noticeable at this point, and although it doesn't change significantly there has been a more obvious semitonal inflection.) The discrepancy between my world and the world of the work is so exaggerated as to be completely dissonant. In real terms, the discrepancy between my existence and this man's existence are also 'brought home', as is the discrepancy between the intents of documentary record and art.

In trying to think what might induce this particular significance for me I can suggest several contributory reasons: this moment is preceded by the first footage to feature animals en masse, without human presence, and the men are also the first to show a very noticeable 'group' awareness of the camera; the men come into shot gradually and – unusually – they walk across the shot rather than remaining in one position while they complete a task; they move nearer until they are in close-up, and this sense of changing perspective is also unusual. Aurally, by this stage in the work the electronically projected sound has become my world – I have lost the ability to think in gradated terms of loud and soft. I have long ago abandoned any conscious attempt to find, or create, a relationship between the music and the film. Instead my attention is split – continually traversing listening and viewing, but never synthesizing the two. However, the music is very much closer than the film. It is, literally, inside my ears. The film is further away. I am not expecting any connection between myself and the other place in the film. When I find one, it's a shock.

I could go on interpreting, but there is obviously no decision on Phill Niblock's part to make this particular moment stand out. The lack of any narrative intent, or any association between the two media, puts the onus on the listener/viewer. The possibilities are immense and, as Bachelard suggests, 'since immense is not an object, a phenomenology of immense would refer us directly to our imagining consciousness' (Bachelard, 1994, p. 184).

An image of another place can provide a metaphor for a break in the wall.

An image of a break in the wall can be a metaphor for another place.

Every metaphor has within it a potential for reversibility. The two poles of a metaphor can play the role of the real and the ideal alternately. With these metaphors, the most time-worn expressions, like the flight of ideas, can take on a bit of material substance, a bit of real motion.
(Bachelard, 1988, p. 55)

Notes

1 A gallery of emblem books can be found at http://education.umn.edu/EdPA/iconics/emblem
2 Electronic sound here includes the electronic projection of recorded sound (of any kind), the digital or analogue manipulation of recorded sound and the synthesis of sounds through electronic means.
3 Although the painting is probably more of a collaborative effort, it is generally agreed by experts that Leonardo da Vinci's involvement was significant. But, anyway, this is not so important to my metaphor: the 'Leonardo' I refer to was never flesh and blood, he is my by-line for a construct I have put together; he's a fictionalized artist whose (apparent) motivations validate my somewhat quirky reception of *Annunciation*, a painting executed (mostly, we think) by a man whose name was Leonardo da Vinci.
4 For a detailed exploration of metaphors for the mind see Draaisma, (2000).
5 *Wings of Desire*, dir. Wim Wenders, 1987 (more information at www.imdb.com).
6 It is not only in fictional reality that film attempts to give us wings. In the BBC series *Supersense* (1988, dir. John Downer) specialist camera techniques enabled the viewer to experience flight from the bird's perspective and this kind of 'as if you were really there' filming has become the mainstay of much natural history documentary work.
7 You can tune in and space out at spacemusic.com
8 *Modulations*, dir. Iara Lee, 1998 (more information at www.imdb.com).
9 I wrote an extended piece on this particular work, in relation to narrative and space, in a previously published chapter. I'm resuming briefly from a different perspective. The original chapter is 'Stepping Outside for a Moment: Narrative Space in Two Works for Sound Alone' (in Emmerson, 2000).
10 Study of a sleeve, pen and ink, 7.8 × 9.2 cm. Oxford: Christ Church.
11 'Only the slightest impulse is needed to activate this lightness that prefaces his whole being. It is easy,

and very simple: striking the heel lightly on the ground gives us the impression of being set free. This slight movement seems to free a potential for mobility in us that we had never known, but that our dreams revealed' (Bachelard, 1988, p. 29).

12 'A clear awareness of being able to fly develops in the dreamer's soul' (Bachelard, 1988, p. 20).

13 Pierre Schaeffer's theoretical work on classifying sound 'objects' according to a complex system of typology is still of great significance to the 'acousmatic' school of electroacoustic composition. His three significant publications are *A la Recherche d'une Musique Concrète*, (1952); *Traité des Objets Musicaux*, (1966); *La Musique Concrète*, (1967).

14 For a clear discussion on how this affects listening, see Pierce, 'Hearing in Time and Space' (1999). The 'precedence effect' requires a loudspeaker to be behind the (human) speaker, so that it is further away from the audience. 'If the amplification isn't too great, the audience tends to hear the speaker's voice as coming from the speaker's mouth rather than from the loudspeaker' and, as Pierce goes on to clarify, it also encourages a visual association with the speaker's moving lips.

15 Whole repertoires are selected with that 'in your face' proximity in mind. Information provided by the British group Icebreaker is clear in outlining political and practical requirements for would-be composers:

> Since the band aims to deliver energetic performances that will appeal to a broad audience, pieces which are predominantly loud, aggressive and fast are preferred to those that are perhaps more introverted. ... The music is always amplified, enabling the blending of instruments that don't balance acoustically. The mix is essentially static, however ... .
>
> (Example from promotional material previously posted on Icebreaker's website in 2002)

16 Per quanto riguarda il clarinetto dal vivo, anche quello si potrebbe muovere nello spazio dal punto di vista acustico, ma io ho una grande attenzione per il rapporto tra strumentista e suono, e in genere mi sembra che, soprattutto in un pezzo dove ci sono suoni riprodotti da macchine (cioè senza una corrispondenza visiva), è più giusto mantenere la corrispondenza spaziale tra suono e immagine dello strumentista. (Ceccarelli, email correspondence with Katharine Norman, March 2002. Trans. Katharine Norman)

17 I will use the word 'tape' throughout to refer to the electronic part. More often today this is in reality a CD or computer file, but the word, harking back to the reel-to-reel tape machines that were the first widely used means for playing these types of work, has become almost generic to indicate pre-recorded 'non-live' electronic music.

18 La mia lunga esperienza di lavoro sullo spazio sonoro mi ha sempre più convinto che ogni spazio possiede un suo suono particolare e che questo stesso spazio influenza in modo sostanziale la musica. Questa consapevolezza mi obbliga in ogni mia composizione a pensare a come effettivamente 'suonerà' un certo ambiente e a come sarà, come 'vivrà' la musica dentro di esso.

... Noi sentiamo il suono attraverso lo spazio e quindi sentiamo esclusivamente il suono dello spazio sonoro e mai direttamente la fonte sonora 'pura', che in quanto tale non esiste.

19 For instance, as in the experiments by Ames in which a restricted peephole view encouraged observers to think they were seeing a real chair, when in fact the 'chair' was a collection of unconnected pieces of wire hanging in front of a painted backdrop (see Gombrich, 1960, p. 248).

20 Harvey is acutely aware of the metaphoric significance of electronic sound, remarking elsewhere – in relation to his opera *Inquest of Love*: 'My initial idea was a sound of the sort only electronics can produce, a long static sound in which one could live' (Harvey, 1999, p. 54).

21 See John Chowning's chapter 'Perceptual Fusion and Auditory Perspective' pp. 261–75 in Cook (2000) for a detailed explanation of auditory perspective cues.

22 They share this tendency with Stockhausen's *Trans*, in which the near motionless activity of the ensemble, playing extremely long, sustained notes, is disrupted intermittently by the amplified sound that shuttles back and forth (in fact, the recorded sound of a weaver's shuttle). In both cases time, and space, is of the essence.

23 After I completed the first draft of this chapter I sent it to Jonathan Harvey who pointed me to a passage in his book *In Quest of Spirit* (1999). To my amazement and encouragement he there describes a dream of flight (pp. 54–55). Later, in relation to live electronics, he remarks, 'When they lack connection to the familiar instrumental world, electronics can be overwhelmingly alien – other, inhuman, inadmissible, dismissable (like the notion of flying in a rational world)' (ibid., 1999, p. 62).

24 As in 'a garden enclosed is my sister, my spouse, a fountain sealed, a well of living water, a garden with the fruit of apples' (Cant. iv. 12, 13).

25 The painting measures approximately 7×3 ft – which makes the figures pretty much life-sized in terms of a viewer's perspective, looking 'into' the depth of the painting (and, of course, assuming that angels are of human proportion).

26 In 1435 and 1436, Alberti published *De pictura* in Latin and *Della pittura* in Italian, which contains the earliest known geometric and optical analysis of linear perspective. The book was of great influence (and is cited by Leonardo da Vinci in his writings on perspective). 'First of all, on the surface on which I am going to paint, I draw a rectangle of whatever size I want, which I regard as an open window through which the subject to be painted is to be seen' (Alberti, quoted in Edgerton, 1975, p. 42). This 'open window' principle is often wrongly attributed to Leonardo da Vinci himself.

27 There has been some discussion on whether Leonardo da Vinci did in fact have unusual visual abilities, from those seeking explanations of how – unaided by technology – he could have made such minute and accurate observations of, for example, the flight of birds. For instance: 'There is no doubt that the nerves of his eye and brain, like those of certain famous athletes, were really supernormal, and in consequence he was able to draw and describe movements of a bird which were not seen again until the invention of the slow-motion cinema.' (Clark, 1988, p. 191).

28 Some paintings *require* a sideways look, perhaps the most famous example being Holbein's *The Ambassadors* in the London National Gallery, which employs anamorphic perspective to play a visual trick. There is a good online page about this painting at http://webserver1.oneonta.edu/faculty/farberas/arth/ARTH214/Ambassadors_Home.html

29 The version I am talking about was specifically released on video for 'home' performance, although it is essentially the same format as his performed works.

30 Difference tones are aural artefacts caused when two slightly detuned pitches are played in unison, or more noticeably when across octaves. The artefacts represent the difference in pitch between the two, and so are inharmonically related to the played pitches. This précis of a detailed explanation by David Soldier indicates the physical nature of this auditory hallucination:

> The fundamental pitches stimulate mechanoreceptive cells, the so called 'hair bundles' in the cochlea of the ear, by deflecting a mechanically sensitive 'hinge' on the cell ... With the addition of a second frequency, the cells vibrate not only at the frequencies of the fundamentals and their harmonics, but also at the frequencies of sum, difference and combination tones. ... The hair bundle's new 'hallucinatory' vibrations are transmitted through the ear's basilar membrane, activating other hair bundles in the region of the cochlea responsive to the new frequencies. The auditory nerve, and the cerebral cortex is therefore unable to differentiate between 'real' played frequencies and those arising from this special characteristic of the frequency responsive cells in the ear.
> (David Soldier, leader of the Soldier String Quartet in the liner notes to Niblock, *Five More Quartets*, Experimental Intermedia Foundation 1993, XI 111 ['Further notes by Dave Soldier in his day job capacity as an assistant professor in the departments of neurology and psychiatry at Columbia University'].)

Part 2

Sounding ... worlds

Chapter 3

With no direction home

GET LOST

Let me confide that I have very little sense of direction. When I go for a walk I tend to keep going until I reach halfway (often a difficult concept), then turn on my heel and meander back home by a different path. It *usually* works out OK. Naturally, this approach is best undertaken only if you have no particular place to go and no particular desire to stick to a predefined route. But even an aimless walk still involves a choice at each corner; it's simply a matter of following intuition. That way, arriving home can always be a surprise.

> *The sound of the scouring*
> *Of the saucepan blends*
> *With the tree-frogs' voices.*
> (Ryokan in Watts, 1990, p. 208)

A music made from the sounds of the world can instigate a transcendent, composed listening that re-encounters the familiar as something wonderful. Frogs and saucepans continue oblivious – *listening* is the 'medium' that is composed, and it is the listener who is transformed. But listening arises from individual perception, not from the sounds themselves. Nor does listening make any moral judgements with regard to sounds; no sound is of itself 'good' or 'bad'. The natural sounds of birds, tinkling brooks and insects are appealingly mellifluous, but the raucous clamour of post-industrial society can have its own visceral attraction. And here I am only talking about the content of the sounds, rather than any meaning we might weave from extra-sonic connotations. Likewise, the various approaches to composing with recorded sounds from the 'real world' are not mutually exclusive or hierarchical: they can encompass the abstraction of the Schaefferian *objet sonore*, the ecological concerns espoused by R. Murray Schafer, the apparently passive indeterminacy of Cageian listening and more besides. All these various theoretical approaches have charted ways of mapping the territory yet, even if they are not already attempting to do the engraving themselves, many have been unwittingly inscribed into traditions by the dogged enthusiasm of academic outreach (which, by definition, rarely reaches too far beyond convention). But a good theory is a temporary abstraction for testing out ideas, or a way of thinking: it's a place to start from, rather than end up in; there's no need to make a method of it. But, regardless of all that, listening can be a substantial matter.

But is there a way of expressing listening through sounds in time, comparable to film's monopoly on seeing through the moving image? Film narrative certainly speaks through images of real things, 'from life'. Although a film requires a ridiculous amount of equipment and intervention to get it off the ground, on watching the end result it feels to be just you – and you just *looking* – at a world in moving pictures. Simplistically put, the images are reflected back on you – an individual – and on how you *see*. How often do you pull up a chair in an auditorium to just be aware of you, just *listening* to a representation of the world, in moving sounds? Can the end result of a sonic work be (or feel to be) a map of the world where sounds reverberate towards you – an individual who listens?

In Krzysztof Kieslowski's 1991 film, *The Double Life of Véronique*, the eponymous heroine receives an unidentified cassette tape in the post. On listening repeatedly to the recorded sequence of mystery sounds, she gradually identifies specific places and actions that lead her towards a station café, where her anonymous admirer awaits. This enigmatic film questions what is real at every turn, starting from the premise that the French Véronique and her alter ego in Poland, Weronika, are unwitting doubles, whose lives follow strangely parallel courses. And, as you might expect, the film is replete with visual allusions to reflection and doubles. But in devoting a significant portion of a film to a reading of sound, Kieslowski also brings images of listening to the fore. And, after all, listening could be heard as the neglected mirror image of looking – cinema's usual obsession. But the recorded sound images are just images – pale reflections of the objects that made them – that lead the listening heroine to her physical goal. As usual, listening is a supporting character to sight.

MAPPAE MUNDI

⊙ CD[7]

You got enough to tag along? I hope so, because a map is a composed intermediary that intends to be read: there need to be at least two people involved in making sense of it. Although I'm relying on you, I'll admit that the sound recording wasn't much good for the purpose. Most maps (you see) are visual representations that tell us what to 'look out' for. This is natural, since landmarks are stable and, in human terms, lasting objects, while soundmarks – a term coined by composer and sound ecologist R. Murray Schafer – tend to change more rapidly over time. So the conventional map[1] does its visible work without a murmur. And nobody complains, although if in reality the world fell completely silent, we would stop and shake out our ears in disbelief. But it is not the sounds or their absence that I want to chart here, but listening.

Although some of the first maps in existence were simply written lists of directions, maps more usually represent an area compactly, in a reduced, diagrammatic form. The map is an explanatory tool that assists a journey from A to B, whether the territory is the surface of Mars, the intricacies of the human genome, or simply a conceptual means to think your way around a problem. Obviously, maps are not solely practical guides for physical travel, they can also enlarge our personal horizons and help us understand things we may never see (or hear) in reality ourselves. We may never go there, but we can still imagine how the journey might have been. You can imagine listening to silence too, although it is a country you will never visit.

In the late 1200s, probably whilst holed up in a freezing cathedral in Lincoln (an area of England so bleak and flat as to belie today's knowledge that the world is round), Richard de Bello carefully inscribed an ornate 'mappa mundi'. This large map, which became known as the Hereford map, offers one way of seeing the world; its vellum surface is crammed with drawings of mythical creatures, descriptions of monsters and strange semi-human beings, and the whole thing is optimistically topped with a detailed rendition of the Last Judgement.[2] Is this effusive cosmology drawn, in any sense at all, from life? Richard's travels didn't amount to much more than a few trips between various ecclesiastical establishments. But although his world-view might have been restricted, his inner vision ran riot, nourished both by reports brought back by explorers, and symbolism brought forth from medieval Christianity. For Richard, as for his contemporaries, the monsters were very real. Even so, accurate images are hardly necessary for following this particular map's direction, where it's the underlying sermon that counts, for or against your personal salvation. (So – however inaccurate its proportions – the mappa mundi is still a route-map of a kind.)

Today the world tends to extend outwards from our own domain. Our relationship with contemporary maps is often avowedly self-centred. An arrow or a blinking light proclaims 'you are here!', and that – along with 'which way's "up"?' – is enough to start our trip to the cathedral. But it wasn't always that way. Medieval maps often placed Jerusalem, the Holy City, in the middle and heaven to the East – this was a familiar orientation (a literal turn 'to the east') in a society where the individual was not as prized as now. Yet some knowledge that we share with Richard, cloistered in his medieval cell, is that both map-making and map-reading can provoke powerful journeys of imagination. If I spin a globe, unfold a street-map, or spread out a nautical chart between us on the table, I immediately bring a possibility just that bit closer. Reading a map is never an objective activity, since it is an aid to envisaging how a place – real, imagined or desired – might be, in reality. Running a finger across a printed meridian I commence the fiction that I might know the wider world, in all its detail. Yes, even the most dreamy perusal of a map of an unknown place is an attempt to put one's self in the picture. Like Richard, we sometimes pin back our ears to hear travellers' tales from afar.

⊙ **CD[8]**

Incidentally, those same medieval explorers who brought back the tales of incredible beasts and peoples that decorate Richard's mappa mundi also created their own preferred map, which came to be known as the portolan. These portolans charted the ins and outs of a coastline with obsessive, filigree care, but usually neglected to describe the interior at all; it was hardly of concern while you were bobbing about at sea, trying to navigate in zero-vision. For both monk and explorer a great deal remained unseen, and was taken on faith as being (they hoped and prayed) just beyond their view.

But I am spending all this time poring over historical details, and there's no real listening going on. You are waiting for all this sound to speak up for itself? If mapping – on paper or in the mind – is inherently visual, how is it possible to reverse the situation so that listening becomes the first port of call, and looking is deemed inessential for the moment? How can we do it?

⏵ CD[9]

In reality, it is usually quicker to describe the world in visual terms – tall trees, rocky outcrops, green, the sea in the distance, and scuddy clouds above. With our speedy vision to rely on, why would we bother with unseen birds and distant planes? We take this perceptual preference for granted and chart our environment accordingly. And when we make that chart, we gaze out from the middle of our world – life is a panorama that rotates around our sight. When sight fails, literally or figuratively, the world stops turning.

> Here is another feature of the acoustic world: it stays the same whichever way I turn my head. … The view looking that way is quite different from the view looking this way. It is not like that with sound. New noises do not come to my attention as I turn my head around. … Perhaps there is some slight shading of quality, but the acoustic world is mainly independent of my movement. This heightens the sense of passivity.
> (Hull, 1990, pp. 82–83)

The world is what we, via our senses, make of it. Just by perceiving the world, we create a map that is peopled with symbols, similes, comparisons, and other interpretations. (See that woman over there? She looks just like my mum.) Through our mapped listening we may or may not identify the vestigial sounds of a late-night stroll in Dublin, a dusty street in Havana or the sea on a wild Northumberland shore. It depends on our experience – did you recognize any of them? How did you recognize them – and by how much? All our attempts at mapping the territory create an imaginative palimpsest through which we reveal as much about ourselves as the world we try to describe. Like poor Richard (still in Lincolnshire, shivering towards heaven) perception inevitably peers out from the window of experience and cultural context. And, in this spirit, perhaps all works of art are *mappae mundi* of a kind. But while mapping and looking walk hand-in-hand, listening still stumbles along belatedly. How can we stride out confidently, when we're not sure where we are just yet? It takes time to get your bearings with sound.

So is it due to lack of practice? We are not used to thinking about listening to sound in our lives, so how can we make listening into art? Perhaps listening as a means of expression is difficult to rely on. Certainly, in real life, we rarely even sketch a map through listening and then invite someone else to read it. But I would expect no less of

Hildegard Westerkamp, whose entire work as a composer is focused on the sounds of the natural environment, what they might mean, and how we might listen to them:

> This is a typical sound.
>   We have the very high, peeping sounds of the birds that are way up in the trees. Can you hear them? ... they're very quiet. And then you have the sea planes ... that's Lighthouse Park.
> (Hildegard Westerkamp, in conversation with the author, April 2002)

Have we just forgotten how to listen? Perhaps there were times when we did listen more acutely: R. Murray Schafer feels that 'the elaborate earwitness descriptions in works like the Bible and *A Thousand and One Nights* suggest that they were produced by societies in which sonological competence was highly developed' (Schafer, 1977/1994, p. 154). But it seems that, nowadays, the developed world tends always to look first and listen later – if at all. The television announcer who warns you about 'disturbing footage' is suggesting that you might want to avert your eyes. You can turn your head away, you don't have to look. But once you start listening, you cannot avoid the starving child's anguished cry or the scream of marauding hyenas. How often are you warned about those? And, of course, this is why 'noise pollution' is so defined and is such an aggravation: the unwanted sound is inescapable and outside our personal control – and yet we can't help but listen.

But map-reading leaves room for personal interpretation. Are you with me? Certainly we can huddle over the map together, planning that walk on the coast. But perhaps you see yourself marching along with the wind at your back, and the song of the sea in your ears, while I pessimistically envisage trudging along a bleak sea wall, clutching the street-map and hurrying to find the house before the weather changes. Even in your mind's eye, you can never quite duplicate my journey. Similarly, we each bring our Self to listening – everyone's idea of noise is different.

A one-to-one map of the world

In 1971 R. Murray Schafer founded the World Soundscape Project (the WSP), basing it in the Communication Studies department of Simon Fraser University, Vancouver. Along with a group of like-minded researchers, among them composers Barry Truax and Hildegard Westerkamp, he set out to chart the sonic environment and make an archive collection of recordings and studies of sound. The research that has arisen from this project ranges from sociological studies to musical composition and continues to inform many studies of listening and the sonic environment. Among these studies, and similar related studies internationally, are a great many visual maps of sound environments.[3]

In 1996 the WSP, under the aegis of Cambridge Street Records,[4] published a fascinating two-CD collection, charting the soundscape of Vancouver through both recordings and soundscape compositions. Archive recordings made around 1973, and released then as *The Vancouver Soundscape*,[5] are complemented by a group of composed works, made in 1996 from Vancouver soundscape recordings, and a documentary comparing the changing soundscape, featuring Truax and Westerkamp. Although there are an increasing number of recordings of soundscapes, in part due to the ease and relative inexpensiveness of disseminating CDs, this collection is unusual because it listens across time, and from a variety of perspectives. With its mix of composed responses to sound recordings, documentary and straightforward archive material, it offers a range of mapping techniques. Some are more directive than others, but all draw attention to our listening relationship with the soundscape that surrounds us, as much as to the sounds themselves. And the members of the WSP unashamedly take an overtly activist stance, drawing attention to those sounds which, it is generally accepted, pollute and disrupt human experience – air conditioning hums, traffic density, ugly electronic sound signals and so on – as much as those (not always natural) sounds that evoke sonic well-being and pleasure. The message is that the presence of the unwanted man-made sounds could have been avoided if more consideration had been given not only to listening, but to listening as part of a more holistic perception of the environment. When Hildegard Westerkamp points out that the tourists taking a trip on the seabus have to 'listen to this sound for the ten or so minutes that it takes to cross – visually spectacular – Vancouver harbour' she is deploring the schism between visual and aural perception as much as the level of noise.

ⓓ CD[10] excerpt from 'The Changing Soundscape' (from *The Vancouver Soundscape* CD)

Archives such as the World Soundscape Project, and a growing selection of small online collections of field-recordings and 'soundmarks', make a point purely by being there as museums of sound. They map a territory that has shrunk, and they draw our attention to a need for preservation, as poignant reminders of what we should take pains to keep, or may have already lost. Cloth-eared perambulists, we totter around noisily, while failing to notice that sounds have disappeared. For instance, the British sparrow has declined significantly in numbers over the last 8–10 years – one survey suggests by as much as 59 per cent in the South-east of England[6] – and one suggested reason for this decline is that the level of ambient noise has prevented the birds from communicating with each other. My own piece, *London E17*, made in 1993, opens with garden recordings in which the sounds of chattering sparrows were omnipresent. Now, in 2003, those sounds are far less noticeable in the aural landscape.

So, recordings of lost or endangered sounds create a nostalgic map of the past that subtly nudges us towards a listening that can inform a moral belief. Much of the fervour concerning the preserving of 'threatened' sound environments arises from an ethical stance that regrets post-industrial humankind's unthinking effect on the natural environment as a whole – although, of course, sound ecology[7] charts the sounds and environments we should nurture not *only* on ethical grounds, but also because they are beautiful, widely accepted as enjoyable and uplifting aspects of human experience. But, put more neutrally, sound archives map the course of historical change itself, and sometimes change is neither for better nor worse but is merely revealing. An archive sound recording can be as fascinating as a historical map that shows landmarks that have long since disappeared underneath layers of new building or through natural changes in the landscape. Perhaps preservation for the sake of it can be unnecessary or misleading, even damaging: another suggested reason for the sparrow's decline is the artificial reintroduction of the sparrowhawk, for whom it is natural prey.[8]

A field-recording need not be of 'nature' – animals, wildlife and the like – but often is. These kinds of sounds are exotic to city-sated ears, and sometimes a rather questionable exoticism has a part to play. Like the intrepid explorer, the field-recordist often goes out 'into the wild', employing the language of the hunter – 'on safari', 'capturing sound'. These terms are ironically transliterated to that most passive of occupations – listening – with subverted activist enthusiasm. The hunter brings back the prized game, unusual and from foreign parts, and transplants it from the wild and untamed 'jungle' to the domestic interior, where it can be displayed on the wall (via loudspeakers). And, quite understandably, field-recordings are often made away from home, when on a visit to a strange and compelling environment where strange new sounds accost the listener from every corner. Then the traveller returns, goes online and tells stories.[9] On the homepage of the 'Phonography' group, Isaac Sterling provides an intelligent essay exploring what 'phonography' might mean, could mean, and might be becoming. Here is an extract from his thoughtful consideration:

> The simple answer is that phonography (literally 'sound-writing') refers to field-recording. ... Auditory events are selected, framed by duration and method of capture, and presented in a particular format and context, all of which distinguishes a recording from the original event during which it was captured. ... Some useful analogies can be made between phonography and photography. The majority of early photographs were intended to be documentary or forensic, and many field-recordings serve these same purposes. ... [but] a new generation of recordists has emerged, preoccupied with the abstract and formal dimensions of captured environmental sound.
> (Isaac Sterling, www.phonography.org/whatis.htm)

The beauty of the field-recording – of any documentary sound recording – is that this bounded slice of life can be yours, dear listener, to take home and enjoy in the comfort of your sitting room. You can make sense of it in your own way, and in your own time – and away from reality, without the distraction of mosquitoes or pungent smells. I find it a joyous thing that more and more pairs of ears are out there, not only listening and recording the world but also – and this is even more glorious – sharing the results through a simple, generous exchange of attractive or engaging soundscapes. But, as Sterling's words indicate, there is a blurring of distinction between a documentary field-recording and a recording that is subsequently composed in a response to the sound environment (however indirect that response may be). Sometimes the difference is hard to chart but, I think, a field-recording *per se* is not the best map from which to navigate through listening.

Although the field-recording appears to provide a perfectly-formed map of at least a small fragment of the world, of course it doesn't: it is an ambiguous representation, whose maker faces some of the same problems encountered by ethnographers of all kinds. Just by virtue of pressing 'record' when something interesting comes along, a choice has been made. Sound recordists, just as much as anthropologists, have to guard against their own deciding presence if they want an unmediated documentation of a time and place. But of course they can't, and quite often they don't want to. Many sound recordings are, indirectly or not, making a quiet point from behind the microphone. That point is that we should prick up our ears to the sonic environment, cease making noise for a moment, in order to fill the space it leaves with listening. But I also think that sometimes it is easy to get a little waylaid by the moral obligation we might feel towards our sounding world, and in particular towards the fragile beauty of the natural environment in sound. There is a difference between expressing what sound means or can indicate about the world outside, and expressing how listening feels, in terms of the inner world of self.

Perhaps you just cannot have it all. As allegorized by Borges, a map that fully depicted a country on a 1-to-1 scale would be useless and obstructive, best abandoned to 'the Inclemencies of Sun and Winters'.[10] Such a ridiculously accurate representation of reality would reduce the cartographer to a functionary who, while noting every sensation faithfully, had failed to perceive a jot.

If by some quantum leap in technology I could secretly record the sounds outside your window and play them back to you simultaneously in real time, *exactly replacing* what's there, would you notice a difference? If there was no difference to perceive, then there would be no point in doing it – or, rather, there would be no way of making a point through your listening. For, as Borges quietly asserts through the gentle suggestion of fable, the entirety of reality is impossible to chart; any belief that we might manage to do so misconstrues the power of the map. A map-maker makes choices on what to leave in, what to draw attention to and what to leave *out* – and why. (A street-map doesn't have room to show the lie of the land and a geological survey has little interest in indicating political divisions.) In fact, a good map is, in some ways, a poor representation that makes its viewpoint known through a filtering of information. This still leaves room for each individual cartographer to chart a multitude of different realities, whether they are physical, imagined or metaphorical.

Sometimes that filtering process occurs by virtue of the artefacts – sounds themselves can be gathered into collections that map out a period of time or delineate a particular geography. Listening becomes a process of mapping connections and reading the map-maker's intent. But there has to be a difference between the map and the ground it covers.

Like home, but different

Here, listen now:

A motorized barge approaches, coming slowly towards you. The rumbling of a passing train emerges and then accompanies the boat engine, which continues its slow approach, gets louder, passes from left to right and then recedes: the sound departs just as slowly, taking its time; the boat continues to chunter away in the background, because it is still there. This is representation of a time.

Here, listen again to the same place from another angle – this time in your ears:

◉ CD[11] 'Canalside atmosphere', recorded by Peter Cusack (track 6 of his CD)

Peter Cusack's sound recordings were collected in a small patch of north-east London called the Lea Valley, an area of ungentrified marshland that survives alongside a canal, between a tatty mass of housing and a tangle of local railway lines. I know this place well because I used to live just down the road. But now you know it too. Maybe you could come to know those sounds far better than I can, because I am forever reminded of the actual sights that accompanied them whereas you are there, right now, listening. Actually, this is not a straightforward documentation, but a carefully structured listening adventure. Mostly, that structure has been imposed at the time of recording, by the path of the microphone as it seeks out some sounds and encounters others. Occasionally, the sounds are edited a little to bring them into relationship with another. The mix is subtle, and the effect is, I find, riveting. I never knew the place could sound like that (until I listened). However, it would be evasive, I think, to call this experience 'music'. And Cusack – in other guises a composer and performer of some renown – doesn't: he bills the CD as 'sound recordings', with himself as author. The difficulty (if only in finding a way to describe them) is that these sound recordings are more than archive documentation. They are a map, drawn by an expert listener.

A particular aspect of Cusack's mapping of the sound environment that I find interesting is the equivocal choice of duration. Many field-recordings of the environment are much longer than the average musical work: the world takes time to unfold, and perhaps a lengthier duration also allows time to forget time, and also to forget self. And this is surely why so many of the more execrable 'new age' ambient recordings are CD-length meanders through birds, waves or other unchallenging sonic surroundings. A more didactic approach goes to the other extreme, with sounds offered as neatly labelled 'exhibits'. For instance, a website for 'Listening to Nature – A Sound Walk Across California'[11] lists indigenous birds and wildlife, with sketches (not photographs) of each, accompanied by a brief written description and a click and play environmental sound recording of the animal in question. Although the animals are no longer stuffed and arranged in glass cases, I fear they might as well be in terms of listening.

Cusack is somewhere in the middle. There are short recordings of bird cries and frogs chirruping, but they are just long enough to create a little window on their world. There are written descriptions of what made what sound, but these are brief notes that provide minimum information. And, at the other extreme, even the longer recordings are – at around two minutes or so in duration – too short to become background ambience. You have to listen; you don't have time to zone out. In fact, the locality is often mapped in quite an upfront, directed way. The CD as a whole is an engaging mix of environmental 'nature' recordings and oral history interviews with 'old-timers' who have worked on the canal and have anecdotes to tell. The careful choice of track order, the fragmentary liner notes, a few haunting photos to set the scene, the inclusion of the sounds of people just getting on with life and sharing an amusing tale or two: all these surreptitiously invite you to pause a moment and listen while Cusack maps out his mappa mundi. Although there is virtually no processing or other sonic interference in these environmental recordings, there is definitely an authorial 'voice' behind the microphone which invites us to listen from another angle – even, on several occasions, underwater, from the earpoint of a frog. The experience of wonder from this simple, inhuman, inversion of the world is extraordinarily potent.

Cusack's recordings are a celebration of listening to what is there, in his community – an unexpected police encounter, motorized vehicles, rowing boats, rattling trains, joggers, dogs that bark annoyingly and even a nightingale recorded next to an electric power station (a superimposition offered by nature, not Cusack). The irony of encountering this rarely heard birdsong next to the mundane trilling of a transformer is offered without comment. All you need to do is listen.

A diversion from the normal route

[Bakerloo (brown), Piccadilly (dark blue), Metropolitan (pink), East London (orange), Jubilee (silver-grey), Northern (black), District (Green), Circle (yellow), Victoria (blue)]

Faster now, I'm on the move. The maps are different here. Train schedules measure out journeys in minutes taken rather than distance run, so there's very little to see. And underground – enclosed and without a view from the window to distract attention – all territories are mapped in terms of personal space. Reality contracts, and so does time. I am squashed into a seat that, at this moment, is my personal micro-empire but, a mere three seconds later, will be occupied by another individual whose feelings are equally proprietary. There is barely time to smell the beery breath of my snoring neighbour or to have my elbow nudged by someone's briefcase, before the doors slide open to reintegrate these passing sensations as part of a more extensive reality where I'm merely late for work. Outside, I catch my breath in the real world, and those individuals no longer exist. I am a face surrounded by a faceless crowd. Quick – onwards – alone into the rush hour.

Well-travelled routes, followed and refollowed with unthinking expertise, can engrave another map that leads from one recollected experience to another – indeed from one stage in life to another. And these odysseys of personal memory, perhaps we like to think, help define us as individuals: they map our histories. So for me – as for thousands and thousands of other Londoners – the London Underground 'tube' map can trigger a one-person theatre of memory. As I sit on the train, gazing absentmindedly at the diagram representing one line or another, powerful associations colour every station with its own traveller's tale – no, *my* traveller's tale. The silvery-grey of the Jubilee Line shimmers away to the distant reaches of Willesden, to buy semi-transparent manuscript paper printed from metal plates (themselves anachronistic maps of etched staves and clefs); in the same vein, the Northern Line still snakes darkly and inexorably upwards to dreary oboe lessons in Highgate; the Victoria Line's optimistic bright blue belies the gloom of the ghastly bedsit in Finsbury Park; and South Kensington's yellow-green splice is, regardless of the time of year, a sunny school trip to the Natural History Museum, with cheese and tomato sandwiches eaten outside on the grass, and – from another time – a market stall festooned with strings of hippy beads.

Any novelist will tell you that half the trick is encouraging the reader to become the character but, really, I've gone too far. None of this wallowing is going to be of great interest to you unless I dress it up a bit more or universalize the 'feeling' in some way. Although we might sit down and exchange comparable memories, you can never share my precise feelings for Finchley Road. You may even be a bit embarrassed by my gauche revelations because a personal reminiscence is a self-indulgent map – best not for public use. But I'm enjoying the map-reading process now, looking back (how often do you *listen* back?) over past times. Yet, even if all this remembering is fiction, you don't want to bother with reading my map unless there's something in it for you. And I think that this can also be a problem with both making and 'reading' works made from documentary sound: sometimes they intend to express how it feels, but end up expressing how it was. And these are not the same at all.

Despite the wealth of extraordinary sound environments in the world outside the window, it seems to me, especially from my experience of working with beginning composers, that many first experiments in working with recorded sounds are explorations of home (I certainly include myself in this). Equipped with binaural headphones and a digital tape recorder, sound-gatherers are suddenly introduced to a heightened awareness of their own domestic habitat – and sometimes respond with the enthusiasm of explorers encountering an undiscovered country. Every little detail is fascinating and new, and worthy of collection. Fortunately, the only real side-effects of this particularly healthy altered state are recordings which contribute to pieces that often convey a palpable sense of astonishment at so much interesting sound going on, right before your ears. Kettles boiling, toilets flushing, water going down the plughole; alarm clocks, televisions and radios, computer keyboards; bacon sizzling, coke cans snapping (not to mention coke snorting, on one memorable occasion), footsteps, laughter, talking, phone calls, various bodily noises – all these and many more regularly feature in a litany of everyday listening brought into unexpected focus.

Frequently, I think, for the maker the piece is an extraordinarily evocative reminder of that listening 'astonishment' they felt. They not only wrote the map, but visited the country first. And any listener can sense and enjoy that with them to an extent. But for a map-reader who comes along later in search of routes that lead further, astonishment is limited to this one particular path. I don't think that the astonishment at listening to ordinary sounds afresh necessarily wears off (I fervently hope it never will) but, in order to really develop a composed *listening* to the world, the self-directed voice of the audio diary needs to subsumed within a more profound response.

TRAIN OF THOUGHT

⏵ CD[12] Pendlerdrøm ('Commuterdream'), by Barry Truax (excerpt)

Pendlerdrøm is a composition that explores metaphors of travel through explicit sound associations. At one level this piece paints a familiar scene. The sounds that open the piece are immediately recognizable to most of the Western world as a generic soundscape from a bustling station environment, which is soon revealed more fully through the sounds of tannoy announcements, trains and various electronic beeps and signals. Although entirely invisible, this is definitely the real world.

Footsteps and human bustle (but not much distinct talking)
Voice announcements
Children's voices
Blowing a nose
Laughter
Electronic beeping – (lift, lift doors closing, rattling?)
Electronic chimes … then the sounds of people disembarking into another space
Sounds of trains arriving and departing
Squealing brakes
Pneumatic door opening, and air-brake hissing

I'll bet you knew them all. The daily train commute is one activity where the primacy of vision happily lapses for a while; the boredom of repetition provides time to listen. The commute can be done with eyes closed, and frequently is, since the time begrudgingly spent on travelling is a necessary practicality and there is no 'desire', no sense of discovery, no reasons to journey other than those of obligation and necessity. On the train we are passive, acquiescent and life (like sound) comes to us. We have relinquished control – hoping to arrive on schedule but knowing we can do nothing to ensure it. Perhaps our only desire is that, given a magic wand (or perhaps a lottery win), we too could click our heels and find ourselves back home in an instant. And this desire to evade the clock already leaves a chink open for listening to creep forward.

What Truax recognizes, of course, is that the 'idea' of commuting has little to do with which train you catch, or if you catch a train at all. Those familiar sounds are symbolic of a darker Kafkaesque nightmare of being unwillingly locked into habitual tedium, unable to escape from the eye of time, trapped in a greyness that has no variety but will, on the contrary, be identical for ever – day after day after day. In suggesting ways of re-perceiving a familiar sonic environment, Truax – like many other composers of 'soundscape' work – is also suggesting a transfiguration of our normal response to the mundane. And this can be a means of escape. At two points in *Pendlerdrøm* the sounds of trains arriving and departing are moulded into lyrical drones, tuned to perceivable 'musical' pitches and time-stretched by Truax's trademark technique of granular synthesis. The harmonic choices are consonant, and the natural sonic contours of trains passing through the stations are perfect candidates for a slow reverie. During this brief encounter with listening, time stands still; and when time stands still all obligations disappear. You can be anywhere you want.

> *Pendlerdrøm* (1997) (or 'Commuterdream') is a soundscape composition that recreates a commuter's trip home from the Central Train Station in Copenhagen. At two points, one in the station and the other on the train, the commuter lapses into a daydream in which the sounds that were only half heard in the station return to reveal their musical qualities. It is hoped that the next day the commuter will hear the musicality of the station's soundscape in a different manner as a result of the dream; the rest of us may discover the very same aspects the second time we hear the work.
> (Barry Truax, from the liner notes to the CD, *Islands*)

Pendlerdrøm is a little unusual for Truax, in that the sounds were provided for him by a Danish group, SKRAEP. And, similarly, many composers have made pieces from the source recordings collected by the various members of the World Soundscape Project. Possibly, for a composer, it helps when the sound environment you are processing is slightly unfamiliar to start with, even to you. Not being an involved participant in the original 'time' you are now dealing with as material offers a degree of distance that can facilitate abstraction.

But Truax's piece is, at root, a documentary work that invites a few moments of unexpected, musical reflection yet doesn't intend to stray too far from the real world – it wouldn't succeed if it did. This is a music that composes a narrative through listening, and where a way of listening provides a map to read. The absence of discovery, revelation and desire in the daily commute (in reality or as metaphor) is supplanted by the encouragement of discovery, revelation and desire in our listening response to sound. One map overlays the other.

Alternative transport

I once had a car embellished with 'go faster' stripes, giving it the appearance of a turbo-charged racer. It frequently broke down. I would have preferred stripes of the 'go further' variety. However, although I have no great attachment to cars of any kind, hearing the heavy sound of a car door clunking shut, at night, somewhere in the distance, evokes a certain feeling of nostalgia in me. I don't know why, and 'nostalgia' is the wrong word really. I can't quite place it on the map.

Maps require an imaginative comparison between two different territories, the one on the page and the one outside the window. (Look, there's the turning, can't you see?) For map-reading to serve its purpose you need to make a connection between the real and representation. So there you sit with the road atlas open on your lap, torch wobbling in one hand, while the car bumps over the unmade track until your driver admits – finally – that you're irretrievably lost. Listening for clues doesn't help one iota, when all you can hear is a complaining engine and the hum of your buzzing thoughts. Stop the car and get out for a moment. Stand still. It's night time, and the summer air is full of whirring emanations. Close your eyes, and listen for the way it feels to hear the world. Listen differently from associating (or not associating) the object and the sound. Listen differently from dreaming back and forth between reality and its transformation. Listen – where are we? Unfold a new map of familiar territory and start again. The quality of the subjective feeling that accompanies our experience of smelling freshly ground coffee or of stroking fur or of being incredibly happy or sad is impossible to map adequately in words. These types of unchartable subjective experience – for which the philosophical term 'qualia' has been coined – are beyond articulation. We can't get near: I don't know what it feels like, for *you*, to be sad. But I do know that when we feel sad, we are each aware that it makes us feel a certain way. All we can share reliably is the knowledge that we feel it, and that we can somehow stand 'outside' the window of our sense of being, to *know* that we feel it.

The study of consciousness continues its intellectual struggle to pin down whether qualia are indeed a product of a separate, individual 'self' through which we amass and use perception of the world, or if the notion of consciousness as self is an illusory creation of the brain.[12] I would not presume here to venture into the treacherous waters of philosophical discourse, where qualia occupy a subdivided field of thinking that goes well beyond any general use of the word. However, like author David Lodge, I would draw attention to the connections between the impossibility of articulating qualia and literature's endeavours to 'simulate' them through a lyric use of metaphor and simile. Lodge quotes a passage from Anne Michael's *Fugitive Pieces*, which describes a street after a heavy snowfall. He draws attention to her poetic imagery: 'by describing each quale in terms of something else that is both similar and different – "a salt cave", "a theatre of whiteness", "like frozen waves" – the object and the experience of it are vividly simulated' (Lodge, 2002, p. 13).

Though all but useless at doing what words usually do, these strange conjunctions go some way towards describing the quale of 'experiencing a response to new snowfall' without resorting to simple description, which would conjure up a picture but not a subjective experience. The confusion as to what language is 'doing' deflects our response towards an awakening of the *feeling* we have on seeing a street transfigured by pristine snow. Words go beyond themselves, and beyond describing any individual's 'real' experience (fictionalized or otherwise). As Lodge comments, 'the method of lyric poetry is ... to use language in such a way that the description of qualia does not seem partial, imprecise, and only comprehensible when put in the context of the poet's personal life' (Lodge, 2002, p. 11). This kind of poetic language short-circuits normal sense – and provides an opportunity to navigate towards a subjective experience. The reader does the navigating. I think that there is a way of composing sound that shares this kind of lyric juxtaposition and allows the listener to navigate, through listening, towards their *own* feeling of reality in sound.

Here is an illustrative example:

⊙ CD[13] *Night Traffic*, by Paul Lansky (excerpt)

This ten-minute work maps a musical chart onto a real world sound. The sounds of traffic on a busy highway are tuned to bring out musical pitches, themselves extracted, by digital 'comb-filtering', from the inherent qualities of the recorded sound material. A dark, but strangely familiar, soundscape ensues. But this is no composed toing and froing between representation and reverie. Any travel is the listener's intuitive choice. Musical processes and real-world sounds are fused in a conjunction that is not unlike the 'salt cave' simile that Lodge quotes above, which describes the feeling of experiencing new snow, but has nothing – on the face of it – to do with it at all. To speak of sonic abstraction is meaningless in this work by Lansky, because the subject of listening to *Night Traffic* is the *feeling* of listening itself.

The sonic abstraction of traditional *musique concrète* essentially inserts the *objet sonore* into an abstract musical discourse. Here, listening for meaning is 'reduced' (Pierre Schaeffer's term). Reduction is relative and so implies some kind of comparison. We are still map-reading in the old, familiar way, keeping an eye on the real world outside the window and trying to match things up. But I think that Lansky's work is abstract, in a way that completely undermines intellectual priorities. This piece does not sound like a highway at night, but listening to it awakes that particular qualia – what listening to the highway *feels* like. How? The sounds of traffic appear recognizable – in contour, shape, pace. The representation of traffic is transparent. Similarly the musical framework is a clear 'representation' that is recognizable – pitches, rhythm and so on. Neither of these would work alone; it is in their (literal) confusion that the lyric simile resides. An epic field-recording of untouched traffic sounds would be too literally a 'picture' of a sound. An abstract musical work that presented a slow, aimless voice-leading harmony would be a pleasant diversion. But the two together offer a mutual confusion.

And this apparently straightforward processing of traffic sounds has bugged me for years. I feel I am only just beginning to understand how to read my map of it. It is not a descriptive piece at all. Because it starts as it is, and continues much the same, there are no explicit opportunities for flipping between listening to sounds and following memories or associations. The whole thing is a continuing 'entity' that carries on into the darkness – timeless and immutable. It does not go on with any place in mind. Listening to it is, essentially, simply beyond the trivialities of making associations with a source. Of *course* those are trucks and cars. The sounds become irrelevant: within a short time, listening becomes a purely subjective response to the feelings such sounds evoke.

To be on your own

Another, last, subjective anecdote: at one time I frequented a tiny formal garden whose solitary stone bench proclaimed the biblical suggestion: 'Come ye yourselves apart, into a quiet place, and rest awhile' (Mark 6: 31). In this one-person space, really little more than a couple of glorious azaleas and a miniature pond, I felt completely alone, even though the busy world outside was still perfectly visible a few steps beyond the wall. The world must have been audible too yet, strangely, I can't remember hearing any sound at all.

Imagine that other kind of map, where there is no commitment to disembark at any one station. You can take any road you please. If you wish, you can walk for a long while, or you can just sit still and travel. There is no direction home. Perhaps this map represents a territory that we long to chart on a 1-to-1 scale although, in reality, we know nothing about this imagined land. There are few everyday moments for the kind of reflection that proceeds from listening to a mapping of our inner spiritual universe. Maybe you can take away the view. There might be advantages to a more passive reading of the world. In any case, perhaps a tentative simulacrum is the most we should hope to create from the depths of our Platonic cave. But I do not think that the kind of mapping that transcends ordinary landscapes comes, necessarily, from an acquiescent listening response to the world. As Robert Louis Stevenson once cloyingly remarked, 'the world is so full of a number of things'; but, although a full and boundless experience of listening to the world is one thing, there is a benefit in the bone-clean purity of emptiness, where nothing is known. Perhaps there you can listen to sounds that are white as azaleas and as pure as water in a shimmering pond. But take away even these similes and comparisons (throw away the maps) and then you really know nothing. And that's different again.

> ... the function of negative knowledge is not unlike the uses of space – the empty page upon which words can by written, the empty jar into which liquid can be poured, the empty window through which light can be admitted, and the empty pipe through which water can flow. Obviously the value of emptiness lies in the movements it permits or in the substance which it mediates and contains.
>
> (Watts, 1990, p. 57)

⊙ CD[14] *untitled #90*, by Francisco Lopez (excerpt)

I don't know what any of these sounds are. And I don't know what I mean by that – what are they 'of', 'for', 'about', 'doing'? Behind a screen of processing there are glimpses of – I think, for a while – waves breaking, insects calling, birds singing. For a few minutes I am straining my ears to hear connections. I can't hear them. I can't use them. But there is this loud, insistent, high-pitched tone – not superimposed, but part of it (whatever 'it' is) – that blasts through like ... no – no *similes* please. It is not a sound to identify, or to care to identify. This sound is at such a high pitch (literally and in terms of volume and intensity) that I cannot do anything but be aware that it is something I do not 'know'. This sound is a singular, 'thing' of a sound, but other than that it is unknown. And it goes on for a long while – over 40 minutes in fact (though measuring time is impossible here) – shifting gear a miniscule amount here and there, working towards every crevice of listening and pushing tentacles into perception. This unyielding experience transfixes a moment of listening that goes on for ever and, instead of changing, becomes more and more profound. And there was really no point in writing all that down because, for you, it will have been different. 'It' is my listening. This is a walk without a map. This is listening with eyes closed.

The answer to so many of the questions we usually throw at sound is, in relation to this listening experience, 'I don't know'. Really that answer is echoed by another – 'I don't remember'. Usually the 'I' that listens puts tangible substance to the experience, by remembering objects or states of mind, or how something (not necessarily identifiable) feels. All this bringing back to mind is a way of following the subjective map that listening makes. In this piece by Lopez, perhaps there is nothing to remember at all because the material that makes this piece is empty of associations and full of substance. So it is not 'the sounds of the real world' but *sound* that fills a space with listening.

After the sound has finished it is not a matter of remembering how it felt to listen to it, or indeed if there was anything to hear. *Untitled #90* ceases, and the gaping space of emptiness it vacates is reclaimed almost immediately by the sounds of the real world rushing back in, like pent-up water released into a channel (full of similes), weaving back through the old paths. Listening is already starting to fill up again. This cascade of returning comprehension is wonderful in itself, but the real achievement was to take us away from our self for a while. Any map we might draw to make sense of *untitled #90* would have to be a map devoid of any orientation, lacking all landmarks and bare of any detailed real-world representation. It is not that the real world is banished by this work – how can it be, you can still hear it over the wall – but those brief flutters of vaguely recognizable real-world sound are such a long, long way away.

> I'm fighting against a dissipation of pure sound content into conceptual and referential elements. My music doesn't have a meaning in the traditional sense, there is no message and no intention of communication or expression. I'm trying to reach a transcendental level of profound listening that enforces the crude possibilities of the sound matter by itself; in particular, the openness, the richness of this matter and all the subjective, individual universes that can arise from this kind of listening.
> (Francisco Lopez in interview with Feardrop (France), May 2000, at www.franciscolopez.net)

Lopez's stated intent does not, on the face of it, concur with some of the other approaches I have mapped out here. But on my map they are all distinct landmarks on related paths. One place can lead to another. Every single cartographer who transforms the sounds of the known environment is charting a route towards listening differently. Every map has its own priorities, but every map-reader chooses their own route.

We might chart a world of listening. But, as someone once said to me (and I'm sure you've met this audience member in one guise or another), 'Do you really call that stuff you're doing "music"?'. Well, of course, that depends on how you listen. Here's my suggestion: do not subscribe blindly to schools of thought; follow your ears and intuition. But don't confuse this with lack of rigour. The charts we draw, read and follow through attention to both our own and others' listening relationship to the world can be dynamic and flexible, and can accommodate various shifts of orientation. But they are not an abdication from making music, since they still require thought, commitment – and active intent. Making music from listening, through the medium of recorded sound, is a composed listening that takes some work from both map-maker and map-reader. It helps to have directions of some kind, if you want to go further than halfway there and back again.

So pack a bag, and don't forget: bring your own map.

Notes

1   There are, of course, maps of non-visual territories and concepts – soundings of sea depths, DNA, maps of history, ideas, political divisions – but these abstractions are translated into visual terms, they are not there on the ground. Those maps – such as radar – that are made through non-visual soundings still result in visual objects, while non-visual maps are still a process of envisaging. When I imagine my vegetable plot the taste of each thing planted there might come to my mind, but I also see the ragged rows of leeks and potatoes (and weeds) in my mind's eye.

2   The map is housed in Hereford cathedral, England.

3   For an example see Appendix 1 'Sample Sound Notation Systems' in R. Murray Schafer's classic text, *The Soundscape: Our Sonic Environment and the Tuning of the World* (1994).

4   *The Vancouver Soundscape 1973 / Soundscape Vancouver 1996*, Cambridge Street Records CSR-2CD (1996).

5   'The Vancouver Soundscape', track 15 on CD[2].

6   For more information on the decline of the house sparrow, and for statistical data, see http://www.bto.org/appeals/house_sparrow.htm

7   For further information on the many and varied preoccupations of sound, or acoustic ecology, I recommend a visit to the World Forum for Acoustic Ecology, at http://interact.uoregon.edu/MediaLit/wfae/home/index.html

8   The sparrowhawk was almost killed off in Britain in the 1960s by the use of DDT pesticides in crop-spraying, subsequently banned once their effect on the environment became clear. Perhaps sparrows just had it lucky for a few years. Further information on the effect this may have had on the sparrow populaton see the Songbird Survival page at http://www.songbird_survival.org.uk/fact2.htm

9   Witness this excerpt from an online article, 'What is an Aural Safari?' by Christopher DeLaurenti, posted at the website of a phonography group – http://www.phonography.org/safari.htm

> I emerge from an alley onto a brightly lit plaza. I am the only white person there. Despite scattered fights and squabbles, the police are nowhere to be seen. I roll tape and stride forward, snatching fragments of combat and conversation. A cuddling couple ambles by and smiles. Someone amidst an imposing throng asks me what I'm doing. I'm too distracted, too cautious to say more than 'collecting sounds.' He wishes me luck. A line of mounted police forms down the street. Anticipating the polyphony of hoof beats on cobblestones, I hurry to the horses. My hunt continues. I am on aural safari.

   Tongue in cheek it may be, but there is a rather suspicious overt enjoyment in the chase from this would-be aural Indiana Jones.

10 'On Exactitude in Science'

> ... In that Empire, the Art of Cartography attained such Perfection that the map of a single Province occupied the entirety of a City, and the map of the Empire, the entirety of a Province. In time, those Unconscionable Maps no longer satisfied, and the Cartographers Guilds struck a Map of the Empire whose size was that of the Empire, and which coincided point for point with it. The following Generations, who were not so

fond of the Study of Cartography as their Forebears had been, saw that that vast Map was Useless, and not without some Pitilessness was it, that they delivered it up to the Inclemencies of Sun and Winters. In the Deserts of the West, still today, there are Tattered Ruins of that Map, inhabited by Animals and Beggars; in all the Land there is no other Relic of the Disciplines of Geography.
(Borges, 1998, p. 325).

11 http://www.museumca.org/naturalsounds
12 I loosely paraphrase here from David Lodge's preamble, in his essay 'Consciousness and the Novel', in the collection of the same name (Lodge, 2002). For a more technical explanation of the notion of 'qualia', and the technicalities of its meaning in philosophical terms I recommend the online entry by Michael Tye, in *The Stanford Encyclopedia of Philosophy*: Tye, Michael, 'Qualia', *The Stanford Encyclopedia of Philosophy* (Winter 1997 edition), ed. Edward N. Zalta, at http://plato.stanford.edu/entries/qualia

Chapter 4

The same trail twice
Talking Rain with Hildegard Westerkamp

*The artist's aesthetic musical language and the language of the recorded sounds
and soundscapes meet in the process of composing. And it is the meeting of the
two 'languages' and the ways in which they are balanced that makes out the
creative challenge in a soundscape composition. It is not unlike a traveller's
encounter with a new place. The journey itself becomes the point of balance
between the traveller's own inner reality and how he or she meets the new place.*
(Westerkamp, 2002, p. 54)

Hildegard Westerkamp's composition, *Talking Rain*, invites a listening journey through
the sounds of water, rain and West Coast birds and animals in British Columbia. Some
of the sounds she uses as her material in this work were collected in Lighthouse Park, a
wooded promontory overlooking Burrard Inlet, near Vancouver. This chapter is based
on an interview I recorded with Westerkamp,[1] as we walked in Lighthouse Park itself.
Three days of solid rain had soaked the ground, but the weather cleared up just long
enough for us to enjoy an exhilarating meander through muddy paths, and up and down
rainwater creeks and gullies.

Writing is a path that leads to sound and, although lightly edited, this writing tries to
hold on to the natural rhythm of our speech as we walked along together. Sometimes
the trail runs through the 'ums' and 'ahs', the half-articulated thoughts and the
incomplete sentences that are left abandoned along the way in normal conversation.
Occasionally we just ran out of breath, or stopped to think, or to listen for a moment.

Indeed, during the course of our conversation we got a little lost. We found ourselves
on a new trail, or rather what turned out to be a familiar trail approached from an
unfamiliar direction. But perhaps that temporary strangeness was a gift that made the
whole walk seem fresh and unusual. This is the way with talking, listening and being in
another place.

The sound examples are taken from our walk, and from *Talking Rain* itself.

> HW: You can hear it on the headphones?
> KN: *I wasn't hearing it but ... yes, that's fine.*
> HW: OK.
> KN: *Yes, that's actually quite loud ....*

75

KN: *Is this where you made* Talking Rain?

HW: Yes, a producer on the CBC wanted me to do a piece about rain because they were doing a whole hour of a sort of 'West Coast rain' programme. And so he approached me and said, 'Can we can we make this composition, and can we be *part* of your recording process?' And so, that winter it happened that it wasn't raining very much, and the three of us were trying to find a *day* where we could go out *here* to Lighthouse Park and record rain ... together. And ...

KN: *The weather didn't oblige!*

HW: The weather did absolutely not oblige! And in the meantime I had made my own rain recordings, and I collected together some old recordings that I had. So I had the material. But we just couldn't get to this *day*. So, finally, we just made a date and said 'Let's go to Lighthouse Park'.

And on that morning it rained. And we arrived, and it rained for about another ten minutes and then it stopped! (laughs) ... so we got this ... actually we walked down this same trail.

Meander ... the same trail

⏵ CD[15]

(We arrive at a clearing in the wood, and stop walking to look around)

An April afternoon, after much rain. Lush, verdant forest and blustery, unexpected sea views. A landscape of trickling, rain-fed streams and cool, saturated air. All these provide the setting, and the reason to go on.

We are walking down the same trail that Hildegard took to record sounds for her piece, *Talking Rain*. On that occasion she was accompanied by colleagues from CBC Radio, but during the course of our walk she also describes other times when she has come here with visiting relatives, her mother or with friends. So this is a familiar journey for her, and one that has its own stories along the route. For me it's another place.

HW: Isn't that incredible?

KN: *Green. There are so many different greens there ....*

HW: Yes, it's the moss.

KN: *The benefit of rain ....*

HW: It's just that. I love this place because to me it's the only forest near Vancouver that has some inkling of the rain forest of the West Coast ....

(resume walking)

So we were trying to get some of the rain sounds on these different soft

While we walk along, negotiating sodden paths and the ups and downs of a rocky terrain, I ask her questions about how she made her piece. My questions prompt responses that involve her going back along old paths. 'How did you do this?', 'Where did you go?' I am listening, and at the same time imagining her memories for myself. And while my journey is more than partly to collect new information, Westerkamp's own walk is also a journey down memory lane. At the same time we are two friends trudging along together. We occupy different places, simultaneously.

And sound? We're making it up as we go along. You can hear our feet. The boots squelching on wet ground, and the slight changes that indicate our encounters with stones, bumps, and a slippery moment or two. There's the sound of the microphone knocking against my hand or body as we walk, and the movement of clothing – trousers, jackets, sleeves. There is a great deal of sonic activity and yet, if asked, you would deduce that this was recorded in a quiet place. Because all you can hear is our voices and the rhythm of our walking in an enclosed, still atmosphere. Yes, we were shielded by tall trees and the atmosphere was also quite overcast and windless. But, also, the recording itself was a little composed: the microphone is directional

surfaces, as opposed to the urban, hard surface raindrops .... So they ... there's all this moss here and the different cedar branches and the leaves and ...
KN: *You can smell it.*
HW: Exactly. So, we ended up recording this particular walk here and then we also found a creek. And we walked up the creek and did recordings there, and we did it in a way

and I chose to hold it close to us. We – sounding, sonic, human objects – are filling a place that the microphone defined. And while the microphone picks up our activity, it also excludes the fine detail of our surroundings. A recording never offers quite the same trail as having been there yourself.

But is being there a problem? Do we get in the way? Is our conversation an intrusion within the natural soundscape, or is it even more – is it an eradication perhaps?

Listening is a silent intelligence that directs us to what we think matters. And what matters occupies our attention. Here, I have directed the listening microphone towards what matters to me. I want it to matter to you. I am holding the microphone towards her voice as we walk along. It appears you have no choice but to hear my intention. Am I a composer? Or are we listeners together – following the same trail? Have I invaded your space? Several things are taking place. It is difficult not to sound rather pretentious, because we are not given to talking about sound and its place in our lives.

It is an interesting mix.
Sound, listening and composition.

... I had the microphone in the hand. I had one pair of headphones and the technician had the other pair of headphones and he had the machine so he controlled the levels, but I was leading them, with the microphone. So I was just zeroing in on certain water sounds and things.

And then we'd have conversations in between. So it was like a soundwalk really, with them. And then part of those recordings became materials for the piece. But the producer made – they recorded, they cut – a soundwalk out of it for the programme. So they had the soundwalk that we did in Lighthouse Park as part of the programme.
KN: *With you talking?*
HW: With me talking and us having a conversation and discussing soundscape and rain and the West Coast and this place, and what was special about this place.
KN: Talking Rain *is very much, for me, a piece that's not just about rain.*
HW: Mmm, no ...
KN: *It's about place. It feels like a foreign visit for me, listening to it.*
HW: Yes ... like going into a different place. Yes, and it made me very aware of how different rain is in every place.

HW: Now, I just realized we went a different route here, but that's OK ... there's one place that we should have gone ... the other ... but this is fine ...

HW: This is fine here. I don't know where it will lead us but ...

KN: *We shall see.*

HW: I notice that in Europe, for example, you have rain ... but you don't have the kind of continuous rain, that you have here.
KN: *No, I associate that very much with North America.*
HW: Yes – I mean it just doesn't *stop*, right!? And, on the West Coast here, you can have just continuous rain for days and days and *days*. And so you have a type of lushness that you just don't get in Europe. And, in Europe, I notice, it's very much

that a day will be interrupted with certain rhythms of rain showers. And I remember as a child that I knew that I probably would need some kind of rain cape during the day. I had to take it with me even though the sun was shining. Or you'd have to stop your bike ride ...

Meander ... hearing place

⊙ **CD[16]**

A sea-plane passes overhead as we are talking. Although Hildegard's voice is in the foreground – the microphone is pointing at it – the plane's sound is still an interruption. The background looms forward and halts our train of listening. Things cannot proceed in the way you hope when other sounds have claimed attention.

'Can you hear them?'

Listening to this sound clip now, her looped voice becomes a pattern with an interesting lilt. Perhaps vocal repetition tends to catch our ears because it is relatively unusual in normal, uncontrived circumstances – in particular when the sound is of human origin. The rhythm of her

and you'd just have to ...
KN: *Yes, yes ... be prepared!*
HW: Yes!

HW: This is a typical sound. We have the very high ... peeping sounds of the birds that are way up in the trees. Can you hear them?
KN: *Yes, very quiet.*
HW: They're very quiet and then you have the sea-planes – that's Lighthouse Park.

speech becomes structured; but it was already – there was a listening 'beat' of 'silence when she asked that question.

The answer to 'Can you hear them?' is preceded by a space in which action is required. During that beat of silence I am straining my ears to hear the birds singing way up above us. I am trying to hear what she hears. I am trying to get inside her head. But actually I can barely locate these other sounds while the drone of the sea-plane captures my attention.

'That's Lighthouse Park.'

We are foreign bodies in this landscape. Two intrigued non-natives exploring a different place (although she has been here quite a while) and finding it somehow essentially different from the paths we knew before. And yet it's hard to put your ear to the difference – the wind, the overhead hum of the sea-planes, and high treetops occupied by small birds of an unknown breed. We make comparisons between a place we remember and a new place.

KN: *How tall are these trees would you say?*
HW: ... these are not even really very big trees. I don't know, I can never tell the height, but they're a lot higher than most of the trees in Europe, right?
KN: *I was just thinking that the tallest waterfall in England is about 110 feet ... rather sad compared to these trees!*
HW: True, true! Yes, and there's quite a cliff there right, and the tree goes right above it.

(We resume walking)

HW: You know the piece made me much more aware in detail of the difference between where I grew up and here, in terms of the rhythms of the rain, and the sounds of it. And there's also, of course, the urban and nature aspect in that piece as well; you have the sound of rain on concrete, and a car going through the rain and ...
KN: *That's a big surprise, when the sound of the car driving through rain arrives.*
HW: Well I had a problem doing this piece, I thought, 'My God how do I do a piece that's about rain for the radio, without it sounding like something else, like fire or whatever?' So I had one recording that I'd made around a friend's house: it was raining hard that night and I said, 'Can I just come over and just come round your house and record under the roof?' And so I spent about an hour recording all these detailed sounds around her house – she lived in a very forested environment. And there was one recording, where a

Meander ... in time

⊙ CD[17] opening of *Talking Rain*

It appears to take the lightest touch – just a few steps down the path between a recording and composition – to turn a documented landscape into a new journey. It's a matter of surreptitiously offering a new approach, one that a listener might come across while passing through familiar territory. You know it, you could swear you'd been there already, but you can't quite place the difference.

At the opening of *Talking Rain* there is the sound of tapping rain on a roof in the foreground. It traces one, recognizably musical, path through many

raindrop went down onto a plastic ... er ... garbage can and it went ... *Ta* ta ta ta, *Ta* ta ta ta, *Ta* ta ta ta, *Ta* ta ta ta ... and that's the beginning of the piece. I thought I've got to establish that we're in a composition here!

(Laughs)

KN: *That's something I've thought about a lot with your work, actually. Also in* Gently Penetrating into Another Place *you establish a rhythm with a tapping sound. And it is to do with saying that 'this is music', isn't it?*

other water sounds. Its rhythm invites other sounds to join it as music. And yet this rhythmic musical tapping is also merely the sound of rain on a roof. Indeed, the air is saturated with the sound of falling water. Listen to the rain – or rather to its results, since this is not the sound of a stormy downpour or even a misty shower. This is the sound of water running across roofs, dripping down drainpipes, splashing into gullies. This is the active, descriptive poetry of rain's downward travel. This is Hildegard Westerkamp's composed response to what rain means, to us.

The tapping is a structural signpost that's hard to avoid and easy to become attached to. My toes twitch in time as *Talking Rain* begins. When that rhythm fades, it does so to make room for the unmistakable sound of a car driving through rain. The foreground sound of wet tyres on tarmac is an unequivocal reference. Like the overhead sea-plane that clouded my listening in Lighthouse Park this sound approaches, takes over, and simultaneously defines the essential nature of the environment.

By the time that car's travel has faded, the tapping pattern has become subsumed under a looser 'close-up' layering of unambiguous water sounds. The sound is naturalistic but magnified. It is nearer than usual to my ears. A dripping splatter now becomes a resilient thread of continuous sound. And, as this episode fades, the tapping sounds resurface, renewed by an additional repeating pattern.

Direction. Invitation. Suggestion. Question. Intervention. Infiltration. Interpretation.

These are just some of the compositional activities that tap away at our listening to the strangely familiar. It is how these sounds are put together – composed – rather than how they are changed that leads us lightly down a different path. I know this sound, but something's not ... quite ... the same.

HW: It is. Because I'm continually worried that nobody notices that I'm composing!

HW: I don't know this trail; this is great. This is a new place for me here .... .

HW: Yes, so in *Talking Rain* it became really conscious. I've done it in other pieces but here I suddenly thought I've got to establish that we're in a rainy environment, plus that this is a composition. So that's why the car comes in there, quite early on – because it sounds *so* wet that I thought everybody would recognize it as rain, as a wet environment. That's why.

KN: *So it's not so much a political statement at that point?*

HW: No, not really, no. I mean, it can do that too ... but it led me then into that other section, later, in the city. It made me think that I'd like to go into the city as well. Because the urban environment in rain is such an absolutely different place, and people often hate it, whereas in the natural environment you actually enjoy it, don't you?

> KN: *Yes ... except that we are walking down a stream at the moment; I don't know how much I'm enjoying that with a dat machine!*
> HW: And I don't actually know where we are ...
> KN: *Well ... there's human life down there ....*
> (We stop to listen)
> HW: This is great ....
> KN: *I should be recording this.*
> HW: You want to?
> KN: *I don't hear much ...* (pause walking to record)
> HW: There's something up there, it might come down here ....

KN: *And in* Talking Rain, *you started with a stereo piece, but then made it into a 'larger space', for eight-channel sound?*

HW: Yes, someone invited me to do an eight-channel composition and I ended up not having time to do a new piece. And so I proposed that I would try to make this piece into an eight-channel work. And I wouldn't recommend that to anyone. It's really difficult to do, very difficult. It's certainly much better to compose directly for eight channels, because it's a totally different thing from stereo. But it helped me to learn a lot about it.

> HW: ... look at that!
> (A large fallen tree bridging a small ravine)
> KN: *I don't think I can do that!*
> HW: No, no, we don't want to go across, it's too slippery. I fell off a log like that with the Nagra tape recorder once, because it took me out of balance. This was on the West Coast when I was two months pregnant .... And I fell on my head, it was awful ... but, Sonja's fine!
>
> We had a big storm here – was it last winter or the winter before? – I think it was the winter before. It was a huge storm and that's when some of these trees fell over and had to be cut.

HW: Yes, when we were recording sounds for *Talking Rain* – when it stopped raining we went to waterways ... and I can hear some sound right now ....

> (Sound of feet in water)
> KN: *Here you go.*

HW: Mmm, there it is. A little waterfall.
(Sound of waterfall and KN moving a microphone over it)
KN: *I'm learning!*
HW: Yes, you go really slow. You can just really go very, very close ...
(sound of very close miked water) and if you just move like a little bit ... (sound of water
and overhead plane too, in distance)

KN: *So you would normally record in this compositional way?*
HW: Yes because I don't see it as composition, I see it as listening: it's incredibly
fascinating. And the first time I had an experience like this was in a village where
there was a creek like this. I heard all these flicking sounds and I didn't know where
it was. So, with the microphone, I went searching for it. And I ended up finding just
a little branch of a leaf, like the stick ... what is it, the leaf 'handle'? (Laughs)
The water was kind of flicking around it and had all these different pitches. And
that was a discovery at the time; I had never experienced this before. And the
microphone kind of found it for me. And I thought it was absolutely fantastic.
KN: *You see I have not recorded in this way at all. I've usually made pieces where
I've taken it from my point of hearing rather than searched ...*
HW: Mmm ...
KN: *So this is teaching me a lot.*

(Sea-plane sound is getting quite loud overhead)

HW: A searching microphone: it is very much, again, a listening process, but at
another stage – and that's what I like very much about this kind of work.

(The sea-plane is very loud by now, drowning the water sound)
HW: It has got worse over the years, you see the plane over there ... ?

HW: But the thing that I've got so excited about, especially with water, is that it
details the architecture of that particular place and moment. And that's what gives
us that sound right then and there. As soon as you shift that, you get a different
sound. The water is an instrument, you see? So it's both to do with architecture and
instrument building, and of course it has a connection for me. I used to love
building little waterways as a child.
KN: *Making things go from one place to another!*
HW: On rainy days I'd be outside and I'd be building little channels for water.
KN: *But this is composing, Hildi, without the technology!*
HW: (laughs) Of course, as a child, although I don't remember the sounds of that
time, they were there all the time, yes?
KN: *It is interesting I think, that when you're a child, playing with water is a very
important thing.*
HW: Yes, very.
KN: *And I'm sure the child is thinking of sound.*
HW: I think so. When I played like this as a child, it was always in the holidays.

We'd be in the Black Forest or in the Alps. We didn't have much water where I lived! And so you could always kind of rechannel water ... into another place ...
KN: *Eight channels!*
HW: Right!

And since it often rains during your summer holidays, that's what we would do. My parents would make a point of encouraging us to go outside. Even on a rainy day you'd 'do' something – and I loved it.

(Pause walking, bird sings)
HW: They're way up in the tree tops ...
KN: *You don't know what that is?*
HW: I don't. I have never been with someone who knows what they are. So I still don't know, even though I've lived here for thirty years ... (start walking again)
KN: *You know the sound ....*

HW: When I was doing *Beneath the Forest Floor* I went to Lighthouse Park to see whether I could get some supplementary recordings. I already had all these things from the West Coast, from the real rainforest. And, one day, I thought I would go to Lighthouse Park and just see what's there, maybe some squirrels. But the West-Coast forests are so quiet that you actually don't get that many sounds. But they're there – the squirrels are definitely there. And sure enough there was a squirrel. But what I also found was a group of small, sort of wren-like birds feeding on these roots here. And I was probably only a foot away from the microphone, and from them. And they were fluttering about and, while they were doing that, they were also peeping. And I used those sounds, of the peeping, in what was, at that time, the quietest spot in the park that I knew. (And there were no sea-planes. ...) When I slowed those down, they became part of a sort of very beautiful pitched environment at the end of *Beneath the Forest Floor*.

HW: I just want to see the sign here ...
KN: *'Songbird meadow'* ... *isn't that lovely, it doesn't look like a meadow.*
HW: I have no idea where we are, this is so funny... I've never been in this part, it's beautiful!

HW: And so they were yet another songbird that I had not heard before when I was in the West Coast, but I know they are in the forest there.

> HW: Here, look at this, my God!
> (We stop at an open-air theatre, very overgrown)
> KN: *There's a bird .... You have not been here?*
> HW: No, this is the open-air theatre I'd heard about!
> KN: *Oh yes, there's a stage, seats ... tree seats ... a bit soggy.*
> HW: Imagine a concert here!
> KN: *Yes ... but we're already having one.* (There is birdsong)

> KN: *Look at the moss on top of that!*
> HW: Beautiful ... I don't think there's anything happening here now. But it would be lovely, huh?
> KN: *Ideal for a concert, you should do something!*
> HW: Yes, but outdoor concerts here are too difficult because you never know about the rain.
> But, imagine!
> KN: *Do you know what they do here?*
> HW: I think they used to put on theatrical things here ....
> KN: *... because it's not a natural amphitheatre really is it?*
> HW: No ... no ... let's go down to that ...
> (We starting walking again)

HW: Another thing that happened with *Talking Rain*, that was kind of unexpected for me, was that I began to think about the liquidity in animal sounds. So I had recordings from frogs; frog recordings, some of eagles, some of young ravens –

various, mostly those kind of sounds. And also a sound that I love – a bird that's called the redwing blackbird. You find it in all the marshy areas here, and it has a very beautiful (sea-plane sounds nearly drown her voice) liquid call; and that's also in the piece, and totally unchanged. I don't change all the animals' sounds ...

Meander ... a strange hybrid

▶ CD[18]

The water is trickling past, very close to my ears. There are two streams of sound: the sound of a high-pitched, fast burbling and the sound of water falling into a dip or hole, with low-pitched plops and splashes resonating as it hits the bottom, or rebounds against the sides. At least that's what it sounds like to me, it's hard to tell – and now I'm realizing just how unfamiliar sounds can be when they're let out on their own.

A subtle filtering brings out the higher frequencies. There's a slight sleight of hand (an aural confusion there). Because there are no other sounds – there is no room for other sounds – my attention is on the 'hear and now', the close-up presence of water. When distant bird calls gradually admit the context of the outdoors, and some kind of wider landscape rises slowly around my abstracted listening, I have to decide which path to take.

except for – no, that's right, *all* the animal sounds are unprocessed. They are left the way they are, because to me there was a direct relationship between them and some of the processed rain sounds. That just 'happened' in the process.

KN: *Well, you noticed it!*

HW: (laughs) Yes, that's right. Well, that's what it's about. You do these things and then you notice the connections, right?

KN: *The thing I love about listening to your music, and* Talking Rain *in particular, is that somehow when I'm listening to the rain I forget that there's processing going on for a moment, or rather I'm aware that there's a toing and froing between unprocessed and processed sounds, and a feeling of it being an environmental recording.*

But right now I am up close, near the stream. I am listening to the world from the water's perspective. My attention is bound up with this delicious, enticing, tactile sound. Just this sound.

And from this position, a magic congruity emerges: the gradual infiltration of frogs peeping in a chorus of trilling croaks. Their natural call is at exactly the same pitch and tempo as this trickling water sound. They are part of the abstracted sound, then they are part of the sound of water, then they are frogs. The water parts to reveal them before returning to cover them again. In that moment of transmutation, frogs are suddenly revealed like a gleam of gold in a stream.

And something essential about the sounds and what they say is also revealed through this compositional alchemy. Yes, it's an easy thing to take two sonically similar sounds – their destinies alike in terms of timbre, rhythm, tempo and general contour. And it's also a relatively simple exercise to apply digital processing that will accentuate the similarities and cast a shadow on differences. But it's the nature of the essential meaning of the two sounds that creates the real magic. Inside water, outside frogs. Abstraction, context. Inanimate, animate. But in spite of their differences, the sounds share a wealth of meaningful associations with this specific landscape.

This composed listening travels from shape to shape, and draws attention to aural similarities. The sounds invite a hybrid listening, to the ordinary made strange.

Surely such unexpected congruities please our creative tendency to find imaginative relationships between distinct things that naturally coexist in the landscape. Gazing out over a rolling landscape our eyes alight on that particular group of trees that forms a rounded repetition of the hill itself. There is a pleasure in coming across uncontrived connections.

HW: Which is what we do with listening anyway, yes? I mean we process all the time, and then we're back into listening attentively, and then we process again. Yes, I think it's probably similar . . . .

KN: *You seem to have a consciously light hand with regard to processing. You're very subtle with it.*

HW: Yes, I feel that the processing is only there to emphasize things that are already there. So I'm not really trying to invent anything new. I'm just trying to extract what's there and exaggerate it a bit. And, because I'm delighted by what's there and I hear it in a certain way, I just want others to hear it in the same way!

KN: *You want them to share in your delight.*

HW: Yes, that's it . . . that's basically what it is, you know. I'm never very interested in the kind of sound processing that leads me way too far away from the original sound, *unless* it really makes connections . . . .

HW: OK, now this is the riverbed … more sounds … .
KN: *I'm going to make some in a moment by falling flat on my face … .*
HW: Yes, right!
This is a very nice high-pitched one. This is a nice little river here … .

KN: *I suppose this creek is just here because of the rain, do you think?*

(Water sound)

It's travelling quite fast.
HW: Yes, are you able to move the microphone without making noise? It's difficult.
KN: *Yes, I think so. Most of the time.*
Do you edit a lot of noise out?
HW: Lots – and also the hands, the 'bone sounds' that sometimes become low-frequency sounds. In natural recordings you can actually get rid of them because none of the sounds you want are as low.
KN: *Do you spend a lot of time cleaning sounds up first?*
HW: Ah, a *huge* amount of time. I clean all the time. In a way I'm dusting and cleaning up. Something that happened unexpectedly in

Meander … can you move without making a noise?

⏵ CD[19]

The materials don't perform; they exist (and some of them are temporary). I wasn't performing for the microphone at that moment, and neither was Lighthouse Park. Westerkamp and I hunch over the trickling stream as if we are listening in on private moments. When the microphone is no longer directed at us, we are no longer part of the landscape. Any noise we make is extraneous, and to be avoided. We are trying to have some respect.

And listen, this is how it was, I haven't changed anything. Two people talking, behind the trickle of a rain-fed stream. Our ears on sound, concentrating close up on this burbling of running water.

The sound is just a starting point for composition. Before you even get to cleaning up the sound and considering its nature, the microphone can impart an intense glamour (a Romantic light).But this is beyond reality, and I haven't even done anything to the sound yet. No high-pass filters, no time-stretching or granulation. Just how it was, but illuminated by the microphone. It causes the sound to leap forward and reveal its lustre, and its meaning too – like a torch in a dark place or water running over a dull stone.

Hildegard Westerkamp, and many other composers working with sound in this way, often refer to their work as soundscape composition. A soundscape sensibility involves composing layers of listenings and relistenings, whilst staying quiet. There is no microphone noise in Westerkamp's piece, and no snatching of sounds away from their origins. Abstracted pyrotechnics don't apply. The performance is of a different order.

Is this the appeal of soundscape composition? This aural reinterpretation of the natural sounds of the environment creates a sonic landscape in which the audience is composed of motionless listeners, who listen in from outside as the natural world sings its private song.

Perhaps the soundscape composer tries to move without making a noise.

Talking Rain was that I had all these initial recordings, and was going to introduce rain on different surfaces, in different contexts. I didn't do anything to the sounds I had; they were basically clean recordings. And I started to mix and I realized that some of the recordings were made in the city so there were low frequencies. And when I faded them up, the first sound that you heard was the low frequencies, of course. So, I had to filter these frequencies out completely because I wanted to zero in on the rain. So I had to go back, do all this 'cleaning up', which I hadn't anticipated – should have .... .

KN: *You don't notice it so much at the time when you're recording the sounds.*

HW: No. I was aware that they were sounds that had some low frequencies in them but I had forgotten that, of course, the low frequencies would be coming through.

KN: *Do you have a kind of plan when you're making a piece, a shape – or is it really the materials that dictate it?*

HW: In the case of *Talking Rain* I knew that I wanted to introduce the rain specifically first somehow, and to make sure it was not too easily confused with fire, and to make it clear that we were clearly in a rainy environment. And so, the way to do it was just to take these various recordings of rain soundscapes and bring them all together in some sort of fashion. And then I think I sort of vaguely knew that I was going to go on a bit of a journey inside the rain, by using the processed sounds. If I know the beginning of a piece I start it and then I realize, in the process of going into the piece, I have to do a lot more processing work and cleaning up work before I can get to those things. So, it kind of happens in parallel. I may know aspects of the piece, I may know the general curve of a piece .... .

KN: *And for this piece you were thinking of radio while you were making it?*

HW: Yes, it was for radio .... .

KN: *So you were consciously aware of that? You weren't just thinking, 'Oh I'll just make it' .... .*

HW: ... it scared me. Because I thought, 'How do you broadcast rain on a tinny, kitchen radio?'.

KN: *Yes. And mono perhaps ...*

HW: I was thinking, 'How will people listen to this piece?' And I know my kitchen radio – it's *terrible*! So, what do you do? How do you let a piece actually get through?

KN: *This is very hard, isn't it ... ?*

HW: Yes. That's why it was a big challenge actually and it took a long time for me to actually like the piece. I felt I was just struggling with the material mostly. I liked individual passages and individual sounds ... but I really felt I was ... I felt that it wasn't really a composition that I should be too public about. And then I just noticed that people really *noticed* it.

KN: *Well, many people like that piece. And when I've played it to people and performed it I've had very positive responses. You know, not just sort of the usual thing ... so it obviously touches people, deeply.*

HW: Yes, this has really surprised me, very much. And maybe it's because I had to work so hard to get the piece to 'speak'. And the title itself is interesting because I couldn't find a title. And that's always a problem for me, when I don't find a title. Often I know the title before I do the piece – and then the whole meaning is clear to me, and then I can work. But, if I don't have the title, I don't know what the piece is about. So, in this case I kept thinking about somehow the rain is *saying* something. And I had at one point also wanted to go to some native people and get some of their words for rain – but that failed; I didn't have enough time to develop that. And then I spoke to Norbert [Norbert Ruebsaat] my ex-husband. We used to do a lot of work together (sound of sea in background coming forward) and he is very good with language and I really like his way of working with language. And I played him the piece and said that I wanted the title to have something to do with how the rain speaks, speaking rain. And he said, 'Why don't you call it "Talking Rain"?' (Laughs)

KN: *It makes sense!*

HW: You know, like the talking sticks … so there it was.

KN: *I'm so glad it hasn't got rainstick sounds in it.*

HW: Yes … right!

KN: *Oh look, we're at the sea. I don't know if I want to go all the way down there.*
HW: **You want to go down there!?**
KN: *I don't know … I think I'll fall over. It's too windy!*
HW: **It's too windy … hmm, so we are way over on this side now, interesting … .**

KN: *What is this? Are these trees?*
HW: Yes, those are logs. This is the logging industry losing their logs as they go in the logging booms. And the whole coast is littered with them … they just lie there.
KN: *Are they just left there?*
HW: Yes, it's very typical for West Coast beaches, all over.
KN: *It looks almost like rusted iron.*
HW: That's right … they are very beautiful things, and I really like them. In some of the more abandoned beaches they are piled up several feet high.
KN: *You haven't made a piece with talking wood yet?*
HW: No, but there's a woman who was, in the early days, a student at the Sonic Studio [the studio at Simon Fraser University]. And when I was doing *Fantasie for Horns* she was doing a piece … what was it called? … *Wood on Wood on Water*. And she went to the beach and played them like log drums. And it was a very beautiful piece, actually.

KN: *And I have often thought that perhaps people respond to* Talking Rain *so strongly because water is an elemental sound, and it seems those kind of sounds ... water and wood and wind are very ...*

HW: We relate to them strongly, when we allow ourselves. Yes. And I always find that the attitude to weather in the city is appalling. How people hate rain and snow and ... , oh, but I fall into it myself. You know, I've been complaining to you about the rain the last few days.

KN: *Because the weather hampers your activities, it is annoying in that sense.*

HW: Yes, seemingly it hampers it. And yet when I'm out here in Lighthouse Park, who cares!

KN: *And you can appreciate how beautiful the weather is.*

HW: Exactly! And you know for me, both composition and recording are always processes of discovery. And that's why I do it! It's like building that creek as a child. I'm not interested in being in the studio and creating synthesized sounds, and new sounds. It's not something that I ... it's not part of how I want to make music. That's why I have a hard time doing things with instrumental music, because I'm basically not that interested in it – unless I can find the connection between the instruments and environmental sounds, and undertake a process of discovery with instruments in the same way. For instance, in *Fantasie for Horns* I added the horns. The horn to me is an instrument that was used environmentally, originally – for instance, the post-horn, the hunting horn and that kind of thing. So there was a connection there for me. But I have a hard time composing for abstract contexts. They have somehow to relate to real life, always.

KN: *But also, they have to relate to real life because you're thinking of the listener as part of the work?*

HW: Yes, I think so – because I'm a listener myself. And the listening to sound is very much about that process of discovery, and the discovery in the process of listening itself.

HW: We're discovering a new trail here today. It's lovely.

KN: *Where do you usually go, do you have a favourite?*

HW: Well, there's sort of a favourite route that I take and I know how long it takes. Because one can get lost ... (laughs)

KN: *Thank you. Now you tell me. Well I only have one more tape, so we have to get out in ninety minutes.*

HW: Yes, we will, I promise. I don't have that much to say!

KN: *You were saying, to paraphrase, that you don't like the computer so much; but you are very much concerned with getting inside sound, aren't you? You are timbre and sound aware* ... .

HW: Very, exactly ... you know I like listening to some electroacoustic music up to a point, but I find it very tiring to listen to it when it becomes too separate from everything in my life. When I'm sitting in a blackbox theatre for two hours listening to nothing but abstract synthesized sounds then I get bored. Well, it depends of course on the composition – if it's interesting, well, then I don't get tired. I think to speak through these different sonic mediums we actually keep our ears alerted and awake in a way that's pleasurable. I think it's a question of pacing a concert properly, so as not to get tired by it.

KN: *But you're reaching a big audience that doesn't come from the abstract music world* ... .

HW: Yes, exactly. People who actually have nothing to do with contemporary music actually quite like some of this stuff ...

> Here's another river, a river pathway.

... I mean, I've always felt on the fringes somehow. We probably all of us do.

KN: *Perhaps we need to feel like that.*

HW: Yes. But I have never had a feeling of exclusion, because the one pleasurable thing about being in the studio with environmental sounds is that you are in a sonic landscape that you can relate to. And it's also very private because you are in the studio, so that's where I *like* the studio environment. You don't get interrupted: you can be with those sounds and I think that on some level I like this feeling of being left alone while I'm working, like that.

KN: *I agree. And I sometimes begin to think of sounds in a very tactile, substantial way when I'm working with them in the studio.*

HW: Yes, that's right, and it's very detailed, it's – it's almost like eating. Touching and being touched by sounds.

> Ah ... it's beautiful over here ... .

It's hard to explain to people.

> KN: *It's nice to come across the sea so suddenly.*
> HW: Yes, you see this might be OK down here, not too windy. This is gorgeous ... .
> KN: ... *Hey, we have a friend!* (A dog passes by, panting)

KN: *Do you find you become sensitive to certain kinds of sounds after you've been listening out for them? I find I'm now listening to all the watery sounds* ... .

HW: Yes, also as you walk here with all these rocks coming and going you get this interesting spectral change in the water. One of the things that I find most difficult to deal with is when I try to look for silence. It depends on where you are, but, of course, when you go out recording and you want to get only natural sounds, yet you're near a city, it's very difficult to find. And it becomes aggravating. But, I try not to go out with too much intent when I record because you end up being disappointed. It's a bit like going to India, where you can't have any expectations .... I think that's why I responded so much to the country because recording is very similar.

KN: *You have to be open to unexpected things in fact.*

HW: And I think that's what I really love about recording, and that's what I also love about India – there are these surprises and then you connect to them, and then you work with that.

KN: *The fortuitous ... happenstance.*

HW: And it's interesting that in fact this kind of surprise element – unexpected things and activity – is not only peculiar to societies like India that are very socially full and busy, but it's the same in nature. So, in effect, a country like India on some level is not unlike a natural environment because it – the randomness of it, or the seeming randomness of it – is so strong that nothing is overorganized. I mean usually when you go into a mall you can sort of know what you're going to get, yes, and then the human element will give you some element of randomness ....

KN: *There's no regularity ....*

> HW: Do you want to go up there and look?
> KN: *Yes, yes, if we've got time – you're coming?*

HW: We were *here!* Now I know, we were here!
KN: *We were here before, just now*
HW: That's right! ... we were just ... so this ....
KN: *This is where I changed the tape!*
HW: Aha! (Raucous laughter)

HW: So what must have happened ... when we arrived here again I just thought, 'Oh they have the same name as for the ... different spot. How unimaginative!' And then when I went up the same trail, we actually went up just the same trail we went down and then retraced our steps. Then we went up that complicated trail back up around the water ... !

KN: *Well, I'm convinced. I have no sense of direction anyway, so it could have been anywhere!*

HW: So I have got to know another snippet of this park. It has a lot of trails, and I don't know them all by any means.

Meander ... disorientation

⊛ CD[20]

The sound of water, magnified and impossibly close, becomes an intimate play of pitches, timbres and minute fluctuations. But the car tyres on wet tarmac stretch out towards the real world. From outside in the 'real world' the sounds of frogs emerge from streams of abstract sound as a new, related journey.

Composition is a process of reorientation in which gestures, phrases, timbres are placed relative to one another. Directions are indicated, thwarted, negated or mapped out as unfinished implications. Sounds travel in memory.

Can you hear them?

That's one map of the world.

KN: *It's getting brighter.*
HW: This is the nice part about this environment. As you go more directly to the coast like this, you don't get too much of the rain.

When the materials are field-recordings, then maybe orientation requires a bit more head-shaking. Listening to *Talking Rain* involves poring over a rapidly disintegrating map of the woods, where curling paths blur and cross into musical lines. It's confusing because it bears some resemblance to the familiar. Which path to take? And the rain gets into everything.

Later on in *Talking Rain* there is a swirling maelstrom of sound that seems to arise naturally out of a gradual increase in volume, density and general activity. This is a straightforward and effective musical technique. Applied to recorded sounds it has additional tensions to resolve.

HW: **Ah, we were here earlier!**
I'm curious where we came from.
KN: *We came down there. This is where we descended . . . .*
HW: **Oh my God, I didn't recognize it this way.**
KN: *And this is the same trail again . . . .*
HW: **The same trail the other way around. I've never gone that way!**

The sound of rushing, surging water becomes the dynamic material for a rhythmically fast montage, cut into a layered swirl of loud, low-pitched and dark timbres. A car swishes out of this turbulence but is no longer a defining moment, rather a sudden emergence that cannot compete with this stormy surrealism. In the background a tuned drone circumscribes space and refuses to let our listening out of this enclosed, musically defined enclosure. Although this 'mess' of sound – this *dénouement* – is very much built up in 'conventional' musical terms, its tension, I believe, is the result of an aggregation of gentle conflicts – the frogs that were water, the rain that becomes a car on a road, the close-up musicality versus the trickle and splash of natural distance. These ebbs and flows have offered a map of the world where no path is reliable. Instead, all paths are familiar, and no destination is guaranteed. You are left abandoned in the rain.

KN: *Well, there must be an analogy here somewhere with reversing a sound!*
HW: **Very interesting, so we turned off earlier than we should have, or than I normally do. See I never recognized . . . .**

HW: The thing that fascinates me about Japanese design is the observation of nature in it.
KN: *In the way that it's a really strict stylization of nature.*
HW: Very much so. But it's still connected to nature and that's where I find the fascination – if it doesn't go too far. That shares something with that creek-building that we were talking about, the waterways building from your childhood, you know. Because, playing with building channels for rainwater, as a child, you get into all the detail, and you make your own little garden, yes?

HW: This is so funny!
KN: *Here we are ... .*
(Men passing, voices)
(Feet in water — strenuous climbing)
HW: Are you OK?
KN: *Yes I'm fine. I was just thinking, two female composers travelling upstream. Somehow that's terribly allegorical!*

HW: And, you know, in Europe, where my mother lives, I have a very strong relationship with that landscape. It's very beautiful and she has a small forest right behind her house, and behind it is a field, and then there's the factory [the Westerkamp family business], and some village and more forest. But the forest is so *transparent* in the winter. I was there recently, it's all beech trees, and so you can see right through it. And, you know, I don't remember noticing that as a child. To me it was the ... like a dark forest.

KN: *Well, you were shorter!*

HW: Yes, that's right ... but you can see right through it.

KN: *Do you think it's been cleared?*

HW: No, not really. It has not been changed all that much. It could be that the trees are taller now. And that maybe the branches were lower, that could be it ... and yet I keep thinking, where can you find these darker sorts of places that I remember?

There's part of me that really would like to be closer to that again. I don't know, the older I get the more I yearn for it. It's something that I grew up with. And when I first grew up, after the war, we were in a house where there was a small forest across the street with these very old stone graves from a long time ago. And there was a sort of magic around that, and we used to play there. But there was a sort of freedom you know. I would just walk out of the house and there it was. There was a small street, but there was hardly any traffic.

KN: ... Let's go out here before we have to turn.
KN: *We've been here!*

HW: ... and you'll see the lighthouse.
(Walking, wind)
This is good place to sit in. If it was sunny now ....
KN: *You'd be able to sit and read here.*
HW: Yes ... (walking over rocks, wind, sea)

KN: *I didn't notice the lighthouse at all when we were here before* ....
HW: No, you can't see it from where we were.

It's a beautiful spot. And I interviewed the lighthouse keeper a few years ago. The lighthouse used to have an absolutely gorgeous foghorn that you can hear on the *Vancouver Soundscape*.[2] But now the foghorn has been changed to a 'beeeeep!'.

KN: *There's no one living in it is there?*
HW: No, but there's a lighthouse keeper in the houses there behind.
KN: *So it's not an automatic lighthouse?*
HW: Well, yes, most of it is automated now. Actually the lighthouse keeper is there because of protests. He refused to leave because he said we still need people. And when they automated the last thing, he simply didn't go. And I don't know where it's at now, but he fought ...

Meander ... remembering

◉ CD[21]

Wrapped in the sound, we lean into it and remember other times like this. Other times when we braced ourselves against the wind, with the taste of the sea on our lips and our hair whipping in front of our eyes. Other times when we turned away from an exposed cliff and walked back inland. Other times when the sound of the crashing waves and the blustery gale died rapidly to a distant surge behind us. And other times when this soothing, sea-shaped drone circumscribed the safety of our little tented world at night.

The sound of the wind subsides and puts distance between the 'reality' of that elemental sound and our creative interpretation of what this blurred, distorted signal might mean, signify or even merely feel like. Beauty is in the ear of the rememberer.

Do you hear it?

That's the sound of the wind.

What do you remember?

(Like straining your ears to hear distant birds, remembering takes a moment.)

If the paths that *Talking Rain* offers are remembered fictions and fictional remembrances, then listening becomes an imaginative making up. The listening composer is creatively writing sound.

Down below us the lighthouse keeper refuses to turn his back on the wind and the grey sea. That sound has defined his place in the world for as long as he can remember. For him, it's a reality that he cannot abandon. Perhaps the sound of the booming sea has become so embedded in his consciousness that he cannot imagine a path that trails away from that accompaniment. His role and his experience are fused. Or perhaps I am making up a story for him, spinning it from my experience of his windy look-out post.

HW: ... let's go back now ... here ... and now I just have to make sure I've found the right trail ... (walking, splashing). **Every time I go through this process, but somehow it's harder now!**

(Very windy, walking ...)

KN: *I really like that sound – or lack of sound – when you come away from the sea and you notice the change.*
HW: Yes. It's a memory of camping near the sea – at night when things quieten down and you're lying in your tent, and you're hearing the sea in the distance.
KN: *And you felt safe ... .*

KN: ... *Where are you going? Are we going out ... ah, I see ... .*

HW: Is this what we looked at before?
KN: *Yes, but it looks different from this perspective.*
HW: I saw the fence, I saw the *fence* – we were all the way here before and I didn't realize!
KN: *Well, I was occupying your attention at the time!*

KN: *I think this wood is just lovely, laid out like that.*
HW: Isn't it . . . .
KN: *You want to photograph it don't you, it's so mottled.*
HW: And this is really the winter look of the wood, that rusty . . .
KN: *Beautiful.*

HW: I'm amazed, I've taken you twice on the same walk. I didn't even realize we were going on the same walk!

KN: *Well, we were talking, you were pointed at a microphone!*
HW: It's true, you know – you have a completely different memory of something if you were busy doing something else as well.

Meander . . . the same trail twice

◑ CD[22]

At the end of *Talking Rain* there is a moment where someone – Hildegard Westerkamp? – stops to listen. Everything else stops.

No, that's wrong. There are footsteps – a dissonantly human and recognizable sound that doesn't emerge so much as crunch on stage. And then these footsteps stop, while someone pauses and listens before resuming their journey. And that is the end of the piece. A reminder that this piece is itself an extended moment where everything stops to listen to what rain has to say.

HW: Are you OK here?
KN: *I think so . . . .*

(negotiating a high climb)

HW: This is not too nervewracking?

Male passer-by: Hi! It's rather rough along that way, really steep.
HW: I know this trail. It's the way one has to go once one gets here.
KN: *It's the only choice!*
HW: This walk is such an unexpected pleasure.

This is an easy thing to do. There are many pieces where the composer's (or the apparent composer's) footsteps or voice crop up in the piece. Sometimes it a straightforward narrative and sometimes it's a knowing aside. There are many songs where offstage studio chat at the end of a track teases us into thinking we were in on the game. In a landscape based on environmental sound a human presence is something to identify with. The woman with the microphone substitutes for the man with the movie camera. In other pieces, such as *Kits Beach Soundwalk*, Westerkamp is a constant presence; her voice leads us along with suggestions, reflections and a gentle direction or two. But she is not out there in the field, her voice is a *post facto* addition that imposes yet another presence – either visual and live, sitting on stage with a microphone, or aural and recorded, speaking over the sounds on the CD.

The presence in *Talking Rain* is carefully placed. At the end.

Suddenly, hearing those footsteps cut across my aural path, I realize that we were on the same trail all along. Now it is made explicit that, despite all the different paths and traversals that the piece ostensibly meandered through, there was a guiding hand, or rather a guiding pair of listening ears. The path did not meander aimlessly, although it at times meandered with apparent aimlessness. Let's go this way, try

KN: *Good, for me too.*
HW: I've been wanting to get out for a long time.

HW: **Let me see, let's go there. I think that's the easier one.**
KN: *Up there is a* **trail?!**

this diversion, or follow this interpretation. Listen, what do you think? What do you feel? Can you hear it? That's *Talking Rain*. It's only at the end of the walk, when the footsteps crunch towards a real, familiar soundscape that we realize that what preceded was in fact not new at all – water, rain, forests, animals – this path is well known. But this old path was transfigured by an invitation to listen through a different, composed perspective – water, rain, forests, animals – this path is a new adventure.

It's the same trail twice. It was quite an expedition.

HW: Yes, this is a trail!
KN: *I don't want to do* **this** *one twice!*
HW: Ah, where does it go? ... This is definitely one version of it ... .
KN: *Down there ... .*
HW: Yes, this is it, we're right ... .

Programme notes
Talking Rain (1997) for two-channel tape
Length: 16:00

Rainsounds from the westcoast of British Columbia, Canada are the basic compositional materials for *Talking Rain.* Through them I speak to you about this place. The raincoast. A lush and green place. Made that way by rain. Nourished by rain, life-giving rain. In *Talking Rain* the ear travels into the sonic formations of rain, into the insides of that place of nourishment as well as outside to the watery, liquid language of animals, forests and human habitations, all of which are nourished by the rain.

Talking Rain was commissioned by CBC Radio for Westcoast Performance. It was realized in my own studio, Inside the Soundscape, and was premiered on April 20, 1997. Most rain recordings for this piece were made by myself in and around Vancouver. Thanks to Norbert Ruebsaat for providing his recordings of ravens, eagles and frogs from Haida Gwaii and also for finding the right title for the piece, magically. Thanks to Bruce Davis and Peter Huse for their high-quality recordings made in the early seventies for the World Soundscape Project's environmental tape collection at Simon Fraser University; to Robert MacNevin for his equally high-quality recordings made 20 years later (1991 to 95) for the same collection; to David Grierson for his light footsteps and receptive ears during the recording of our rainy forest soundwalk in Lighthouse Park near Vancouver. Special thanks go to John Siddall, producer of Westcoast Performance for giving me this opportunity and for challenging me to create a radio piece with sounds that must be the most difficult sounds to broadcast!

Talking Rain is dedicated to my companion Peter Grant.

(Programme note from Hildegard Westerkamp's homepage at http://www.sfu.ca/~westerka/)

Notes

1 14 April 2002, in Lighthouse Park, Vancouver, Canada. I recorded two tapes of material. During the second tape we realized that we were, physically, walking along the same paths we had taken earlier, but this time in another direction.
2 *The Vancouver Soundscape*. A double CD providing field-recordings of the Vancouver Soundscape in 1973 and in 1996 – see 'Recordings' for details.

Part 3

Sounding ... voices

Chapter 5

Speak / Listen
Invisible voices in radio, radio art and works for sound alone

A recurring voice: seeking Lotta

I'm desperately seeking Lotta. By the time you read this I may
have found her but, at the time of writing, Lotta Erickson is
still a mystery voice. Right now, all I have is a piece that she
made and called 'Please, Mr Coldstream', for reasons I don't
understand. The piece is on a CD of experimental radio art, but
the cover offers little information.[1] A series of possible
contacts has led from one person to another, with no luck. Email
addresses have bounced, people have moved on, details have not
been kept on file. An Internet name search produced various
references to the CD and an intriguing web page for a Finnish
production of *Grease*. Perhaps she is the young woman who grins
out from a cast photo, but it seems unlikely to me: although I
don't know who she is, I feel that I do know who she *isn't*.
Nobody has heard of her. Except that I have heard her, many
times. I have listened to her and I feel that I've got to know
her quite well. We're on first-name terms, although she appears
to be invisible.

I *believe* her voice is in her piece, which, *I* believe, is
primarily a documentary radio work. A young woman, speaking
English fluently but with a strong Swedish accent, tells the
story of a love affair she once had. She reminisces with the
boyfriend concerned and interleaves their conversations with
her own monologues. I *think* she is in her piece, with her
boyfriend (or ex-boyfriend?). *I* think it is a piece about
remembering. They remember how they met, and what they did, and
how they felt. (Recording encourages remembering; tell me what
happened, speak into the microphone, let it all out — nobody
can see.) Their voices are natural, but I can hear that he is
slightly embarrassed in the way he pauses and stumbles at
times. And surely he knows that he is being recorded?

BROADCAST VOICES

Turn your radio on, and there is a crowd of voices jabbering away at you.[2] Let me introduce just a few members of the speaking chorus: the voice as authority, the voice as confidante, the voice as adviser, the voice as friend, the voice as expert, the voice as reader, the voice as questioner, the voice as listener, the voice as performer, the voice as the link between. All these voices, and more, can broadcast a powerful, defined presence, straight into your ears. Generally, on conventional talk radio at least, they maintain a discrete distance from one another. Although a multitasking radio personality may well finish an interview, then turn to make a link, or introduce a piece of music, she does so by adopting a new 'persona' each time. Her intonation may change quite perceptibly as a result. These aural personae populate TV too but, on radio, their sound is all we have to focus on. We have grown accustomed to their voices, and evaluate their roles with some precision. Or at least we feel we do. Yet, although there are now perhaps as many women's voices as men's floating on the airwaves, certain kinds of personae have been – and perhaps still are – perceived as male.

> [the radio voice of authority] does not mumble or stutter, it pronounces full and meaningful sentences, it says something. As a voice, it is traditionally male, having a certain timbre and intonation that suggests a belief in what it is saying and a degree of authority in saying it. (Dyson, 1974, p. 167)

An authority explores an argument, or is there to throw light on a postulate, or to provide an informed opinion. The voice of authority – whether male or female, sounded or written – assumes that you will listen because it has information that you need to know. Authority doesn't digress into personal reminiscence on a whim or move from discourse to anecdote at the drop of a hat. It is above such things. But if anyone speaks to us, we notice them, *whatever* kind of voice they may have. This much is a truism. And although the toffee-nosed voice of authority frequently seems to jostle to the head of the queue when it comes to paying attention, there are other voices worth listening to. This *should* be a truism too. Authority is often overrated or misused, and it can be just a load of hot air. Trusting an authority without question can be as mindless as assuming that all academic writing must be conducted in the third person, using long, inelegant sentences (with convoluted embedding), and frequent digressive subclauses, in order to achieve an appropriate *gravitas* – just for the sake of making an educated-sounding noise. But you don't need to write (or read) things that way.

About 15 years ago I spent a year working at a large institution for severely mentally handicapped people, some of whom were deemed 'insane' on their childhood hospital records (euphemisms were less gentle then). One of my 'regulars' was a small, middle-aged lady called Joan,[3] with a 'mental age' of about five or six. She was never quiet. Usually she spoke incessantly under her voice, in a half-whispered, rapid monologue which otherwise lacked any expression. It was impossible to understand her words or know whether she was speaking to me or to anyone else. Sometimes I heard snatches of questions or swear words, but all spoken in the same hurried gabble. She always appeared to be tense, worried and fearful. She never looked me in the eye, however much I flailed around with guitars, percussion or silly songs. Then, one day I abandoned tambourines in favour of a delay system using two reel-to-reel tape recorders. I started it going and handed the microphone to Joan. At first she was terrified, and then amazed when she heard a voice. Gradually she talked more slowly, listened and responded to her own words coming back through the speakers a couple of seconds later. And she spoke up – so that she could hear her 'other voice'. For the first time she appeared to be aware that *she* was doing the talking, and that she could be saying something worth listening to.

Vocal transformations and unexpected asides can invert the familiar, and stand it on its head. Boys will be boys, but girls will be boys too:

> In performances, I loved to use the lowest setting on the Harmonizer, a digital processor that lowered my voice, to sound like a man. This was especially effective in Germany. When I spoke as a woman, they listened indulgently; but when I spoke as a man, and especially a bossy man, they listened with interest and respect.
> (Anderson, 1994, p. 131)

Laurie Anderson's use of what she calls the 'voice of authority' mocks the misguided power relationship between how it looks, how it sounds and what it says. The vocal transposition comments on the dissonance between her seemingly 'unauthoritative' physical embodiment (not only small, but a woman at that) and the sound of the voice that appears to issue from it. She thereby challenges our notions of what 'authority' is.[4] Significantly, she remarks that she stopped using this voice after taking singing lessons.

> I began to use my own voice for pieces that contained pointed social criticism. I've always thought that women make excellent social critics. We can look at situations, especially those involving power, and size them up fairly well; since we don't have much authority ourselves, we don't have that much to lose.
> (Anderson, 1994, p. 261)

Anderson's habitual multilayered commentary is such that one would hope this nonchalant admission is itself an ironic call to ascribe authority to a different kind of voice. Similarly I would like to believe that conventional radio's remit has developed to acknowledge authorities of other kinds. But it is a sad fact that the voice of authority is still generally deemed to be the province of the male. If you currently look up 'voice of authority'+ radio on any Internet search engine, the majority of references refer to male radio presenters or personalities, despite the significant number of female broadcasters in reality. It seems that, at times, we still define radio voices without listening. Yet, I think, it is the fact that the vocal personae of radio are *entirely* defined by sound that enables access to a different kind of listening when these conventions are resituated in works of composed sound. This is perhaps particularly effective if the work is not intended for radio presentation and itself raids the possibilities of both 'radio' and 'musical' listening to speech.

Here's a shaggy dog story. The popular music track 'Everybody's Free (To Wear Sunscreen)' offers an interesting subversion of several of these associations. It was written by Baz Luhrmann (the director of *Strictly Ballroom* and *Moulin Rouge*) in 1997, and became a hit after a shorter version was released a while later. The urban myth surrounding this track – in which a male 'voice of authority' recites rather 'cheesy' maxims over a beat – is that the words come from an actual commencement speech delivered by author Kurt Vonnegut at the Massachusetts Institute of Technology. In fact the words were a tongue-in-cheek column written by a Mary Schmich, a writer on the *Chicago Tribune* (1 June 1997). The text was posted on the Internet, with authorship attributed to Kurt Vonnegut, and the myth began to proliferate. Luhrmann was sent the words, contacted Schmich, made the track and got into the charts. The voice on the recorded track is that of Lee Perry, a professional voice-over artist. Interviewed in 2001,[5] he remarked that when the track was subsequently performed 'live', he was somewhat at a loss as to how to present himself. In the end, he wore a dark suit and spoke from behind a lectern. He created a speaking voice which he said 'had lived a little'. The *Chicago Tribune* described his choice of tone as having 'fatherly authority'.[6]

It's worth noting that the *sound* of the voice is more significant to the success of both the text, and its subsequent 'realization' on the music track, than the visual presence of the speaker. The Internet community seems to have sensed this in promulgating the fictional notion of Kurt Vonnegut as author. The author could have remained anonymous, but Vonnegut as author has an almost mythical cult status as a 'voice of authority' in the world of sci-fi writing, amongst American students in particular. Mary Schmich's 'authority' on the matter remains deliberately hidden behind a host of other voices. Just as everyone within a certain cultural orbit 'knows' what tonal music sounds like and 'does' (even without knowing how to articulate this), radio listeners 'know' quite a lot about listening to the invisible speaking voice. We are all authorities on the matter.

```
Lotta is in her piece, with Rob. He is very candid about his
feelings. He speaks to her, not to me, but I can eavesdrop on
the very personal details of his insecurities, regrets and the
emotions he felt then, and now. (Of course, it's all 'then', now
that it reaches me). He, she and I are looking back on that time
they had together. I know that she and he remember different
things and also that they remember the same things differently.
Lotta knows this too. But there is only one point where Lotta
(for surely it is Lotta herself?) and Rob converse on tape in
front of me, and both appear oblivious to my listening
presence:
```

[4:44]
[*Continuing background ambience of voices, phones ringing — an office perhaps*]

She: Maybe I wanted you just to take care of me and love me and . . .
He: [*Interrupting*] Right, right . . . you, you see, yeah . . . I think . . . that's probably what I wanted you to do to me, as well . . . Yeah, that's what I wanted. I mean . . . after all, that's what all men want isn't it . . .

[*Behind this a simple scalic pattern commences, played on a child's toy glockenspiel*]
to be kind of . . . taken care of.

[*Glockenspiel continues but all background ambience disappears abruptly*]

She: I remember that we only travelled in warm countries. He was so cool among all those colours . . . .

RADIO VOICES

The speaking voice on radio is an intriguing paradox. Voices 'off the radio' are ready-made material for composers, and are ripe for parody and collage. But they are also alluring in that they transmit both the 'romance' of disembodiment – an inexplicable mystery – and the chummy informality of being a friend in your ear. Sounds that reach us over the radio waves appear to be magical; they are flying, dislocated, free, and liberated – however mundane their origins.

And such sounds do 'reach out' to us in a way that other media don't. Once we've found that friend in the ear, we don't want to lose her. It is very hard to woo 'regular listeners' from one station to another, while 'regular viewers' are far more fickle. While TV offers different *channels* – an opportunity to go with the flow, change, move – radio *stations* ask you to put down your bags and rest awhile. The technology significantly assists a reluctance to abandon friendly voices – we may flip channels at the touch of a button, but we need to 'retune' our radios. Of course, many radios allow the listener to assign stations to pre-set 'memory' buttons, giving a 'flip' control comparable to the TV remote control. But this generally restricts choices to a few favourite selections – and by assigning those buttons to the stations we 'always listen to' we abandon any subsequent adventures. We only retune our radio listening when we find ourselves abroad.

◑ CD[23] *Frantic Mid-Atlantic*, by Evelyn Ficarra (excerpt)

Evelyn Ficarra's *Frantic Mid-Atlantic* takes radio listening to another country, far beyond simple collage. This piece of radiophonic art is an invitation to turn the dial on what those familiar radio voices mean to us. Her sources are gleaned from American stations, with a few from the UK, and are, for the most part, from the most mundane kinds of news and 'talk radio' programmes. There are fragments from interviews, traffic news, weather reports, news bulletins, phone-ins and late night shows. The voices initially rise out of a distant sea of crashing waves whose white noise has been gradually infiltrated by timbres reminiscent of short-wave radio static (although how often do we *actually* hear that particular radio noise now?). Choruses made from voices 'from the radio' are used to touching, and somewhat humorous, effect (everyone tells the weather or traffic news at once, everyone announces their radio station's name or frequency at the same time, everyone says their own goodbyes). At other times phrases reappear again and appear to comment self-referentially on their roles within radio: 'We're going to continue ... , 'You know, I mean, it's a little disorderly ...', 'We're trying ...'. These voices – none of whom can 'hear' each other – become a chattering cast of 'radio personae' who are familiar friends thrown into new relief by their unprogrammed collisions. What they say doesn't really matter, but how they say it does. A male BBC interviewer questions an articulate, educated High Commissioner with authoritative, weighty insistence. This is interleaved with the interrogation, via an interpreter, of a female Spanish-American. The latter is a nervous witness to a crime; the former is confidently evasive and sly. Some editing on Ficarra's part throws a little ridicule on the male interviewee ('Let's talk about fish' is hauled out of context), but otherwise allows the painful differences between the two scenarios to speak for themselves.

In its episodic coming and goings *Frantic Mid-Atlantic* creates its own narrative tide from layered voices, swathes of static and surrealized Morse code beeps. (We know in our bones that these beeps are coded secrets, but how often have we *actually* heard such messages outside fiction?) The piece has a rhythmic structure that could be heard as a hybrid between 'magazine' format[7] and a kind of overtly musical rondo refrain. The pace is gentle and the touch is light. While rolling waves of noise crash softly on the borders of abstraction, the voices are never fragmented to the point of losing their radio connotations. The content – what they say – is carefully edited to *accentuate* their role as being 'about the radio' while the sound of their voices provides a musical ebb and flow of varying intonations. Perhaps, while they float back and forth across the boundary between information – sense – and sound, we retune between radio, music, radio, music ... .

The final section of the piece offers a typical 'late night sign off' from a particularly saccharine radio host. Her voice is warm and cosy, in your ear; she's right there, keeping you company – but, by now, the insincere intimacy of this radio persona is made explicit. Displaced from her usual context she is vacuous and ephemeral, and nothing more than air.

[*Continuing sound of waves crashing in the distance, subdued noise*]

Well, well, well, here we are ...
In this grey and cool air evening, umbrellas and raincoats are in order ...
And it's a night to snuggle up. And, if you're close to a fire, and the logs are crackling away ...
Remember to put one on for me.

[*Waves crash and fade*]

Lotta and Rob are talking in my ear. On the face of it her work
is a small, inconsequential documentary that has an understated
realism and remains unclouded by too much technological
intervention. The natural-sounding conversation seems to take
place within everyday environments — perhaps from his (their?)
flat, then a café, an office, children — with a few bars of
glockenspiel or out-of-tune piano music added to the final mix.
The narrative thread is provided by Lotta's commentary.

Their simple story seems quite touching and naive; they are
just sitting there, baring their feelings to one another, but
also to me, of course. I have come to care about them — are they
still together, are they in England now, was this just a brief
moment of nostalgia before they went their separate ways?
Sometimes I recollect similar experiences alongside Lotta's
and Rob's remembering. And sometimes I am more jaded, and the
piece seems a rather self-indulgent, self-aware construction
that makes me feel that I have been duped into eavesdropping on
a fake, contrived relationship. Those domestic background
sounds are clearly 'mixed in'. Worse, the very opening is an
arch reference to both the radio programme 'theme tune' and the
fact that technology mediates both sound and how we hear it:
after a few notes of unannounced recorded music Rob turns off a
cassette machine and changes the tape because, as he then
observes directly to Lotta, 'this one sounds all furry'. This
could be real, or acted after the fact. What is the fact? What
is 'real'? Who are they? Things do indeed sound a little furry.

Lotta is in her piece, interviewing Rob. In fact, in the sections
of apparent 'actuality' she is hardly there at all. I can only hear
Rob's responses to those questions which she presumably asked —
'What do you remember?', 'Do you remember . . .?', 'What did you
feel when . . .?' This kind of absence is quite the norm in
documentary radio where an interviewer might ask questions to
elicit information and response, subsequently editing out her own
voice when mixing the programme. The interviewer's role in this
context is to extract content, and then step out of the limelight.
More importantly, the now silent interviewer may be inaudible but
is not absent. She becomes a listener, who brings us, listening,
into the time of the interview. It's as if we're almost there in her
place.

But when Lotta does this her inaudible voice is the missing
half of an *intimate* dialogue between two people. She *should* be
there because she is directly involved. By wilfully silencing
her voice, she places me in *her* position, so that I become the
listening lover to whom Rob reveals his emotions and feelings

of remorse, and even his remembered sexual insecurities. He's
uncomfortable. So am *I*.

HIDDEN VOICES

Well, well, well, there we were ... snuggled up by the fire together. But Evelyn Ficarra's
sugar-sweet presenter wasn't really there for me. An endless wall of blindness came
between us. In order to get close, sight had to be bracketed out of the experience. I
couldn't see her (sitting behind her desk in a brightly lit booth) and she couldn't see me
(lying in the bath with one toe stuck up the dripping tap). But I didn't even want to
imagine her. If there are certain boundaries that a radio persona cannot cross without
deliberate transgression there is one that she shouldn't cross at *all,* and that is from
invisibility to visibility.[8]

There has to be space between us because she is not really either 'here' or 'there'.
Transmission takes (a kind of) time, even without the 'obscenity delay' that most live
radio employs. Once inside a radio drama we may go along with the pretence and
imagine pictures for the characters in a play – too often an approximation of visual
theatre – but we don't want to see the voice of radio presence. Some things are best left
hidden, and there are reasons for this:

> ... while in cultural production, and particularly in mass media, the model for presence is the
> speaking subject, the real significance of presence is caught up in the notion of inner speech.
> For 'truth,' we know, can be spoken only through the technology of language. Despite the
> simulation of interiority by the media, the voice comes full circle – back to language, and
> back to its silence in the anaerobic, anechoic chambers of the mind.
> (Dyson, 1974, p. 177)

The disembodied voice has a presence beyond vision. As Dyson notes, the interiority of
the speaking voice produced by mass media is a simulated one. Certainly the radio
voice in the ear can encourage the feeling that we are listening to our own beliefs and
thoughts articulated (hence our loyalty to programmes that 'speak our language'). But,
while we're not looking, variations on this disembodied voice can slip from place to
place under cover of darkness. That visual blackout is essential to any work for sound
alone; it might be radio, or the electroacoustic concert hall, installation space, gallery –
or just the space between your ears. I have always distrusted that old wives' tale, 'what
the eye doesn't see, the heart doesn't grieve over'. Because when the lights go down,
we still listen. And we can still grieve.

⊕ CD[24] *Hidden Lives*, by Cathy Lane (excerpt)

Hidden Lives is Cathy Lane's 'celebration of all lives lived and forgotten' and explores
ideas of 'women as the curators of memory and of hidden histories'.[9] This work for

sound alone – composed for the concert hall rather than the radio – broadcasts a subtle lament through a host of inner voices that speak invisibly. Whilst drawing attention to the 'interior' domestic territory that women have often, historically, both inhabited and made, the piece also grieves audibly for what wasn't seen, and still isn't seen by too many.

Although the major part of the work is made from speech sounds, the piece begins and ends with the quite 'ordinary' ambience of life on a normal street. This documentary sound, the recorded comings and goings of people walking about, does not communicate 'music' or 'abstraction' but does transmit the voice of 'broadcast actuality' and presence. It is, in that contradictory way that unadulterated recordings imply, the sound of 'how things are' – the truth – 'right now'. It is also the sound of unfettered, exterior space. Both these actualities are now rebroadcast in the concert hall. But it is not long before the resonant crash of a metaphoric door slams shut on one truth and offers an alternative. Space is very much at issue here – this is most definitely not a radio work, since the slam of the door puts us 'inside' the concert hall, participating in a metaphor. Isolated vocal fragments occupy this newly confined space, appearing first in one place, then another. These sounds are miniscule to the point of non-existence, ranging from short sibilants (tss … psss … ssss) to tiny inhalations and shushing sounds. Though very much part of normal speech, these are sounds that are generally unheard, or at least remain unnoticed. But now they are placed in the foreground, buzzing back and forth in our ears, while, in the background, an ominous distortion creaks and groans.

It is not until about seven minutes into the piece that intelligible words start to emerge. Prior to this, the sound world is made from flurries of vocal fragments (all women's voices – this is very clear from the timbre) that gradually build into swishing, repetitive surges before subsiding again. These repetitive rhythmic waves are too fast to be soothing, and have a sense of industry that is perhaps reminiscent of sweeping, scrubbing or polishing. There are fleeting moments where fragments become phonemes and a vowel sound leans towards the possibility of speech. Despite the nature of the sounds – soft, unvoiced, ephemeral – there is a kind of frantic urgency throughout. The imprisoned speaking voice – an identity that has been cut into tiny pieces – is somehow masked or trapped beyond communication, but is most definitely there.

You might expect that words would grow from this striving mass and that fragments would lengthen, bit by bit, into phonemes, words and finally speech. But although they certainly build towards some kind of *dénouement*, this is not how speech emerges. Why not? Well, the community of tiny speech sounds *cannot* speak because it is truly incorporeal – a fact delineated by the dynamic use of space – and is not concerned with direct reference to any exterior 'reality'. These sounds do amass as a single voice, but this is the speechless voice of a disturbed 'interiority'. Here the interiority that radio voices strive to appropriate for speech ('Let me just whisper in your ear and we'll pretend *you're* thinking my words') is itself appropriated to become an interiority that speaks through sound alone. Words fail it. Words require other voices, which is the reason why snippets of speech begin to step forward from behind this wall of vocal disturbance; here, at last, are the ordinary voices of women speaking. Although they are invisible too, they represent an exterior normality. But, because they are both invisible and 'real', they must be 'transmitted' from 'outside'. And this is a reference to the 'non-live' broadcasting voice that sets them apart from where 'we' are, listening in.

[*6:45 onwards*]
[*More than one female voice, layered*]

sleeveless dresses ... fresh eggs ... Mondays ... in hot weather a deodorant should be used ... you will find ... at least a job ... only herself to blame ...
... washed ... baby's breakfast ... dining room ... passage ... 8:30 ... boiled sweets ... kitchen and lavatory ... passage ... sweep bedroom ... bedroom ... prepare baby's lunch ... wash up ... do shopping ... 1pm ... and change ... baby's tea, put baby to sleep ... cleaning silver ... the pram ... 7:30 7pm 3pm ... living room, baby's bed ...

While this is going on, the fragmentary vocal sounds continue to obstruct and colour the texture. But the speaking voices become more and more insistent, mix in lower and higher transpositions, and become louder – and thus nearer – until their words become a ranting cacophony. But wait, rewind a bit: there's something in their tone that is quite revealing. Whether by inspired accident or design, the voices are not *performing* their words in declamatory fashion; they are *reading* aloud. Although I didn't speak up about this earlier (I apologize for keeping you in the dark) the source material for *Hidden Lives* is taken from recordings of women reading from *The Book of Hints and Wrinkles*. Lane describes this wryly as 'a small piece of social history from the 1930s which describes how women should manage both their houses and themselves in no uncertain terms'.[10]

In her programme notes for the piece Lane describes these voices as building up to a 'wall of orders and commands' but I think the passage concerned can also be heard as the articulation of an escalating anger in reaction to unsustainable demands. In speaking about the work, Lane has remarked on how friends who read for her expressed amazement, amused astonishment – and sometimes anger – at the sentiments in the text.[11] And I wonder if you can hear this in their neutral speaking tones that place space between voice and text and say 'This is my reading voice'. Read my lips, but someone else's words. These voices depict and comment, simultaneously.

In reading a text, one invisible voice addresses another; the reading voice meets the authorial voice, and words are shared.[12] But the reading voice also meets the listening voice. When we 'do' reading we are also doing listening to our own interior voice. So there are other implications to get cosy with. When someone (whether Daddy or a tape) reads aloud to us, it's not just that we are listening to someone 'doing reading' for us, they are also doing 'being us'. It's no wonder that we prefer to find the voice attractive, or at least to feel we might just get along. Well-known actors with distinctive voices are often used for recorded readings of novels: the success of BBC Radio 4's long-running *Book at Bedtime* lies in its winning combination of attractive timbre (... and now that nice Martin Jarvis) and popular text (... reads *Pride and Prejudice*, episode 11). You certainly don't want readers to make a big performance out of the activity, and the voices that read in Cathy Lane's *Hidden Lives* don't. They read in an unaffected manner and their voices are well modulated and easy to understand. When they 'do' reading for us, we are perhaps more likely to listen to them, and identify with them, than if they had stood up on a soapbox and yelled. We hear their dignity in relation to their indignation at the text they are encountering. And, after all, it is a piece about indignity beyond words.

And here are a last few words on the reading voice. Other than the important translation from seeing letters on the page, and processing them as text, we read prose without any particular need for visual amplification.[13] The text communicates an entirety and though we may picture how a character or situation looks, our visualization is simply a pencil sketch or a quick snapshot to sum up what was said. And I think that this is another reason why taped books are good for accompanying driving or trying to nod off. It's not just that someone else turns the pages while you're busy turning the steering wheel; it's also that you don't need to concretize visual or visualized images to be fully involved. We don't run a film in our mind, frame by frame, as we listen to a novel on tape. Both our external visual apparatus, and our inner eye, can be directed elsewhere (which is fortunate). But we *are* doing *listening* whether we are read to, or read 'to ourselves'. It is very hard to attend to someone speaking while immersed in a book. Shush, stop it, do go away. Can't you see? I'm trying to read.

Lotta tells the story. Her words are clear and unhurried, probably scripted or thought out in advance. Her narrative tells me the story, and the story that has already happened.[14] This is no 'audio-diary' confession. She is not embarrassed, nervous or shy. The recording quality is impeccable; she wants to get it right. More significantly, when she speaks, the background ambience fades to almost nothing and she is just there in 'dead' air, outside its world.

This convention is widely used in 'magazine format' radio, where documentary segments are corralled together by written 'links'. We go 'back to the studio' for the familiar presenter's voice. (Perhaps the written equivalent is the return of a different typeface each time.) Reassured, our listening ambles off obediently, taking geographical and metaphorical displacement in its stride without noticing, over much, that it is responding to direction. But this presenting voice — always the same voice, situated in a neutral, very 'present' place — keeps coming back to talk to us and keep us on track. It is the same voice every time, and frequently the same voice 'at the same time next week'. It's an old refrain.

So Lotta is presenter. But her voice transgresses the boundaries of this role too. While her interviewing presence may be virtually silent, her presenting voice says too much. She's explaining her side of the story to me. She has stepped

out of the background into dead air to tell me secrets, which
Rob can't hear (she refers to him in the third person). Her
links are not a means of getting from one place to another. The
content is personal, intimate and anecdotal. Rather than create
objectivity she draws me into an illicit relationship with a
presenter who is involved rather than disinterested. Her voice
does not comment on the story, her voice *is* the story. She wants
me on her side, and she presents her side immaculately.

CLEAN AND UNCLEAN VOICES

Cathy Lane's *Hidden Lives* rails against a text that extols the virtue of cleanliness but
surreptitiously uses that virtue to keep women invisible, locked in their homes by
routine tasks. Well, that was the 1930s and things may have changed a bit. In Lane's
subtle reading the text becomes both a cipher for those things that haven't changed, and
a celebration of those things – and people – that have. Today, sitting at a laptop in my
1930s-built home, I didn't even make the bed, let alone scrub the step. But cleanliness
is still a metaphorical worry when it comes to sound. The live radio announcer's one
aim in life is to get through the whole performance without a hiccup. To cough or
splutter is to admit human weakness and thereby unintentionally to embody a
disembodied voice. And to retain its superior 'other-worldliness' the radio voice of
authority needs to be suspended in 'an abstract and idealized' space (Dyson, 1974,
p. 180). When BBC radio discussion programmes are aurally invaded by the sound of
offstage drills (as quite often seems to happen), a boundless space for sparkling wit
encounters the brouhaha of a less than perfect wall. There is embarrassment all round.

   Dyson's exploration of the 'radio voice' is confined to tracing the genealogy of that
well-spoken voice of authority. This voice (whether male or female) is, of course,
clean-cut; it speaks in a clear, educated manner, with a confident tone.[15] A 'good voice
for radio' in this very particular sense is one that indicates trustworthiness and
reliability *as a result* of its clean enunciation. However the enunciation must remain
'invisible' in the listener's conscious evaluation of these character traits. It can be a
nasty shock when this voice turns up in the wrong hands; it's no coincidence that 'Bond
movie' villains, and similar characters, are well-spoken individuals (and, in American
movies, often played as stereotypically British 'upper-crust').[16]

   When it comes to post-production in radio, not to mention other recorded media, the
'clean edit' is a vital complement to the announcer's clarity of enunciation. Sound
editing can become an obsessive quest to wash away troublesome grime. The dark
secrets of the edit are so well hidden that, in common parlance, 'sound editing' refers
solely to the cutting and splicing of recorded sound in time whereas, in reality, it can
often involve precise manipulation of the recorded material to 'remove error' by means
of digital filtering or reverberation. Such techniques are usually used quite crudely in

speech radio to compress away unwanted background noise but, significantly, pop music stations with DJ presenters seem more fastidious, desiring to erase all signs of a space other than the one created by the music.[17] A 'good' edit ensures that the text is clear and uncluttered, and able to speak on its own terms. A 'good' edit is 'invisible' to the reader or listener. The 'good' radio edit enforces the disembodiment of speech but remains inaudible. You cannot hear the joins. No listener should even consider the possibility that a hard-pressed production assistant spent an irate 30 minutes on someone's nervous throat clearing. Edit and enunciation go hand-in-hand into this perfect world of mainstream radio where everything appears to be cut and dried. (Clean is good – invisible and absent; unclean is bad – visible and present.) But let me mention some ways in which these two 'voices' – edit and enunciation – can speak up through their subtle subversion. The two are omnipresent and cannot be got rid of: clean or unclean they are always there, the one in the technology, the other in the voice. Even the live microphone 'edits' the enunciating voice by accentuating various aspects of its timbre and paying less attention to others. But the squeaky-clean enunciation that still characterizes the 'voice of authority' is now ironicized (and alien, to many people). Producers now relish 'unclean voices' as communicative in a very precise way: to the British, Scottish accents are currently deemed 'trustworthy',[18] 'estuary English'[19] appeals to youth audiences, and minority and/or regional accents promote inclusivity (at least, that's what it sounds like). Radio trips over itself in an effort to leap over class-conscious boundaries yelling, 'Hey, listen. I'm not that posh you know'. But though the lepers of received pronunciation have been banished, the reappropriation of regional enunciation on mainstream radio is still somewhat self-conscious: those regional accents must be *noticed* in order to do the trick – they have to be heard to make a noise.

Everyone is trying to get down and dirty – but the voice of authority has not really left the building. A nice Scottish radio voice with 'sultry' or 'husky' tones remains a disembodied one.[20] Achieving disembodiment is one thing, but re-embodying the incorporeal voice requires a bit of an act. It involves painting on a bit of stage make-up, accentuating the positive through the unclean voices of editing and enunciation. When Barthes speaks of the 'grain' as the 'body in the voice as it sings, the hand as it writes, the limb as it performs'[21] he is calling for the corporeal presence as an antidote to the disembodied purity of the technically 'perfect' singing voice. For him, cleanliness is not necessarily next to godliness: the embodied singing voice is transcendent *through* the very sounds of its embodiment – the presence of the throat in the roll of an 'r', the 'patinated' vowels that show the 'wear of the language'. The re-embodiment of disembodied sounds requires one to go from the sublime to … this guy I used to listen to, called Bruce.

As an insomniac graduate student, far from home, I spent many a wasted, late-night hour listening to phone-ins on local radio. I really enjoyed them. I had a particular soft spot for Bruce, (no doubt syndicated across America) who dispensed wisdom on anything from roof cleaning and résumés, to how to get off the booze or on to TV. His steady stream of callers greeted him like a neighbour. I was fascinated by the trusting, bizarre, and sometimes desperate, folks who called in, and their various problems and

... hey, I just liked his laid-back drawl: 'Well, well, well, here we are again ...' But what was it that made him so 'ordinary'? Why did people trust him? What did he do that made his little constructed world so convincing? How could he be 'just like me' to so many individuals? I got hooked on the cracks between his words – the way he was so *audibly* 'human' – he sniffed, creaked in his chair, snapped open a can of coke, rummaged for a cookie, flipped through papers, pressed and punched buttons, frequently fumbled with either his words or his technology. He made no secret of being in a radio studio, and I swear I heard him put his feet up on the desk. We were all in on the act.

And those 'offstage' sounds, that nobody edited out, became the accompaniment to the personal anecdotes that he snuck in now and then (another dirty trick you're probably familiar with). In addition, because he was thinking on his feet, his speech had lots of 'spacers' – all those sounds we use to fill gaps, the 'ers, ahs, hurrumphs, mmms' of our non-verbal communication. Who gave him a creaky chair? Why didn't he drink out of a plastic cup? Did he really need to rustle all that paper and hit all those buttons? Did he really have to make such a racket? Of course not. But extraneous noise did not appear to be edited out (though the programme was certainly not live by the time it reached me) and his voice luxuriated in the grunge of paralanguage. The two unclean voices, edit and enunciation, were working together to give a semblance of corporeality to a radio voice. By these means Bruce and his ilk – they are such stereotypes that we make shows about *them* – invite you to come on in and pull up a chair. But beware of letting strangers into your home; they may notice the dirt and use it to their advantage.

⏵ CD[25] *Geekspeak*, by Pamela Z (excerpt)

In *Geekspeak*, Pamela Z walks right in and pulls the rug from under her victims' feet. She subverts the voices of edit and enunciation to dish the dirt on some other stereotypes. Her subjects are not incorporeal; as with Bruce, the 'dirt' of paralanguage is used to flesh them out and create a fictionalized presence, but here these same processes heighten their lack of substance in other terms.

Geekspeak's recorded sources are the speaking voices of several employees in the Laboratories of Xerox PARC, Palo Alto. These male Californian computer experts are interviewed *in situ*, and give their opinions on various computer operating systems and terminology. Their voices become the material for an apparently jovial piece of sampler-chic. But even though it may be lightweight and humorous on the outside, *Geekspeak* comments insidiously on the darker implications of some disconcerting binaries. And it does so by means of some disarmingly ordinary tricks. On the whole, words remain perfectly intelligible, and the verbal content is exposed, rather than being turned to purely sonic ends. However, the content is edited into short phrases and repetitions, and forced to participate in musical games. The piece cheerfully dismantles grammatical sense and thus draws attention to the non-verbal communication of diction, accent, turns of phrase and vocal mannerisms. It doesn't take a huge amount of effort to get the point and smile (or wince, depending on your own situation).

[*Opening – counterpoint, one voice entering after another*]

Bit baud byte Bit baud byte Bit baud byte Bit baud byte Bit baud byte ....
   Currently written as 32-bit able Currently written as 32-bit able Currently written ...
     Quite an operating system Quite an operating system Quite an operating system ...
      the basic ... the basic simple definition of a geek ....

[*sotto voce mumble*] howdihowrightyeah/(breath) ... I ... I ... don't know how to articulate it really ...

Of course, they *have* articulated it, pretty much; they dug their own hole as soon as they opened their mouths, although Pamela Z certainly helped them to jump in. In more than one sense, this piece is about undermining how people define themselves – in both verbal and social arenas – and the difference between defining yourself, and being defined by others. These voices inform us that they are articulate and expert at one level, but are perhaps inarticulate and lacking in insight from another point of view. In their obsession with clarity, machine-reliability and system optimization, their sights are set on the sterile perfection of the digitally clean binary world. But, as Laurie Anderson has said, that's 'just not enough range'.[22]

The piece continues along a deftly constructed episodic narrative, during the course of which the speakers voice their own definitions of a 'geek' or a 'nerd'. Later on they are evidently invited to consult the dictionary. I say 'evidently' because the voice that asked is silent, edited out. They read (and we hear them 'doing reading', as in Lane's piece) with obvious surprise.[23]

[*Layered speech, reading voices*]

Geek ... the carnival performer ... person that bites chickens heads off ... geek eats chickens heads ... nerd eats pizza! ... [*reading*] biting a head of a live chicken or snake ... the origins of the word aren't terribly pleasant!

As an underlying provocation, the work interleaves two genres, and it is never quite clear which one is in parentheses.[24] This is a documentary radio work (the material is recorded interviews, and the subject matter is organized into a narrative) and it is music (often edited into rhythmic patterns). It is affectionately teasing (looped speech fragments become amusing riffs) but also pokes cruel fun (the repetition makes the speakers sound ridiculous). In formal terms the piece is cleanly constructed (episodic 'counterpoint' or ostinati interspersed with solos) but in production terms the sound is unclean (the sounds often contain room noise, the edited cuts are 'crude', and the voices are not particularly 'good' for radio).

These are patently location recordings: there is quite a bit of room ambience in the signal and, at times, the background hum of machines and some 'offstage' human activity is quite prevalent. Speech is of priority, and background noise is neither loud nor brought forward to participate. (Non-vocal 'noise' is only used once as an overtly illustrative foreground element – the turning of pages when the dictionary is consulted.) For the most part, the more undefined noise in the signal is just 'there', untreated by filtering or compression. But noise is in the way; though apparently just a bit of barely noticeable grit, its presence blurs the edges between zero and one on a number of counts. Editing accentuates it; it becomes audible at the beginning and end of a sample and its timbral profile 'speaks' through its looped repetition. In Lane's *Hidden Lives* the meticulous editing of spoken words created a metaphorical veil, from voices suppressed through the 'deverbalizing' of speech. But here, noise communicates over and above perfectly intelligible speech. It adds its unclean veneer to the oververbalized 'precision' of technobabble and provides a surreptitious interpretation: jargon makes a noise in order to exclude the uninitiated, who perhaps should get back to their sweeping. Sadly, for Pamela Z's victims, cute and rather imprecise sampler loops undermine any pseudo-Masonic posturing.

There is also noise in the speakers' enunciation in the first place, or rather in their lack of performance. These people are talking, in a relaxed manner, caught in their natural environment. They are confident, and not even particularly self-consciousness in front of the microphone (possibly they weren't aware of its presence). They are generalized by disembodiment (you can't put a face to them) but particularized by their different vocal timbres. And, of course, these utterances are also used as instrumental voices. The use of deliberately trite 'counterpoint' (the opening being a prime example) sees them marshalled into responding to a musical baton and 'coming in' at the right time. This ushers natural, speaking voices onto the stage. Once there, they become stereotypical characters in a play on more than words, and the lights can be very unforgiving. One speaker has a distinctive manner of speaking that is so apparently relaxed that he has a constant underlying 'drawl'. But his fast, monotone delivery contradicts this and reflects the hyperactivity of his obsessive enthusiasm. When his voice is looped, the drawl becomes a comical ratchet sound ('quite an operating system') that turns listening from words to timbre. Elsewhere the same voice's monotone delivery is mocked by merely presenting its speech as a stream of relentless verbiage. This strategy is interesting, because it is clarity that gives the game away. In both the examples below phrases have been spliced together, to give the impression of natural continuous speech. In fact there are not that many splices, and joins are largely 'invisible', with words or phrases shortened or gaps 'filled in' with other words:

[00:58]
[*solo*]

> my definition of a geek would be some one who finds a machine er ... really esoteric like logical to be really fascinating construct and likes to and understands it see what its limits are and see exactly what it en..entails play with it and to the extent that they probably find it slightly more fascinating than conversation with most people.

Here there are no loops or contrapuntal layers but there is radio's concern with clean edit and clean enunciation. He is indeed the (defining) voice of authority, to his own ears, at least. Of course 'he' is a constructed persona caricatured by this alliance of edit and enunciation. This cartoonish quality is barely noticeable on first pass since the speech appears convincingly 'real' in a documentary sense, and this part of the piece seems skewed towards a more straightforward radio presentation. A join at the end is revealed not by a 'bad' edit, but by a shift down in intonation. This provides a cadential touch that is comic both because of the words themselves, and the fact that it shifts attention back to musical construction ('more fascinating than conversation with most people' is in an emphatic and slightly pitch-shifted voice). Just a short while later the same persona provides a neat illustration of his own definition:

[3:16]

Mac ... no question
Originally written as 32 bit able ... didn't have the ability to handle 32-bit data passes in the ROM ... no, sorry, the *machines* had the ability to handle it before the operating system did and then they eventually had to go back and write an operating system 2cx where you had to buy a little enabler patch 32-bit mode the way that they designed the system software is that you could tell the system to not look in the ROM ... but just to look somewhere else in the system you know you just rewrite it in the system and they change the pointer to where that particular data is

[*Continuous speech goes on for several more minutes ...*]

... Although I do dream of computers and I had one really weird dream where I was trying to move my arm by double-clicking on it.

So, if in the first example the content is only touching on incoherence, with a comic twist to finish, by the second he's off on a geekish roll, and there's no real stopping his peacock display. When other voices enter, the monologue continues relentlessly in the background, repeatedly pushing to the fore. Although he's not exactly talking rubbish, it does seem a bit grubby for our listening to match his obsessive fervour, given the content. This second monologue, which goes on and on and *on*, is not an unaccompanied solo throughout. When it begins, the other voices contribute underlying repetitions of a previously heard bit of mumbling and then voices gradually enter with variations on 'I was toast', 'toast ...'. leading into a 'chorus' on the theme of 'toast' (computer-geek slang for having messed something up or having got into trouble). Later there's a cruelly elegiac 'slow' episode: 'Cool little box ... ... it was so beautiful in that it was all ... structured ... cool little box ... ... just a cool thing in itself ... how cool! [*growing volume and enthusiasm*] just like ... how cool ... the most exciting thing in modern ... Cool! ...'

A solo male performer, given to swaggering a bit and performing in a fast, rhythmic monotone. A posse of on-stage (male) friends who listen, and encourage with an interjection here and there, and who chip in with the chorus. An unbreachable barrage of words, with its own rules of grammar and street-cred argot. He's toasting. He has all the bits, bauds, and bytes on his side. He knows just which pointer goes where. You know, I think I've heard this somewhere before. Perhaps this nod to that most misogynist of musical forms is just a subtle 'rap' on the knuckles, a gentle way of dishing the dirt on what computer geeks (or any other type of 'geek') are doing when they show off all their fancy words. But, don't forget, in this particular case a woman pulls the strings. And nothing could be less intimidating – we're laughing.

Did I find Lotta's voice? Perhaps it's sufficient to hope so.
Lotta Erickson speaks through and in her piece. All these
created voices — interviewer, presenter and reminiscing lover,
are 'Lotta'. They break their own rules of engagement by
ganging up together in one persona. In doing so, perhaps they
comment on the impossibility of a reliable documentary of
memories and feelings, or of describing either without peering
through the present at the recorded past.

They join a host of invisible voices that can speak in different ways: documentary
voices, musical voices, invisible and unseen voices, unseeing voices, suppressed
voices, authoritative voices, reading voices, speechless voices, the voices of editing,
enunciation, disembodiment, re-embodiment and the voice that hears it all. And all
these voices – how they can speak, and who can speak through them – are open to
interpretation. You just need to listen.

Notes

1 Because I can't find Lotta Erickson to ask her permission, I can't include an excerpt from her
   work here. The work is *Please Mr Coldstream* and it was released on a CD of radio art which
   accompanied an issue of the London Musicians' Collective journal, *Resonance,* entitled 'Retuning
   Radio', vol. 5, no. 2 (November 1996). At the time of writing you can still order this issue from www.
   l-m-c.org.uk/resonance/vol.5.2.html – if you cannot find it, you could try soundingart@novamara.com
2 The voices in this essay are English-speaking voices, and the radio references are to English-speaking
   radio, both British and American. This is because I have chosen to speak through my own experience,
   and these are the voices I know – but, of course, there are other voices too.
3 This is probably not her real name – names can reveal too much – but at least they help to create an
   internal image of a small woman with an indistinct voice.
4 'The Salesman', track 2 of *The ugly one with the jewels and other stories* has an example of this kind
   of ironic social comment. Laurie Anderson's processed voice enacts the puerile, competitive
   backbiting of the salesman calling into head office:

   [Anderson in 'voice of authority' mode]: Uh, Frank? Listen ... Frank ... you know I hate
   to say this about Brad, I mean we both know he's got a heck of a job ... yeah ... right ...
   we both know that Brad just isn't pulling his weight ... and I'm not just saying this
   because we're up for the same Safeway account ... .

5 *I Love 1999*, BBC2 TV, 3 November 2001.
6 See *From column to song: 'Sunscreen' spreads to Chicago* by Mark Caro, *Tribune* staff writer, 31
   March 1999, available by searching at www.chicagotribune.com
7 For an interesting (and inadvertently amusing) example of this see the programme structure of the
   Hong Kong Business Association of Hawaii's radio programme at http://www.hkbah.org/radio_
   program.htm (click on the link to 'Program Format'). I hope you enjoy the music too.
8 An example from the parallel universe of TV: *Morecambe and Wise*, the popular UK comedy show,
   once featured Angela Rippon, a nationally known TV newsreader, as a guest. (*Morecambe and Wise*

Christmas Show, BBC 1, 1976). At that time, newsreaders always sat demurely behind a desk. In the sketch concerned Rippon read the news for a few minutes, before breaking off to come out from behind her desk to commence a high-kick dance number. The transgression still provokes amusement, and is endlessly re-shown (and purchased), which perhaps gives some indication of just how fixed and stereotypical the newsreader role remains.

9 Programme notes by Lane for performance of *Hidden Lives*, in the programme booklet for the International Computer Music Conference, 2000, Berlin.

10 Ibid.

11 During Lane's presentation at 'Sound Practice, The First UKISC Conference on Sound, Culture and Environments', Dartington Hall, UK, 16–20 February 2001.

12 Being read to in bed is another situation in which the listener has eyes closed so that the reading voice is 'unseen' and disembodied. Paul Lansky's piece, *Now and Then*, is about the very activity of reading stories out loud. He says: 'Common wisdom has it that it is never too soon to read to children. Even before they can speak they enjoy the regular, soothing patterns of speech – it must be a kind of music to them. ... *Now and Then* is a musical encapsulation of the sound of this activity' (Liner notes to *Homebrew* by Paul Lansky, BRIDGE BCD 9035).

13 Obviously there are genres in which visual and textual media are integrated, but here I mean prose.

14 'We believe that narrative consists not in communicating what one has seen but in transmitting what one has heard, what someone else said to you. Hearsay' (Deleuze and Guattari, 1987, p. 76).

15 As an example, see http://www.castaway.org.uk/male.htm – *Castaway* is an agency that offers a range of clients with good voices for radio, describing one (male) actor's voice as, 'Rich and deep, gravelly yet sexy. Authority with a light touch'. And another (male) as 'a friendly Scottish voice with strength, vitality & enthusiasm'.

16 In a directly self-referential and subversive nod to the broadcast voice of authority's implications 'Side-show Bob', the well-spoken villain of the popular cartoon series *The Simpsons* is voiced by Kelsey Grammer, who himself plays the eponymous star of the comedy TV show, *Frasier*. Frasier is a radio phone-in psychiatrist whose radio persona ('the voice of Seattle') is the epitome of well-educated, trustworthy authority; of course, the whole show is built on lampooning this characterization in relation to the disasters of his 'real' life. Similarly, 'Side-show Bob' is a parody of the intelligent villain persona. Parodies of two genres are entangled in their own self-parody. And don't forget that cartoons are another medium that relies heavily on the ability of the voice to transmit nuances of character. (In a parody of yet another cultural icon, the final words each week on *Frasier* are 'Frasier has left the building'. They call Elvis – that other now disembodied voice – to mind. And, as with Elvis, though we don't see his bodily presence in the flesh, some of us like to pretend he's still out there.)

17 Of course, editing frequently crosses into producing, and the line between the creative preparation and actual creation of new material becomes difficult to demark.

18   Robotic-sounding voices are not pleasant to listen to so we set out to develop a synthesised voice that was as human sounding as possible. Scotland is often chosen as a location for call centres because the Scottish accent has been said to engender trust and is popular with many people.

        We have already recorded a Scottish voice from a fairly generic Scottish speaker. It is more of an Eddie Mair, Scottish newsreader-style accent rather than a regional one that people might find difficult to understand. We are also working on younger and older and male and female voices. (From an article on voice-synthesis software, published in *Scotland on Sunday*, 27 May 2001).

    See http://www.rhetoricalsystems.com/press/010527_scotsun.htm for the full article.

19 'Estuary English' is a colloquial slang in Britain for English with an uneducated accent, specifically from the Thames estuary area in Essex. This accent has become so fashionable that people have been known to fake it in order to sound 'right'.

20 http://www.speak-voices.com/ displays online promotion for voice-over artists: two examples: 'Funky charismatic presenter with a husky voice' (woman) and 'Very experienced commercial voiceover. Her voice also lends itself to menu and promo reads, as it can be cool and sultry sounding, but adding warmth with great ease.'

21   The 'grain' is the body in the voice as it sings, the hand as it writes, the limb as it performs. If I perceive the 'grain' in a piece of music and accord this 'grain' a theoretical value (the emergence of the text in the work), I inevitably set up a new scheme of evaluation which will certainly be individual – I am determined to listen to my relation with the body of the man or woman singing or playing and that relation is erotic – but in no way 'subjective' (it is not the psychological 'subject' in me who is listening; the climactic pleasure hoped for is not going to reinforce – to express – that subject but, on the contrary, to lose it). (Barthes, 1977, p. 188)

22 From the lyrics to *Lower Mathematics*, 1986:

      Now, in my opinion, the problem with these numbers is that they are just too close – leaves very little room for everybody else. Just not enough range. So first, I think we should get rid of the value judgments attached to these two numbers and recognize that to be a zero is no better, no worse, than to be number one. Because what we are actually looking at here are the building blocks of the Modern Computer Age.
      (Anderson, 1994, p. 135)

23 And for a good read about *that* kind of geek I recommend *Geek Love*, a novel by Katherine Dunn.

24 Though commissioned by New American Radio *Geekspeak* was first presented as a performance at SoundCulture '96 festival. This work steps into that interesting (and increasingly common) transgressive space between experimental radio and music.

Chapter 6

Figure-toi …
Listening to *Sous le regard d'un soleil noir* by **Francis Dhomont**

Sous le regard d'un soleil noir is concerned with schizophrenia and the confusion of perceiving the world in an unusual and often frightening way. It seemed only appropriate that my exploration should engage in vocal counterpoint. Sometimes traditional forms offer subversive routes; it's just a matter of context. Each voice can be read on its own, or you can choose to embark on horizontal journeys that leap from voice to voice and pursue other allusions. There is space between the words, and sometimes that absence is intended to speak. And there is a **bold** story too, of a fragmentary kind. How you read this piece is up to you and, for this reason, I haven't given that many clues. Reading, like listening, is a personal endeavour.

Dhomont's work is in eight movements or 'sections', and is over 50 minutes in duration. Each section is separately titled, and discrete in itself. This discussion includes an exploration of the very opening of the first (*Pareil à un voyageur perdu*) and the whole of the sixth movement (*Citadelle intérieure*). These extracts are both on the accompanying CD.[1]

FIGURE-TOI …	PICTURE …	SPEAK …	LISTEN …
[A listening to the opening of movement 1] CD[26] *Pareil à un voyageur perdu* (section 1)	[A remembrance of listening to Francis Dhomont]	[Francis Dhomont in interview]	[A listening to movement 6] CD [27] *Citadelle intérieure* (section 6)
All of a sudden, a voice speaks. A man's voice, which occupies a specific point in space and time. Someone is present, but apparently invisible. So – because people are not generally invisible – we must be in the dark. Or at least, that is one way of perceiving reality that makes sense.			
You are **listening** to a work for sound alone. There were no introductory flourishes. There was not even an ambient space – an empty stage – to herald a commencement. There are none of the conventional signs.	I am **listening** to the sound I **recorded**. I don't remember there being this much of it. *Picture …* Here we are, starting out on our voyage. We are sitting together on a sofa, in a large hotel foyer. It is quite busy.	*FD: … Is it near enough … do you want to listen first to what you* **recorded** *on it, to see if it's OK … with headphones?* *KN: I don't have any … it's working.* *FD: OK, good … shall I move a bit nearer, it's working?*[4]	
This is the opening of **Francis Dhomont**'s *Sous le regard d'un soleil noir*:	I have asked a question about *Sous le regard d'un soleil noir*. Now he is speaking, and I am listening. An interview (an interhear, perhaps).	**Francis Dhomont:** When I compose, in general, I always have an idea first, a concept, and very often – almost always – the title. The title is very important. For me, the title sums up the general idea, and is a 'motto' for me … it's a way of thinking.	This is one way of listening to it.
A male voice speaks, without preamble.			Two objects. And between them, a moment of nothingness. This is a

Figure-toi ... Figure-toi ...	*Picture ... picture ...*	
Listen. He says it **twice** – a repetition, already! *Figure-toi ... Figure-toi ...* A man speaks, without preamble. Listen carefully. This isn't quite a repetition; something was different. A voice is speaking, to you ('toi'), the solitary listener – the single-figure audience with whom it has an informal connection. This voice knows – by speaking – that you are there, alone and listening. It doesn't take long to endow a voice with a persona; just a couple of words or so is sufficient to create the gender, age, nationality and probable state of mind. In addition, a crowd of other possibilities are hinted at through **nuances** alone. So just those two words can project an image in our darkness (slightly different for each of us, no doubt). Of course, this complex and insubstantial picture has absolutely nothing to do with visual appearance.	The sonic world about us is a counterpoint of many voices: chatter in the nearby bar; people who pass by either at close quarters, their heels clicking, or far away, their conversations merging into a blurred fog; luggage trolleys rumbling across marble floors, followed by the thump of suitcases. And there is music in the distance, and occasional bells from phones and elevators. There is so much unwanted noise **surrounding** us. And that is just the *sound* of the experience. We had worried that it might be difficult to talk, but perhaps what we meant was that it would be difficult to listen (an un-sounded implication). But once we've started there is not too much distraction, and very soon there is no distraction at all. All that activity fades into a low murmur as I concentrate on his voice and on what he's saying.	strange, but familiar, way to begin. (*Figure-toi ... Figure-toi ...*). It happens **twice** – but this isn't a repetition. First there is the sound of something closing shut with a reverberant finality. Is it a door that shuts me out, or one that shuts me in? Then the same sound, differently: the original sound is split into two halves, and put together in reverse order. Now a surreal door opens (uncloses?) in reverse onto a surreal world. ... there is a moment in the sixth movement, which I spoke to you about, where there is a door, which opens, and one hears a crowd ... that is to say many people, speaking. And this becomes very different, it becomes very low. And that is for me the perception one has of schizophrenia. This crowd of people that is **surrounding** him is perceived other than how *we* perceive them. At another moment the door opens again, and there, on the contrary, the sound travels upwards to such a point that it is completely distorted. In my thinking this is in fact a musical element – to go towards low pitch, towards high pitch. And it is also a way of saying, 'I no longer perceive things like the rest of the world; I no longer perceive truth, reality. I am "de-realized".' 'Déréaliser' – to lose reality. It is one of the symptoms, the traits of schizophrenia – one loses a direct sense of reality. [Later on a very real door will open on a very real crowd of chattering voices. But, for now, there are only **nuances** of what is to come.] This sound is not quite 'real', in that it is only partly familiar. But how can that be? It is either real or unreal. We either know or we don't know. Either here or there. One or the other. To know otherwise would be insane.

You know that this persona is male (the voice is always a real giveaway). The speech is measured and unhurried, and the timbre of the voice is **deep**: he is commanding, authoritative, informed on something. Yet, at the same time, he is quite encouraging, even with a compassionate tone that comes, perhaps, from age and **experience**. This persona hasn't said much yet, but is worth attending to, so you will listen. He knows this: you can hear it in his voice.

Figure-toi ... Figure-toi ...

Why repeat this phrase? But, listen again. This isn't quite a repetition; something was different. Although words are reiterated, by the same voice, the two enunciations are quite different from one another. They are *made quite different* from one another. It falls to the listener to perceive the sonic distinction.

The first '**Figure-toi**' is an announcement. The volume – though quite loud enough to impress – does not conjure up a grand declamation. There is an **evocation** of significance through intonation alone. Reverberation provides distance and slightly accentuates the higher frequencies. There is perhaps a tinge of remoteness.

When someone talks to us, we tend to listen. Our inclination is to make sense of speech. We lean into it, bending our ears towards meaning. We turn our sail towards the sounds that speak to us and let them fill the forefront of our **experience**. Yet there is still a background to provide a context, even if it is just the sound of the sea. An inner sensibility decides which sounds are to be attended to and which are mere tangents to the main curve of our listening. We trust that sensibility to be making an appropriate choice. We **filter** background from foreground.

The ear detects depth from such indices as a reduced harmonic spectrum, softened attacks and transitions, a different blend of direct sound and reflected sound, and the presence of reverberation. (Chion, 1994, p. 71)

Picture ...

I have placed the microphones as near to him as possible, but not too close: I want to capture his voice more clearly

---

... in *Sous le regard*, the **deep**, 'profound' voice is that of a philosopher, a friend who is dead now, who had a superb voice. When I was thinking of who could say that text, it was his voice that I wanted. And as he was intelligent, a philosopher, that was very good ...

.. there are quantities of texts that are thrown out, put aside. And when I find those texts that have sense and sound, I look at them. There's no problem. And then I will edit them ... And sometimes, for example, I won't preserve more than two or three words from a whole phrase. Because that's enough, the sense is sufficient – one understands it quickly. If one says 'fear' ('peur'), one doesn't need to say 'I am frightened'. ... That means that in the collecting of texts, you can retain just the **evocation**, the general sense.

Sous le regard d'un soleil noir and

This is a piece that deals with gradations of knowing otherwise. Out of that second half-remembered door that is not yet real, a voice arises. It is a small, pathetic sound that speaks. There are words, but they are beyond our comprehension. As soon as the door opened, we heard this murmuring persona, already talking to himself, or just hoping that there would be someone out there in the dark. It is just one voice – there is only one rhythmic speech pattern going on, and there is no echo – but then again it is several – it is tuned to several pitches. The sound has been **filtered**: part of its essence has been stripped away, yet – as a result – part has been drawn forward to reveal inherent pitches. We might assume that some kind of harmony is intended. So is it music or sound? Male or female? Who knows if it's one or the other?

Her voice is subsumed beneath a dry scrabbling that has a metallic timbre (this is one approximation, but you may have other associations). Perhaps something rattles frantically at the door (let me out, or let me in?). But this inanimate persona behaves in an animal way, with scuttling gestures that move rapidly back and forth in space, mimicking visual movement.

	than the others that might engulf it, but I also want to catch an approximation of the way that I am actively *listening* to the **voice** right now, not just the way that my ears hear it. If I were to turn the microphones away from him, point them instead at a shoal of tourists who may have just swum into hearing, then he would be **a lost traveller** – one of many.	*Fôret Profonde* are the two pieces that are most difficult to project. They are difficult in concert because musical sound can move about, the **voice** … no. … of course, that's the situation with speakers – or with headphones, that is good, that would be quite appropriate, that was how I made the piece [with headphones].	The gestures are fragmented; they appear to pause for thought, making decisions. Her muted **voice** is there between them, in the spaces. On the one hand, it is possible that they are one and the same: perhaps these scrabbling sounds are the frantic machinations of a mental activity that goes beyond words. Maybe we are listening to her unconscious thoughts. And, if so, she cannot know what we infer from this, since she is unaware. Or perhaps, on the other hand, she *is* aware of these agitated beings as separate from herself. There is a moment of muffled intelligibility: 'à l'extérieur' – barely discernible. Is she hearing them, beyond her? If so, she is either with us, or we are with her. Though it is not necessarily one or the other.
This voice is out there, a little apart from us.	Now, we are seated in **close** proximity, and I can get some help from watching his face. Later, I will only have my recording of the sound to tell the story.	… diffusion, when it's well done, it works well. In general … one is in the dark. It is necessary to bring the voices **close**. That's to say to have the speakers very near to the audience. One doesn't want speakers at a distance when there are texts that ask for a voice 'in the head' … one can do it – one can do it if one thinks about it, but it's difficult.	They – we? – are trying to get out of there. The sounds approach us: there is an increase in volume as they hurtle through time. They (or she, or we – **whose voice is it?**) have an end in mind, a horizon in view. They are coming closer. The goal is the door. Here.
This section is entitled *Pareil à un voyageur perdu* ('Like **a lost traveller**'), and indeed the second 'figure-toi' is an 'invitation au voyage'. Low frequencies are more apparent, as is movement – both in terms of pitch and space. The voice is **close** to us, and the reverberation now heightens the pitch contour of the words. The speech is slower; this is possibly achieved by technological means since the natural resonance of the voice is also slightly lower in pitch than that which precedes or follows. However, it is not unrecognizable. Speech can be imbued with an amount of sonic processing before we greet it with confusion or disbelief. The reverberation is appropriate for a small space, an intimate space perhaps, and the sound travels slightly, moving to the right (with headphones, moving 'into' the right ear). Movement of sound is significant, in particular over headphones: we notice it. Or, rather, movement alerts us to our own stillness in relation to the sound: we notice the separateness of our Self. So we are	At some point up there *his* voice became *the* voice, and I'm on the way to netting *my* recording of it. **Whose voice is it?** Did you hear the question I just asked? Are you listening to my voice now, as you read this, or yours? Perhaps it's your voice that recreates the *sound* of the words on this page. I hope you don't mind me addressing you directly.	And although I may also do this with a piece that has no text, with a piece with text I am preoccupied, interested, in the development through time (this is music: time and music are bound together) … and how this can be developed musically, and in the case of a work with text, how this can be developed from the point of view of general sense, and if one can have a real	[Now a very real door opens on a very real crowd of chattering voices. Later there are only nuances of what was to come.]

evolution that goes from one point to another: a thing, a work in which the listener understands new things, little by little ... like that. And I reflect a great deal on how to achieve that.

This sound is quite 'real', in that it is familiar. But how can that be? It is either real or unreal. We either know or we don't know. Either here or there. One or the other. To think otherwise might not be insane.

You might feel that you've heard that before. This piece is full of unfaithful repetitions.

With the alterity of the 'unconscious', we have to deal not with the horizons of modified presents – past or future – but with a 'past' that has never been nor will ever be present, whose 'future' will never be produced or reproduced in the form of **presence**. *(Derrida, 1973, p. 458)*

This crowd is too vividly present for a context where unreality has become the norm. There are many individuals, speaking to one another. Here they are, like an excited audience, squashed into the bar with their glasses and programmes in hand. They are uncomfortably close together as they talk **nonsense** and listen for a signal that the interval is due to end. Everyone is speaking, but nobody is communicating anything as an individual. The listener (she, you, me, we? – it's getting to be quite a crowd) is

---

involved with the sound's **evolution** in time, in that it has introduced its presence into the space of ours. A voice spoke, up close, beside me – in the space where I 'am'.

Figure-toi ...

What is happening between the voice and the sound of the voice? Listen, while I try to explain what I mean.

Reverberation puts his voice in a place. The voice is clothed with another, separate **presence** that echoes, and thus confirms, its existence. The reflection provides an aural mirror for the voice but also, in its timbre and duration, indicates the dimensions of the place. We – in our darkened, limited perception – like to think that there must be something out there. This is a voice attached to a bodily presence.

By being in a space, the voice is made 'real', even though the reverberation is not exactly realistic. (In a minute, this semblance of **reality will fall apart.**)

Picture ...

He is speaking, and I am listening. I am trying to understand. I am putting in some effort because French is not my first language – far from it. This is not a language I am familiar with. So listening is currently a more-than-usually conscious process of relating sound and sense. I am acutely aware of both the distinction between the two, and the necessity to reintegrate them back into a whole. I need both. If I lose one of my two oars, I will be locked into rowing in circles on an opaque sea of **nonsense**. But, even so, I will know that it is *not* nonsense. And this could be truly horrible because I will *know* that he is making sense, but it is just that I will **no longer perceive** it under the surface. **Reality will fall apart.**

In my thinking this in fact is a musical element – to go towards low pitch, towards high pitch. And it is also a way of saying, 'I no longer perceive things like the rest of the world; I **no longer perceive** truth, reality. I am "derealized".' 'Déréaliser' – 'to lose

Sounds have a natural contour for their existence and subsequent demise in time. Clap your hands in a cave and wait for the echo to fade away. You can anticipate an approximate duration from your real-time analysis of the sound. It's called listening, and we're all undercover experts. Half the time we don't even know that we're doing it, it's an unconscious judgement; and perhaps that's one reason why our creative sonic manipulations can proceed at such subtle levels and still have effect.

'Figure-toi' **disappears** too quickly. In both cases, the decaying reverberation around the words is curtailed. It is not gradually damped down in volume or covered up with another sound, it is faded out – rapidly. And this is very abrupt: after he has spoken the sound merely hangs around for a moment, like the vestige of a thought, and then it's pinched away to nothing. Rien.

Figure-toi … Figure-toi … .

There is a silence between the two iterations of 'figure-toi', and another after the second iteration and what follows.

Listen to it; there's a void you cannot avoid. It has several **possible meanings.**

will be alone in my boat, under the glare of a black sun. And the smallest confusion may bring that state about:

He has a cough. I am sidetracked into worrying about whether to get us a drink or not, and how to express this. In my preoccupation, my mind switches back into 'normal listening' and my ability to understand French **disappears** for a few seconds. When he replies I have absolutely no idea what he's saying. Instead, the sounds of language are cleverly processed **allusions** that, I know, should make sense.

But, of course, it can be delicious to paddle aimlessly in the shallows, as long as we're near the edge.

When somebody puns on a word we are momentarily ensnared in a contrapuntal net of meanings, but we know where we are. For a pun there are at least two **possible meanings**, each dependent on

reality. It is one of the symptoms, the traits of schizophrenia – one loses a direct sense of reality.

In this work I tried to be a schizophrenic. I tried to imagine what kind of perception of the world a schizophrenic has. We are all of us a little threatened, no? Life is not clear for us, one can see things in one way or another, and sometimes it's divided – 'divisé'. Just as Plato's text says that perhaps there is difficulty for Man in perceiving the world, there is difficulty in perceiving the truth. Then there are several places in the movements where there are **allusions** to that.

not privy to their discourse. Is this an intermission?

The voices subside into a murmuring, background throng. They move downwards. Sonically they are transformed into a different level of sensitivity by a process of filtering that gradually numbs perception. They are not transposed to a different pitch by a swooping glissando. Instead, high frequencies disappear by stealth, so that fricatives, consonants and plosives are gradually rubbed away, leaving only the darkness of incoherence. And yet, disconcertingly, the volume has not yet been dimmed significantly. So they are still near us but have merely faded from consciousness. For the time being.

The scrabbling recommences, this time tethered by a low resonance from the fading crowd, or perhaps a distant closing door. The attempt reverberates to nothing. Then comes a more determined and aggressive recommencement, a contrapuntal scrabbling now, that builds up from nothing to a swelling fury, escapes the low-pitched grounding of reverberation and is filtered to gain the higher ground. And they arrive, bursting through an unsounded door (or perhaps they are the door) to reveal the crowd, now seen from a different viewpoint. Now the voices are alien, a filter has allowed only the high frequencies through, and the result is distant, mediated audibly by someone or other. There is no depth to the sounds that reach us, only hissing and cracking of the ashes of speech. And rapidly these disintegrate into distortion, then a white-noise splashing in the highest frequencies, which dissolves and ….

I believe that it is important in a musical work – even if it is in a completely different musical language than the traditional language – it is necessary to have a structure, necessary to have a thought. It is not sufficient to make sound.

… There are other pieces … … that are truly a discourse, like a novel, like a work of theatre. These are things that have a sense. Very often, in electroacoustic music, I really have the impression that there is no sense there, there is only sound. So sounds … Of course I love sound. I find … I am a lover of sound, but not on its own. Not … a sound, it is very good but … **sound *and* sense.**

… there is complete emptiness. Worse, like a bare light bulb in a prison cell, a solitary sine wave illuminates a void to reveal its true awfulness. There is nothing human to be heard there is only sound. The sine wave is pitched on a high B natural, beyond the range of a human voice. Other, microtonally close, pitches accumulate around it and a regular oscillation rotates in the background. If it was dreadful to encounter this inhuman, unflinching sound, now there is an implication that something inexplicable will evolve in a world that is not surrealized, but de-realized. When a sharp-edged attack announces the first clearly discernible word in the movement – the first time language has had **sound and sense**, it's as if she confirms our feelings:

What happens *between* those two iterations?

The effect of that abrupt envelope, that cuts the 'natural' (that is, expected) decay of the reverberation imposed on the first 'figure-toi' is to throw the silence that follows into relief.

different possible scenarios, both of which come to mind for a moment when we hear the phrase. We are torn between the two and left appreciating difference rather than meaning.

A pun requires a little time travel: we backward-engineer our 'processing,' of the sentence to separate the available possibilities, and relish the unusual experience of a divided sense. So we allow ourselves (we are in control) an imaginative nuance that is largely absent from our listening to our own language – the language that we both own and which owns us (it thinks our thoughts for us).

There is amusement in it for us; there's no threat – we can throw the differing senses from hand to hand, weighing the options. Our sensitivity to the distinction between **sound and sense** is heightened, enjoyably. And, of course, we have to hear it: if we see it written

Without a fading decay to fill the void, the 'holes' in sound – silence – come hurtling forward. Silence should not be heard; in fact it cannot be heard (and I mean silence, not the unintended sounds of 4'33"). But here is an abyss, loud and in the foreground. This is a real silence: this is blank tape. *No* sound is transmitted. The effect is particularly apparent when listening over headphones, but even over speakers there is a moment of sudden nothingness where **sound and sense** are audibly sucked away. For me, no amount of creaking chairs or coughing

		'Peur'	I said 'she', but there are others now, including a male voice. This is a small explosion of responses, by different voices, in different places, with different inflections. But the fragmented identity is united in one respect: Fear.
		KN: … I don't know if it's the same in English for this text but **'Figure-toi'** is 'intimate' – as one would talk to a child, or perhaps a friend … yes? FD: Yes. It is a free translation, in the way that many have translated Plato. It's a translation that I had in a French book, and which was … to the taste of my philosopher friend who says the phrase. And moreover he worked a little on the translation, and then I reworked some of the elements: I repeated things 'Figure-toi, figure-toi' etc. It's the 'mise en scène'.	It is the halfway point of the movement. We are neither here nor there. As the voices fade into an echoing space, there are perhaps other unspoken questions. **What will happen now? Where am I? Am I alone? How long will this be for?** The sine wave material slowly resurfaces again, unperturbed. It is stronger, augmented with a looped pattern of synthetic pulses, which are high-pitched and artificial. The precision of exact repetition is here disturbing in its persistence. It is foreign in this sonic world which has progressed through change and unpredictability and has not, as yet, asked us to be aware of pitch, rhythm or harmony in any musically structured way. This pattern has an invasive claim on our listening because it is like a 'transmission' from another place: it sends out a message in a Morse code
can placate it. Perhaps there is only one thing more disturbing than too many voices, and that is no voice at all. *Figure-toi …* Listen to silence. The first time we hear that silence we have no idea how long it will last. If I were to hit pause on the CD player, you wouldn't have a clue. He has spoken, and we are listening (for various imperative reasons): but now we are listening to absolutely nothing. What do we *do* during that brief (but we do not know that yet) silence? We ask questions. **What will happen now? Where am I? Am I alone? How long will this be for?** Perhaps rather than asking these existential questions anew, we are made aware of their continuing and continual presence. If movement of sound alerts us to our Self, perhaps a sudden absence of sound throws us back to the chatter of the unconscious. Silence is an absence that makes conscious the murmur of indiscernible voices that, nevertheless, belong to us. Deleuze and Guattari postulate that this internal activity – which they call indirect **discourse** – contains the whole of language. Thus language, and speech	down the pun is lost; the word is fixed with a single meaning. *Picture …* He's talking to me. I listen, hear sounds, come up with a selection of probable words – given the context – and make astute choices, or guesses, or mistakes. I'm confused, but when he repeats a word my ear grabs hold of some familiar consonants and I've got the sense of it. I'm back in context. Even if I wanted to, I would not have time to open my dictionary. I am too busy listening to another, internal, voice, that's 'doing French into meaning' for me (for it isn't, quite, translation).	*... one suspects that the reception of meaning is as much, or even more, a* When one hears a schizophrenic's **discourse**, one is very surprised. One wonders at what they say – they are	

that we cannot crack. We lack the key necessary for **decoding**. Yet we cannot help but listen as it scutters about from ear to ear, repeating a phrase that has structure, is important (there is repetition – please listen) and evidently has a system – but is beyond words.

I call semantic listening that which refers to a code or a language to interpret a message: spoken language, of course, as well as Morse and other such codes. This mode of listening, which functions in an extremely complex way, has been the object of linguistic research and has been the most widely studied. One crucial finding is that it is purely differential. A phoneme is listened to not strictly for its acoustical properties but as part of an entire system of oppositions and differences. (Chion, 1994, p. 28)

That B natural begins to absolve itself. Now there is a B at a lower octave, warmer and sustained. And this is joined by fragmentary clusters, now chords, as accordian-like timbres offer E natural, F sharp, G natural, an occasional C. There is hope of a resolution to a world in E minor, but nothing is fixed. The texture has the aimless purpose of an orchestra tuning up (an orchestra that is tuning to a B rather than the conventional A – but

---

and writing, arise from an indirect discourse of babbling voices, from which we make our Self.

... the collective assemblage is always like the murmur from which I take my proper name, the constellation of voices, concordant or not, from which I draw my voice. I always depend on a molecular assemblage of enunciation that is not given in my conscious mind, any more than it depends solely on my apparent signs. Speaking in tongues. To write is perhaps to bring this assemblage of the unconscious to the light of day; to select the whispering voices, to gather the tribes and secret idioms from which I extract something I call my Self (Moi). (Deleuze and Guattari, 1987, p. 84)

In this way we fumble through the dark silence, wondering what he will say next and, indeed, what *we* will say next. And, while we wonder, he moves forward – silently – and speaks again:

Figure-toi ...

What is being said? What is being meant? What is expected of us? Listen for sense now.

'Figure-toi'. The first time that comes we do not know what to expect, except

---

mad! But are they 'mad' or do they have another way of perceiving things ... But that isn't to say that the person doesn't think. His manner of speaking is, above all, to translate his thought. That's not the same thing. Well ... this is what I suppose; I am not a psychiatrist ... but ... I think there are some things like that. It doesn't require a big thing to pass from one state to another.

... in *Sous le regard d'un soleil noir* I had the idea, starting out from the reading of ... er ... what's it called in English? [in English] 'Knots'.

KN: *Er ...?*
FD: *Noueds ... knots ... the little book.*
You know it ... the little book?
KN: *Ah, yes,* **Knots.** *I've read it.*[5]

FD: And it was this that gave me the idea, the desire, to work with these texts. But I wasn't familiar with the author, Laing, and I wanted to know his work. So I bought the books, above all *The Divided Self*, and it was that really – reading this book – that brought the piece together in my mind.

But, for me, it is always an almost interactive process between reading and experimentation.

Later I will need to write all this down, in English, and then there will be yet another voice to contend with. George Steiner (himself trilingual) offers an opinion that a bilingual speaker is not necessarily a good translator, the 'frontier between the two languages is not sharp enough in his mind' (ibid, p.119). In the bilingual mind the voices are perhaps too tangled, indistinguishable from one another. They all make sense, together, as an undefined mass of **knots**.

Picture ...

We need frontiers, edges against which to come to a stop – a point at which we recognize distinction, and difference. We need a place to tie up our boat. This is in French. C'est en Anglais.

---

process of internalised mimesis, of reconstructive decoding, as it is one of immediate hearing. (Steiner, 1975, p. 125)

that we expect something (a tree, house, woman, time ...?). Without any clues as to what to picture, we are abandoned in murmuring silence, unable to comply. But then, 'Figure-toi ...' again. The second time he speaks we remain in anticipation but have an idea of the silence that may follow (we are experienced now) and await further developments.

There is an imperative here, something that must be done. That's to say, grammatically speaking 'Figure-toi' is in the imperative. The imperative is always in the present: do this – *now*. Moreover an imperative is an unusual speech form because it is an 'illocutionary act'. This is an **utterance** where 'saying' is the same as 'doing' (see Crystal, 1987, p. 121). For instance, in saying 'I swear that I told you ...', the words 'I swear' are illocutionary – to say 'I swear' is to *do* swearing. An imperative, such as 'figure-toi', is illocutionary also in that to say an order is to give an order. This has nothing to do with what the order actually *is*. So

When he unexpectedly said something in English, I ran aground on his foreign accent. There was a familiar word with an unfamiliar timbre. This is perhaps the opposite of a pun, and more disconcerting because now there are two sounds – my sound for this word and his sound for this word – and one meaning. There are too many voices, but it's the meaning that's lost.

(So ... in fact the myth of the cavern, in **Plato**, is not exactly the same.) It was simply an association with the position on Man's perception of what surrounds him, and how he perceives the world. How he perceives his world, and how the schizophrenic perceives the world.

... yes, I think about timbre ... and also about pronunciation, and the accent. For example, in Québec I sometimes

Again, when he pronounces 'Platon' ('*Plah-tohn*') in French my internal sonic database is thrown into confusion for a moment, and then aggrieved – this is not *my* **Plato** ('*Play-toe*!'), the philosopher with the English accent. The **utterance** has fractured something previously familiar into two. Plato has betrayed my limited perception.

who's to say what's right and what does it matter as long as we are in tune?). There is a sense of preparation as the pitches hang around, providing a place of security where things are made safe. In music, many nonsensical things make sense: a chorus of voices is quite appropriate, and counterpoint is a trivial thing; a repeated abstract pattern need not be significantly disturbing; a harmonization does not necessarily imply fracture, but rather a coming together and strengthening of intent. So we are removed from the raw threat of the scrabbling activity at the opening and the frozen horror of the pulsating sine wave. We are released from encountering sound in that moment-by-moment basis in which listening creates questions and feeds a constant flow of inward 'confusion'. Now we are hiding down there in the orchestra pit, reassured that we are listening to music – and not just 'music' but 'tried and tested' pitch and harmony. It can't last: as this music continues it does not progress in any real sense, other than taking time. It is trapped in a slow revolution of harmonic colours around one set of pitches. This does not bode well. This could be merely a new kind of prison.

Things continue in this manner for quite some time before a male voice starts to speak. Previously we were listening in on someone's world; perhaps we were in there identifying with them. Now a distinct persona talks *to* an audience: he has looked up and seen us. This is the first voice in this movement to communicate outwards. Or at least it appears that way at first. The pitched 'music' has not stopped, but this persona **cannot hear** the music that surrounds him any more than an operatic character is 'conscious' of his orchestral accompaniment. For the character itself to perceive a separation between the two would be to lose the plot. And, like a diligent accompaniment, the rotating sequences of fragmentary chords and pitches are – without changing in the slightest – becoming illustrative: he tells us of the burrow he has created while the sounds throw their dark covering around him.

Everything appears to be making sense. Unlike the voice that opened this movement, the timbre of this voice has not been changed significantly. There are no echoes, save a slight reverberation that puts it in a place, and there is no harsh filtering to accentuate, or remove, the frequencies that define humanity. There is no distance at all between it, and us and there are no other voices to crowd the issue. Sonically, nothing could be clearer.

have difficulty in finding a voice for French texts that doesn't have too much of a local **accent.**

And there is a relationship with the part of *Sous le regard d'un soleil noir* where one arrives at a moment, at a perception of the world, which is expressed, noticeably, by a **distorted** text. ….

---

these words are unmediated, in terms of both tense and intention.

Figure-toi … Figure-toi …

Why would someone repeat this phrase? Isn't it enough to sound an order once? Might I suggest (another illocution, that) a way of hearing some other voices **between sound and sense**?

'Figure-toi', the first time, is the very first sound we hear in the work, and we are unprepared for it. There is no conductor's upbeat to a work for sound alone, no violinist lifts a bow, no singer inhales, no pianist sits poised above the keys. There is no possibility of that significant moment of stillness that comes twixt the lifting of hands and opening chords. Now *that* moment of stillness before the piece begins is an illocution in itself. Listen.

'Figure-toi'. The words say one thing and mean another. Perhaps there are other imperatives in that first enunciation of 'figure-toi …': be quiet, settle down, and make yourself ready. Silence the activity in your head. Hush

An **accent** puts *noise* between sound and meaning. It 'interferes' by drawing attention to the sound of speech. But this is a subjective noise, in the sense that it arrives inside one person's head, but not another's. We notice an accent that is not *ours* (we do so like to *own* our voices) but we **cannot hear** our own accent. An accent is outside our experience of producing the sound of speech. But once we perceived it in other voices, it lies strewn atop the stream of speech, **between sound and sense**: whether we regard it as a drift of petals or a disfiguring patch of oil is a matter of personal opinion. While an accent may indicate all kinds of values to do with social class, region, nationality or age it perhaps says most about the person who notices it and contrives to skim off these nuances. There can be a separation now, between what a spoken language sounds like and what it doesn't (or '*shouldn't*') sound like. An accent prises apart sound, opening a chasm between known and unknown, between mine and yours. The sense is perfectly comprehensible, but the familiar is **distorted**.

It doesn't do to write it down. Gunther Kress describes how we 'ignore the sound of an accent and 'normalize'

now. The other imperative is one that I have been trying to underline. Listen: there is another meaning under the words. Picture (you must)/Listen (to me). Both commands are reinforced by the timbre of the speaker's natural voice and the subtle manner in which the sound has been placed in time and space. Our listening is sensitized by the reverberation; we are made aware that what we should be doing now is making a space for listening.

speech in order to spell correctly, and this a learnt, rather than a natural, ability. He gives an example of a child writing down a recipe, dictated in a heavy Northern England accent that was foreign to the listening child. Among several other similar 'mistakes', the child writes 'walnut croosh' for 'walnut crushed', the former being closer, sonically, to the accent heard (Kress, 1997, pp. 124–25).

... So in the passage on the burrow, there, the Kafka text [movement 6], I reverse the words. I made an inversion of the words to make a text that one comprehends but one doesn't comprehend ... if one changes the words two by two, one rediscovers the exact sense of Kafka's text. For me, it was a way of suggesting how the language of a schizophrenic is not empty of sense, but there is a sense that **we don't understand.**

And this persona is secure: he tells us something in confiding, calm, tones. *He* knows that he is making sense. Unlike the murmuring crowd that jostled reality earlier, he speaks to us alone. His words are jumbled – in an ordered manner. The sentences have been split into parts, and the parts have been reassembled with pauses between them (if you remember, we've been through that door before).

We know that he reveals his secret. The problem is that **we don't understand.** The meaning of each sentence is obscured, although nothing in *his* tone of voice appears to be aware of this failure to translate sound to sense. The voice is not processed, but our relationship with words is. And there is just a hint of a reflection in that knowing accompaniment, whose harmonic shards collide in incoherent combinations, offering a partial tonality.

It is a world not quite mad enough to have lost all reason. (But are we not mad or sane, one or the other?) There are still words, but to heal the fractures created by their displacement would require revisiting the text – that is, we would have to go back in time and listen again. That would be more like reading than listening to music, where **time passes,** regardless. And yet

Picture ...

Yes, it often happens that I reprise, revise a work after a year or two, or even three or four years. In certain cases it's impossible, in certain cases I am too far away, I am no longer there in that work. In other cases I have many notes, I keep many of the musical elements also, and therefore I can go and research all that and rediscover the spirit of the piece. But, in general, when I rework a piece I *know* what I am going to rework; I know what I want to change. So although **time passes,** I still

Time passes, then 'Figure-toi', again.　**Time passes.** I'm still listening to the

want to change the same thing.

Yes. Yes, I believe that one can take it on several levels. That's to say that one can think about Plato's text in the sense in which he wrote it – one could think of it as the presentation of … how man in general perceives the world – in a very **limited** way.

And sometimes, for example, I won't preserve more than two or three words from a whole phrase. Because that's enough; the sense is sufficient.

there is some space between each group of words for us to try and figure sense out of the world. We don't have long enough: the scrabbling sounds reappear and their activity and volume masks what we were attending to. Their recommencement precedes the words 'de dehors' ('from outside'). And, incidentally, the first time those scrabbling gestures occurred, right at the beginning of the movement, their interruptions revealed a moment of muffled intelligibility 'à l'extérieur'. Is he hearing them, beyond him? If so, he is either with us or we are with him, although it is not necessarily one or the other. We've heard these sounds before.

And are we outside or inside? At this point we are not at liberty to say: we are trying to attend to a voice whose speech seems rational but isn't. While we try to reassemble sense we are, at the same time, struggling to keep an aggressive, all-consuming distraction 'outside' of our listening. Hence the piece – in both its sonic strategies and the very subject of the words – illustrates our own listening predicament.

Is the scrabbling sound that eats at our listening worth attending to? Perhaps its role now is illustrative: it is a programmatic depiction of the manic

---

But now we're listening to a voice, no, a *man* who is asking us – telling us – to picture something. After the first 'figure-toi …' we did picture something after all, without being conscious of it: we conjured our version of a man who is going to tell us something. We grasped our own meaning from the air. But we do not know what to picture consciously, yet. We stumble into a cave, even before he talks of Plato's myth of the cave, and cannot perceive what lies ahead. And we are made ready for the metaphor because we are currently experiencing its theme.

Figure-toi … Figure-toi des hommes qui vivent dans une sorte de demeure souterraine en forme de caverne possédant une entrée qui s'ouvre largement du côte du jour. A l'intérieur de cette demeure, ils sont, depuis leur enfance, enchaînés par les jambes et par le cou, en sorte qu'ils restent à la même place, ne voient que ce qui est en avant d'eux, incapables de tourner la tête en raison de la chaîne qui la retient.[2]

[**Picture** … Picture men living in a cairn-like underground dwelling, with an entrance opening widely unto the daylight. Inside this dwelling, they have been chained at the legs and neck, since childhood, in such a way that they

sound of his voice. It's an interesting voice, but I have no idea what *kind* of French accent he has. I'm not privy to that, still contending with the nuts and bolts of a foreign language. His accent is beyond my comprehension; its voice is masked by an internal voice that keeps reminding me 'these are sounds which make up words in the French language'. I hope I'd be able to tell if he was getting bored. He'd be too polite to yawn I think. It can be enough to hear a tone of voice, but my perception of this is **limited** at the moment.

Picture …

We are engaged in vocal counterpoint, he and I. Listening and speaking, and sometimes the two together.

struggle to build a safe burrow in the ground. Or perhaps it depicts the fury and determination of some slavering invader, trying to gain access to this burrow. Perhaps it is both. Perhaps such abstracted sounds are not to be trusted as illustrations since they leave us choosing between conflicting allusions. But, whether the sound is inside or outside the burrow, both allusions are impregnated with fear.

Earlier on in this movement this gesture had achieved things. At the outset, it dragged a muffled, filtered 'inner' voice into an 'outer' place. To do this it rose in pitch, through filtering, changing timbre as it hauled itself upwards towards the light, thereby gaining access to a shockingly convincing room: it arrived at a door that opened with audible reality on to a crowd. And then it scrabbled up even further, to burst into another space where voices had become unreal, before pursuing its climb to the heights of a single, inhuman, B natural sine wave.

Now it is more aggressive, with more lower frequencies at the start, and more 'verismo' reverberation that accentuates its presence. It is still on a mission. They – she, he, me, you, we? – are trying to get in, or out, of there. The sounds approach us: there is an increase

KN: And even though one doesn't use all the **texts**, it's important to read them all ... it's in the music.

FD: Yes, yes ... absolutely. It is very important to have a ... to live a little with them.

Yes. The work of art, for me, is not simply a case of taking what exists and saying 'this exists' – a little like Cage, saying, 'There, here it is, one has nothing to do but listen'. By doing this, of course, Cage changed the way we listen. But I believe that the 'plastic' arts – literature, music – must be a 'human' work. That's to say, they have 'human' **thought**. Art, the arts ... in the

remain in the same place and see only what is in front of them, incapable as they are of turning because of the chains that restrain them.]

listening
Francis Dhomont
Figure-toi ... Figure-toi ...

Whatever it is that speakers have in mind, in speaking they are bound by the logic of sequence in time. ... For writing, the limitations of sequence ... are far less significant, and in many forms of writing they are replaced by processes of complex syntactic design, such as the subordination of one clause to another, embedding, for instance. (Kress, 1997, pp. 15–16)

twice
nuances
deep
experience
Figure-toi ...

evocation
close
evolution
Figure-toi

presence
reality will fall apart
disappears
possible meanings
sound and sense
Figure-toi ...

what will happen now?
where am I?

I have some questions written down but they seem irrelevant now. As he speaks his words anticipate my queries or throw up new currents that I would like to pursue. This is not a reading and there are no fixed **texts**.

Sous le regard d'un soleil noir gives time to its subject, and to its texts. Plato, R.D. Laing, and Kafka may be the sources for this dark exploration of schizophrenia, but the texts are a starting point for a deeper interrogation of sound, sense and listening to voices.

Francis Dhomont reads these texts aloud. We are listening to his voice. But by this I do not mean that they are merely spoken by him, through one or other human voice. More than this, they are interpreted, experienced and recreated through this new work, through his **thought**. This is a new kind

in volume as they hurtle through time. They (or she, or we – whose voice is it?) have an end in mind, a horizon in view. They are coming closer. The goal is the door. Here.

This time it does not open. This time we are locked in. Or are we locked out? Thwarted, the gesture continues, becoming ever more frantic. The sounds fly wildly from place to place, shaking the locks of a hundred different doors. Then the lower pitches are gnawed away. The timbre strives upwards, accentuating the higher frequencies, scrabbling towards metallic edges, going beyond purely sonic associations with soil or water to an abstracted animal chewing, gobbling: the sound of an unconsciousness trying to reach outside itself. And while it goes on, following a doomed trajectory, a muffled voice murmurs in the background, submerged and indiscernible. Then a clear and authoritative voice cuts through this muddle. Here is the voice that started it all – this is the sonorous persona that led us into the cave at the beginning of *Sous le regard d'un soleil noir*: He is an outsider who is not part of the torment that continues around him. He enunciates the words that also started this movement, although then they were indiscernible and uttered by a

recorded

Francis Dhomont

surrounding

deep

evocation

voice

close

evolution

no longer perceive

allusions

sound and sense

Figure-toi …

---

of reading undertaken through the composition of sound. It goes far beyond words.

listening
recorded
Picture … Picture …

surrounding
experience
filter
Picture …

a lost traveller
close
whose voice is it?
Picture …

no longer perceive
reality will fall apart
disappears
allusions
possible meanings
sound and sense
Picture …

decoding
knots
Picture …

---

am I alone?
how long will this be for?
discourse
Figure-toi …

utterance
between sound and sense
time passes
Picture …

Figure-toi … Figure-toi …

twice

nuances
filter

voice

whose voice is it?

presence
nonsense

whimpering, muted voice. He speaks of inside and outside, of eating and being eaten, and of emptiness. Perhaps he has been listening all the time.

His words appear to be accompanied by a distorted repetition, filtered but completely intelligible. The timbre of this echo has the hollow lack of substance we associate with a voice on a telephone or radio: it communicates 'this is being transmitted'. But to whom? And behind this there is the echo of an echo: that submerged female identity from the opening is now speaking clearly. He explains, and she (her voices made multiple by filtered harmonization) repeats his explanation, perhaps in some kind of muted acceptance. Her voice is cut off abruptly, in the middle of nothing ('rien'). This is the final word. His voice has gone. Her voice has gone. But behind them that submerged voice had continued and now continues for a few moments before closing its indiscernible communication. Finished.

There are no voices left, but it isn't yet over. While we were concentrating on the words – the speech that claims attention – a rhythmic pattern returned,

key		
sound and sense	Plato	**discourse**
what will happen now?	utterance	**Knots**
where am I?	cannot hear	**Plato**
am I alone?	accent	**accent**
how long will this be for?	between sound and sense	**distorted**
decoding	distorted	**we don't understand**
cannot hear	time passes	
we don't understand	limited	**time passes**
	Picture …	
time passes	thought	**limited**
	Picture ..... yourself	**text**
		thought

with familiar synthetic, high-pitched pulses and a repetition that still speaks of an intelligence tapping on the wall of its prison, trying to be heard. But we still have no **key** to the code. The repetitions become louder and louder until the pattern fills the present and is all-consuming. It is the only thing audible now. It is all there is to listen to. Inside, outside, here, there, one, other. Suddenly, at its loudest point, the pattern is curtailed without warning. Although it had not finished, that is the end. After this abrupt cessation of an untranslatable signal, there is nothing.

On est à l'intérieur.

KN: . . . One has need of a key . . . and a door.

FD: Yes, absolutely. . . . that's it. One has need of a **key**. But that isn't to say that the person doesn't think. His manner of speaking is, above all, to translate his thought.

Sous le regard d'un soleil noir is the history of a shipwreck.[3]

. . . **one understands it quickly. If one says 'fear', one doesn't need to say 'I am frightened'.**

Figure-toi . . .

Notes

1 The recordings, texts, and English translation, are provided by kind permission of empreintes DIGITALes. See Appendix 1 for the full texts and English translation.
2 This text is from Plato's *Republic*, as it appears in the work.
3 From liner notes to CD.
4 The material in this column is taken from an interview by the author with Francis Dhomont, made in Havana, Cuba in September 2001. The English translation was made by the author.
5 Laing (1970).

Part 4

Sounding ... edges

Chapter 7

BEYOND THE LIMIT AND THE LINE

Transgression, Proliferation and Immersion

featuring the ENDNOTES[1]
(appropriated listening)

```
/NB: put 5 blank lines between each subsection here — decrease
by 1 line each section (need some room)/
```

INTRO

This essay considers some of the consolations of listening out for noise. Three noisy anecdotes follow (with a song on the way).[2] There are no definitive conclusions, just some different considerations of the space between noise, technology and electronic music.

And this writing is noisy. Perhaps it'll do your head in, or possibly stretch your ears. Noise is a leaky pollutant that cannot be confined. The opening of the next chapter is a parody of this chapter's introduction. But the next chapter also provides the endnotes to this chapter. Even though you know the score, you'll have to decide which of those trajectories to follow, or whether to flip from one to the other.[3]

⊙ CD [28]
(guitar, swooping strings, slow brushed cymbal beat)
Ooh, oooh. Make yourself comfortable
Ooh, oooh. Make yourself comfortable
Ooh, oooh. Make yourself comfortable baby
(brass wah wah, swooping string cadence)

NOISE Example ONE[4] (see definition below)
There's a noise at the end of the track. The CD writer on my computer is faulty. Whenever I burn an audio CD the last track is followed by an enormous glitch. I have attempted several possible solutions to no avail. I've made various test CDs to check it out: each time I play the last track, wait for it to finish and then, after a few moments, there's that ugly burst of noise again. It's the bonus track from hell. In the time between the end of the track and the glitch I anticipate both options: I long for the sound of silence – with increasing desperation – but always get distortion. I've grown accustomed[5] to feeling unease.

In the fold between 'Is this music?' and 'Is this noise?' there's some room for manoeuvre. It takes a moment to decide, 'This is'. During that length of time there is an expectation of one kind or another. Perhaps we may hum a distracting tune ... .

(ooh ooh etc repeated by backing singer — SV doubling herself.
Female, soothing, behind the verse)
I've got some records here to put you in the mood
ooh..oooh make yourself comfortable
The phone is off the hook so no one can intrude
ooh..oooh make yourself comfortable
I feel romantic and the record changes automatically
ooh..oooh make yourself comfortable   baby

NOISE Example TWO (see definition below)[6]
There's something up with the machine, *it doesn't sound quite right.* Sarah Vaughan's
Golden Hits CD – the one I hum along to while I'm cookin'[7] dinner – has started
misbehavin'[8] in the kitchen. The first couple of songs are fine, but after that the
playback starts doing the hop.[9] Instead of ironic crooning, she's scatting wildly and
uncontrollably. Perhaps it's appropriate that Sassy should escape from 1950s pop, but
she's uncomfortable in the ghetto-blaster, and my omelettes are suffering too.
Everything is all shook up.[10]

In the fold between 'Is this human?' and 'Is this machine?' there's some room for
confusion. It takes a moment to decide, 'This is'. During that length of time there is an
expectation of one kind or another.

Sweetheart, we hurried through our dinner *(first two lines
doubled in close harmony)*
Hurried through the dance
Left before the picture show was through
(solo)

NOISE Example THREE (see definition below)
And finally, a diva who won't stop singing – the aggravatingly present Ms Kylie
Minogue. I caught two minutes of her latest video the other day and now I . . . can't get
the song out of my head.[11] She's lurking in my subconscious, beyond reach of my
ability to stop her. (Yours too?) Indeed, whenever I stop thinking, her whingey little 'la,
la la la' voice pipes up in the background. This noise won't cease, and I don't seem to
have any say in the matter.[12]

In the fold between 'Is this me?' and 'Is this not me?' there's some room for flipping
the pages. It takes a moment to decide, 'This is'. During that length of time – a hiatus
that has a familiar refrain – there is an expectation of one kind or another.

```
Why did we                        (duet)
Hurry through the dinner
Hurry through the dance?
To leave some time for this
To hugahug and kissakiss ... now
```

Now this is no time for after-dinner relaxation. Upstairs in the studio I've got a pile of discarded silver plates with a side order of digital distortion. And downstairs in the kitchen, the Divine Miss V is skipping barefoot through a host of imperfect palimpsests. And inside my head, vacuous pop-packaged Kylie has most definitely outstayed her welcome. There's far too much. Noise.

```
Take off your shoosies dear and loosen up your tie
ooh ... oooh make yourself comfortable
I've got some kisses here, let's try one on for size
ooh ... oooh make yourself comfortable
I'll turn the lights low while you
            make yourself comfortable baby
ooh ... oooh make yourself comfortable baby
(cresc)
```

NOISE (some deafening definitions)
(see Example 1, above) 'any sound, esp. loud or harsh or undesired one' (*Concise OED*)
(see Example 2, above) 'irregular fluctuations accompanying but not relevant to a transmitted signal' (*Concise OED*)
(see Example 3, above) 'unwanted or meaningless data' (*Encarta World English Dictionary*)

(last two stanzas repeat)

Noise is merely too much information. Noise is already rampaging inside your head, rollicking across the cross-wired connections between half-remembered songs and other people's words. There are so many footnotes and references, numbers and examples. Are you flipping sick of flipping the pages? Perhaps you're irritated by those noisy endnotes that make no particular sense (so maybe read them later from a different perspective).

Oh shssh!

Settle down?

Make yourself comfortable........baby!
(louder)
(pizzicato upward scale to end)

No, listen baby, don't you dare. Be uncomfortable, be distracted, be confused. Beware of seductive B-movie sonic platitudes. Be aware that technology gives us not only the gift to hear ourselves as others hear us,[13] but also the tantalizing possibility of feeling noise more keenly than before, and revelling in the sensation. However low you turn the volume, switching off is not an option. Are there no limits?

```
/place significant quotations between horizontal lines, to
delimit them (your noise is other people's information)/
```

Noise is especially relevant to our expectations of listening to music. And in relation to electronic music, noise has a privileged position: the technology we use to make sound enables us to produce a great deal of noise – we can create unpredictable results, beyond our ability to understand them entirely. We dream of transfiguring our understanding, and in doing so reinventing meaning for noise. Even after 50 or so years of making music with technology we still speak in broadly futuristic terms, although more often now we seem to investigate 'new ways' of making content (algorithmic, physical or genetic models, stochastic behaviours) rather than being preoccupied with 'new sounds'. Perhaps there is a magnetic attraction between the means to make noise and artists concerned with the meaning to be made from noise. Noise attracts practitioners who want to make noise count.

This writing is a noisy attempt to think out loud. I make no claims to present anything larger than an idiosyncratic consideration of noise in some of its sonic, perceptual and confrontational guises – specifically in relation to music, electronic music and its technologies.

TRANSGRESSION
there's noise at the end of the track
'any sound, esp. loud or harsh or undesired one'

In the fold between 'Is this music?' and 'Is this noise?' there's some room for noise as transgression.

What is noise? Noise is a disruption to the current flow. Noise sends us skipping back and forth between tracks, between endnotes and the body of the text. Noise is the unexpected glitch. Noise is a song you heard by accident and without desire. Noise is in no particular order. Noise is an annoying subtext and deliberate (/or non-deliberate/) mistakes. Noise is unwanted aggravation. Noise is beyond our control. Noise is thwarted expectations. Noise is overload. Noise is an in-your-face attack – an affront to reason! Noise is every crappy love song you've ever heard, playing simultaneously on a thousand turntables, and all of them turned up high.[14] Noise is also a quietly intrusive revolution – gerunk, gerunk, gerunk – every time the record goes round. Noise is an invitation to think different (the noise of my computer is an intermittent advert for itself). Noise is tactile. Noise is a weed. Noise is pornographic (it obsesses over arousal). Noise is one statement after another without purpose, a relentless aggravation. Noise is 'any sound or combination of sounds' (*Encarta World English Dictionary*).

```
/if time, perhaps reread last para, replacing 'is' with 'can
be'? (Know your limitations, and then leap over them)/
```

```
Transgression does not seek to oppose one thing to another, nor
does it achieve its purpose through mockery or by upsetting the
solidity of foundations; it does not transform the other side
of the mirror, beyond an invisible and uncrossable line, into
a glittering expanse.
(Foucault, 1988 p. 69)
```

Where is noise? Noise is in our relationship with ordinary things, in both the message and the medium (quote it again, then let's move on.[15]) Noise is in the gaps – it is not just the glitch after the music that's noisy, but our anxiety in the space between the two. Noise is in the struggle between what we want, what we get and how we try to rationalize the difference. Noise is there when we want to hear Sarah, but hear instead Sarah and a dodgy CD laser performing a coy duet – animate and inanimate. Are they together or apart? – we so *want* to give them both intent. Noise is a machine with a will of its own. But 'we cannot bear to think of ourselves as the dupes of an aimless and indiscriminate mind' (Gould, 1987, p. 256) so noise has to be the sound of a machine that thinks for itself (and that's uncanny – wait and see). Noise is in the interference that resides within us; it's a previous experience that silts upwards, of its own volition – a remembered Kylie moment, or a deeper desire. Noise is in the conflict between acknowledging the presence of noise and attempting to repress the perception. Though we may try to push it back down, noise is an inveterate scribbling that reveals a hidden message, underneath the surface.

Transgression is neither violence in a divided world (in an
ethical world) nor a victory over limits (in a dialectical or
revolutionary world); and, exactly for this reason, its role
is to measure the excessive distance that it opens at the
heart of the limit and to trace the flashing line that causes
the limit to arise.
(Ibid., p.73)

Why is noise? Well, there's the rub, grind, crackle, buzz, glitch, and general row. There's the subjective question (is it noise to you?). Perhaps noise is there to worry at the limits we assign for music: it looks back and stretches out a hand – 'Come on, there's *more*'[16] (not forgetting that percussion music once made an awful noise). Noise can be there as a pleasurable perversion or an interesting itch. You know you want to go after it. Perhaps it even turns you(r listening) on? Noise can be at once the information overload of our lives and our attempts to assuage it. Noise expresses itself. Noise can be the audible scream of our internal signal paths – a metaphor for the 'too muchness' of thinking about being alive. Noise takes us over, against our will. Noise alienates. Noise is there to get in the way. At the end of the day – or chapter – noise can scratch a stylus across familiar grooves.

Transgression contains nothing negative, but affirms limited
being — affirms the limitlessness into which it leaps as it
opens this zone to existence for the first time.
(Ibid.)

What isn't noise? (There's nothing negative about being negative.) Noise is not the opposite of music: it is not the opposite of anything at all (if anything it's the opposite of *nothing* at all). Noise is not defined by loud or soft, although it can be either. Noise is not cacophony: it is unplanned but not necessarily unpleasant.

Of course, all that preceded, and all that will follow, is just a possibility.

Beyond watching the performer (the merits of vacuum-cleaning)

```
I happened to be practicing at the piano one day ... and
suddenly a vacuum cleaner started up just beside the
instrument. Well, the result was that in the louder passages,
this luminously diatonic music ... became surrounded with a
halo of vibrato ... And in the softer passages I couldn't
hear any sound that I was making at all. I could tell, of
course — I could sense the tactile relation with the
keyboard, which is replete with its own kind of acoustical
associations, and I could imagine what I was doing ... It
suddenly sounded better than it had without the vacuum
cleaner, and those parts which I couldn't actually hear
sounded best of all. ... [W]hat I managed to learn through
the accidental coming together of Mozart and the vacuum
cleaner was that the inner ear of the imagination is very much
more powerful a stimulant than is any amount of outward
observation.
(Gould, 1987, p. 67, my italics)
```

Glenn Gould's various transgressions as a concert, and non-concert, pianist continue to produce a sublime noise. Here was a pianist who stopped giving live performances, had a compositional approach to studio recording, and himself composed a trilogy of sound documentaries that has had lasting influence. Gould as pianist had obsessions that were born of a sensitivity to the relationship between technology and noise: technology in the broadest and most literal sense, as a technique for both the production and manufacture of sound; noise in an inclusive sense to allow for both 'unwanted' sonic artefacts and the intellectually perceived noise from 'obstruction' imposed by the performer. He was extraordinarily attuned to the various nuances of physical and perceptual noise that are part of a musical performance, but was somehow bent on separating them from the experience of listening to music 'itself'. He transgressed.

```
Technology had positioned itself between the attempt and the
realization.
(Foucault, 1988, p. 354)
```

Hardware transgression: Technology itself can be a noise that comes between. The technology of the piano was a noise, and produced a noise that Gould didn't want to hear. But if keys are struck, sound will resound in mundane air, and the performer is bound to a directly literal process of physical cause and outward effect. But the outward effect does not necessarily match the internalized performance of the music – like the reading voice that coexists with (but does not require) sounding speech. By substituting the noise of the vacuum cleaner in lieu of the piano sound, Gould allowed himself the physicality of performing music alongside the internal realization without having to accept the imperfection of the sound produced. He evaded cause and effect; or, rather, he extended effect inwards, beyond the limit implied by the piano, his technology. A cruder, uncontrolled technology – the vacuum cleaner – masked the sound of outward performance with a noise that wasn't worth listening to in the first place.

Aural noise also softened the intellectual 'noise' engendered by having to rely on a piece of hardware made of wire, gut, ivory and wood that 'got in the way' of internalized performance. The same preoccupation with idealized musical performance, and a dissatisfaction with the actual 'noise' offered by the instrument – merely a tool – led Gould towards sound processing and manipulation. These additional tools provided a means to extend the limit further, and so transcend physical reality through transgression:

```
... if I gave it a bass cut at a hundred cycles or thereabouts
and a treble boost at approximately five thousand, the murky,
unwieldy, bass-oriented studio piano with which I had had to
deal earlier in the day could be magically transformed on
playback into an instrument seemingly capable of the same
```

sonic perversions to which I had already introduced Maestro
Scarlatti.
(Ibid., p. 354, my italics)

Error transgression: Gould often practised and memorized his repertoire away from
the piano, only turning to the instrument in the final stages of preparing for a
performance or recording. By practising away from the piano, he not only avoided the
noise of the instrument but also the noise of the fallible human 'technology' of the
performer – and this flesh and blood technology at times fails and leads one to make
mistakes (an instance of noise creation). By not performing live in concert and turning
instead to a studio-recorded 're-composition' of performances he circumnavigated the
weaknesses of human performance (physical and intellectual) and enabled both his
instrument, and himself, to be capable of 'more'. And perhaps this enables his listener
to be more capable as well.

It would be most surprising if the techniques of sound
preservation, in addition to influencing the way in which
music is composed and performed (which is already taking
place), do not also determine the manner in which we respond
to it.
(Ibid., p. 99)

Listening transgression: How can Gould's listener get 'inside' the performance to the
same extent that he did? Playing Mozart alongside the vacuum cleaner provided Gould
with 'the effect that you might get if you sang in the bathtub with both ears full of water
and shook your head from side to side all at once' (Gould, 1987, p. 7). The analogy is a
bodily, tactile, physical one. But it also speaks of blockage, muting, of being shut off
from the outside. It speaks of an experience that is not collective but individual, and a
song that's heard through an internalized 'transmission' of sound. In relation to speech,
Douglas Kahn notes that 'at the same time that the speaker hears the voice full with the
immediacy of the body, others will hear the speaker's voice infused with a lesser
distribution of body because it will be a voice heard without bone conduction: a deboned
voice' (Kahn, 1999, p. 7). This is a literal fact with regard to speech (or singing) but
perhaps it also translates to our listening to performed music. Sitting at the piano is very
different from sitting in the grand circle, in both practical and social terms. We are always

at one remove – we cannot *be* Glenn Gould, even temporarily.[17] The liner notes might perhaps provide a directive to start up our vacuum cleaners each time we listen to Gould's recording of the *Goldberg Variations*, but that wouldn't quite do the trick. We wouldn't have access to either the physical sensation of fingers on keys, feet on pedals, vibration through body or the internal clamour of nerves, memories, feelings and intentions that contribute to the physical realization of a performance.

The recording is just sound, and the sound is just a recording – running a finger over the grooves while it plays won't help on this occasion. But this 'just sound' is not 'just piano'. Gould was notorious for his vocal 'accompaniments': in nearly every recording, the sound of the piano is echoed by his humming and grunting, an audible 'singing along' that rises up and breaks the surface intermittently (just think how many sound engineers must have lost sleep over this …). This noisy artefact of the externalized strivings of interpretation – the struggle to birth the music through his mind and soul to audible existence – is real and physical, but it is a mere trace of another noisy struggle between his intent and its realization, ultimately, through bodily movement. But perhaps Gould's humming does not interfere with the recorded sound of the music so much as act as a proxy for the vacuum cleaner. Both noises interfere with the way in which we listen by masking the sound of a mere piano being played. And perhaps this interference encourages us to turn to another noisy perceptual struggle going on within us: we are hearing the piano timbre, straining to both catch and avoid Gould's vocal mutterings and, somewhere along the way, we're listening to the *music* – which is both within and *beyond* the sound emanating from the record. These are perhaps indications as to why his studio recordings do not lose out, but rather gain, from this 'reintegration' of the noise of performer presence. Perhaps this obstruction 'at the end of the track' is useful in drawing attention to a difference between music and its realization.

PROLIFERATION
that machine's got a mind of its own
'irregular fluctuations accompanying but not relevant to a transmitted signal'

In the fold between 'Is this human?' and 'Is this machine?' there's some room for noise as proliferation. Proliferation is a kind of noise with a metaphor whose unobserved growth wells from beneath until it cracks the surface. Those things that proliferate – viruses,[18] rumours, mass panic, chain letters, recessions – are subject to a process that is, or is generally perceived as, at some level beyond individual control or even beyond human perception. Most often, this process is 'noisy' in that it's associated with undesirability, or at least disquiet, because proliferation is a generative production that appears to be unconcerned with a single controlled trajectory. It does not appear to develop in a direct response to any human endeavour – we may we set it in motion but we conjecture, rather than predict, its outcome. So as a means of generating art (though not necessarily as a means of generating the materials of art) proliferation transgresses a limit: the intention to proliferate is deliberate, but the reproduction is a mindless multiplication whose machinations do not spring from a single, or even a collaborative, consciousness. Proliferation in art makes for intellectual noise because it asks for us to get our single-minded heads around the mindless nature of the process in relation to perceiving its product as art. And, often, the perceived absence of individual human intent or organization, and our encounter with this realization and acceptance (or not) of the anarchy implied is exactly what such art is all about. Generative, viral processes abound in experimental sound-processing software. As improvising performer David Lee remarks succinctly 'Chaos theory has been embraced with open arms by artists because it validates structures that are too complicated to be explained. Art compounds complexity to effect an overall simplicity' (Lee, 1992, p. 5).

Proliferation discourages regulation and encourages 'the beyond'. But to go beyond implies a movement that continues after an *expected* line of demarcation; this is an extension rather than an opposition. To use one of Deleuze and Guattari's preferred terms (and processes), proliferation acts as a metaphorical 'rhizome' that spreads by a branching root system across an endless plane.[19]

```
[Gould] is not just displaying virtuosity, he is transforming
the musical points into lines, he is making the whole piece
proliferate.
(Deleuze and Guattari, 1987, p. 8)
```

Deleuze and Guattari (who did not own up to who wrote what, thereby imposing a satisfyingly noisy anonymity[20]) were referring to Gould's tendency to perform pieces at a breakneck tempo. By streaking *beyond* the expected (and accepted) tempo for its genre – a culturally defined norm that is certainly capable of fluctuation – Gould's performance dances ecstatically towards a new finishing line. But this 'beyond' performance does not negate previous interpretations, performances and listenings; it can only be 'beyond' in comparison to them. Gould's flight urges us to go beyond our expectations, but not to forget them. And with a virtuoso technique that almost goes beyond what is 'humanly possible', he becomes a pinball wizard, a man-machine whose transformation of the work creates proliferation by running at speed ahead of the limit. But the line, where all self-control and self-consciousness is lost, will always keep moving towards a new horizon. Meanwhile, our listening proliferates: the noise of beyondness is our internalized comparison (not an opposition) of the known and the new. And it's our understanding of the work that proliferates towards new 'capabilities' for music.

/place my listening in italics, to isolate personal response
(because it's most irregular)/

Beyond human assumptions
(it's behind you)

Sean: 'That's the thing, what's regular?'
Rob: 'You can go too far, but then that's for you to decide.
We've found ourselves thinking at times that we might have
gone too far. But we've always been in our own space — it's
hard for us to imagine where that datum or line of reference
lies.'
(Sean Booth and Rob Brown, aka Autechre, *Sound on Sound*
interview)

⏵ CD[30] 'bine', track 6 of *Confield* by Autechre
*For three seconds or so, there's the promise of an elegy for solo strings: distant
wavering pitches, one low, the other higher. Two unnamed stems, slowly
intertwining. Spreading outwards, not upwards or onwards. There is barely time to
make yourself comfortable before the noise assaults expectations ... someone's
warped idea of a drum machine in the foreground, it's incredibly fast and its
behaviour is completely frenzied and unpredictable. Sometimes there's a beat to
follow for a few seconds, then it's too disordered and rapid to comprehend as more
than a fast brrrr, click, thud, swish, flip. It's unthinking, aimless and out of control.*
   It's a machine gone mad. But going mad is only human. So is there anybody there?

Presence proliferation: We associate the performance of instrumental music – its
bringing to completion – with an individual (or a collection of individuals performing
'in concert') on stage. Significantly, the term 'instrumental music' draws attention not
so much to the nature of the sound required as to the necessity for *people* to be present,
in order to make it happen. There is persistent dissatisfaction over the concert
performance of electronic 'tape music' (another noisy term – what does it mean now?)
most often voiced as 'I want something to see' but with the subtext 'I want someone to
be seen to *do* this sound'. For an audience comfortable with the flourishes of concert

experience (of whatever genre of music), a human being tweaking a mixing desk or staring intently at a laptop is an incongruous and poor substitute. We want physicality, and even a lip-synching pop diva who drops her mike is preferable to nothing. But conversely, a non-demonstrative performance becomes a discomforting and subversive act that provides a 'no-input' visual mockery of what might be expected (several 'no-input' musicians – like Sachiko M, who makes use of the mechanical and electrical sound of a sampler, rather than using any sounds stored within it – regularly sit virtually motionless on stage).

If you want to avoid making statements through performance, and to concentrate on making them through sound it's difficult, since even a single individual on stage can make a distracting noise in the undergrowth. The 'climate of anonymity' prized by Gould indicates an urge to cut straight to the chase – the stuff of listening to music. So perhaps anonymity is the key. Quite a few musicians currently making experimental electronic music work in collaborative groups or, perhaps more often, in twos or threes. They conjoin in more or less stable configurations, frequently colliding for specific projects. It is often not a case of 'where one ends the other begins' but rather the collective 'us' of single-minded individuals working together – either in real-time collaborations or through less integrated exchanges of material.[21] In this context, the musician/maker becomes a confused and proliferating entity too. With two authors who write as an ambiguous fused 'voice', there's neither one nor the other. There is an absence of presence that appears to be another solution to erasing the 'oneself' of the performer in favour of the 'itself' of the work. There's nothing left to see here. So let's move on ....

```
De:Bug: What are you doing on stage really?
Sean: Just doing tracks.
(Sean Booth, of Autechre, 'The Ultimate Folk Music' web
interview)
```

Uncanny proliferation: Although Autechre's track, 'bine' still peddles associations with 'fake' human performance, this is a different drummer-machine whose simulacrum of virtuosity has no truck with pinball wizardry. Both its rhythmic processes and timbres judder against the limit for 'instrument' and move towards further transgressions – towards the beyond human, the beyond 'drum-like', towards the hypersentient, and hypersonic. The music skids violently between man and machine, towards the unconceivable – and that's gotta hurt (because it's too difficult to bear). This machine thrashes uncontrollably and blindly at the limits of its own capabilities. It appears to be willing harm upon itself, yet neither brakes nor breaks. Squealing, thrashing, flapping, bashing, squelching, banging ... this is horrendous, and there's nobody driving the thing.

Or is there? With an essay by Ernst Jentsch as his starting point, Freud appropriates the notion of the 'uncanny' (in German, *unheimlich* or 'unfamiliar'). Jentsch is of the view that 'one of the most successful devices for easily creating uncanny effects is to leave the reader in uncertainty whether a particular figure in the story is a human being or an automaton' (Jentsch, *On the Psychology of the Uncanny*, cited in Freud, 1990, pp. 347–48). His concern is for the fictional uncanny – the puppet that comes to life, or the automaton that appears human. Freud, however, works towards a psychological interpretation of the uncanny as being the familiar wrought somehow fearsome in the psyche. Broadly speaking, for Freud the 'horror' of the uncanny is acquired and relates to an inherent appreciation of duality: 'When all is said and done, the quality of uncanniness can only come from the fact of the "double" being a creation dating back to a very early mental stage, long since surmounted – a stage, incidentally, at which it wore a more friendly aspect' (Freud, 1990, p. 358). Either way, uncanniness speaks of fear and being frightened – and this is a noisy experience that attacks clear-mindedness and floods consciousness with terror. The frenzied machine in 'bine' is undoubtedly monstrous, but its persistent duality – human or machine? – has an uncanny ambiguity, doubly exacerbated because it is, as music, neither an external fiction nor the listener's own mental creation. We're still not quite sure.

Listen, there's been some terrible mistake.
... there are occasional seismic jolts where the whole thing skips a beat – or maybe just skips a couple of samples as one slab of this stuff is spliced to the next. The volume bursts up a notch, or there's a disruption in the pattern. When this happens the patterns don't match; they're slightly skewed. There's no attempt to hide this botched attempt. Attempting what?

```
It has already begun, and all of this refers, cites,
repercusses, propagates its rhythm without measure. But it
remains entirely unforeseen: an incision into an organ made by
a hand that is blind for never having seen anything but the
here-and-there of a tissue.
(Derrida, 1991, p. 168)
```

If things 'go wrong' there must have been some thwarted expectations. There must be a mind in mind. I want to hear a mind ... but there's a gap. This isn't Bach. This is not a three-part fugue. This wild flight spreads on a different, microscopic scale of invention. In these random and violent shifts of tempo, pattern, timbre, nothing lasts, nothing aims, nothing fades – is this towards a 'breaking down' or a 'breaking through'? Here is something that has been pushed towards its limits, and towards the line between achievement and catastrophe. But is this a failure? (And is this a line?) Beyond a certain point, catastrophe is, I suppose, one kind of successful conclusion ... but it's a double bind.

Double proliferation: Is there something more frightening and uncanny going on in the background? While the machine in the foreground beats listening around the ears with extrovert mania, there is another, uncannily fearful noise. It is easy to forget that 'bine' also offers some softly spoken sonic tendrils that intertwine aimlessly in the background while all this activity is going on. These are the real monsters, who once again thrive on anonymity and a lack of a single identity. For Jentsch, the true horror of uncanniness in fiction succeeds when the reader's attention is 'not focused directly upon his uncertainty, so that he may not be led to go into the matter and clear it up immediately' (Freud, 1990, p. 336). And this is exactly what 'bine''s slow, string-like timbres do. Not only are they anonymous – what timbre is that exactly? – but they are apparently aimless (but then again, perhaps not). Here are quite a few expectations of identity and direction, none of which is fulfilled. But nobody bothers worrying unduly about such ambiguity when the foreground is occupied by a percussive noise that proliferates its aggressive shoots of thwarted, ephemeral and transitory rhythms.

But listen; perhaps these tendrils are the uncanny 'double' of our wanting (a mirror of our internal intertwinings and desires). We want them to have soul because they behave as if they should. Perhaps a gradual realization that they, too, are automata – or just might be – is the psychic breaking point for this piece. We want our world to be human, because we do not want to be alone with a machine. The possibility of listening to music with no human intent at all does not bear thinking about.

Yes there is no real point in it either. I quite like that.
[Derrida] is not really trying to define or pursue anything
specific. It just kind of breaks what's available. It is quite
like the way that humans think anyway.
(Sean Booth, web interview)

Unseen proliferation: A proliferating virus *does* perform – but through an unthinking organic cell-dividing biological process that expands exponentially. If proliferation is mindless in its reproduction that's not to say that it is inorganic in its *modus operandi*. This spreading motion (because proliferation is a constant movement outwards rather than onwards) is organic at a micro level, and functions beyond the ability of human sight. The viral disease that invades and infiltrates does so beyond unassisted human perception, and even beyond the compass of the single-cell bacterial scale. A virus makes its liquid, viscous traverse on finer routes than our cruder, human 'regular' scales of reference can fathom. Its activity cannot be contained easily (or at all) because we cannot pick up its noise unaided. It is everywhere and alien.[22] But, nevertheless, its propagation makes a noise through the symptoms that indicate its presence, and also indicate to us the uncanny depths of the microscopic world within us. This 'inner' body is both familiar – it is ours – and unknown – it is other. It is an anonymous body that we contain, but that is also quite beyond us.

At this micro level the viral procedures of proliferation are unseen – no, unsee*able*. But this does not mean that we are blind. Autechre's 'bine' is 'unseeable' in terms of gestural performance since these wild rhythmic patterns and flailing timbres are playable in pushbutton, mouse-cursor terms, but untranslatable through human movement. Of course, those gestures can be mimicked – through projected images perhaps – but the result would be an interpretation, and this is compromise. This work performs its gestural metaphors in a more immediate sense and, I think, avoids the need for sight. To quote Virginia Woolf's equally ambiguous *Orlando*, it goes straight to 'the dark hollow at the back of the head when the visible world is obscured for the time' (Woolf, 1977, p. 201). But, on the way, it might light up the hairs in your ears.

... but I can almost feel the edges of this sound – like razors, unfinished and jagged. There is some 'body' to it; it has a physical presence that invades ... underneath the skin ...

'Bine' does not travel to arrive, but it moves on. The sound conveys its own physicality: because, although there is no human referent to this tactile, tensile mass of sound, it *does* have a presence analogous to the movement of some kind of body. The rhythms and the patterns of its activity imply motion, and striving – but it's much more than that, I think: 'bine''s behaviour is defined by movement, flux, propagation; the physicality that this behaviour produces is directly transmitted to the physical listening body, unmediated by anything but air. You do not envisage a sound-producing object. On the other hand, the sound is an object that seems to inhabit rather than reach the ear, through a 'surgical' invasion that cuts through the surface of listening without resistance. The sound is loud, but it is not loudness alone that leads to it taking command: because there is no 'need' for a performer (actual or envisaged) there is no noise between the body of sound, and the body that listens. You don't perceive a boundary. It feels as if it was always there.

We use machines to extend our own behaviour.
(Marsden, 2000, p. 15)

IMMERSION
can't get you out of my head
'unwanted or meaningless data'

In the fold between 'Is this me?' and 'Is this not me?' there's some room for noise as immersion. Immersion plunges an object into liquid, which then seeps into every crevice and every possible space. An immersed object is full up – there is no question of a *need* or desire for more. Immersion is a willingness to accede to baptism, renewal or escape. Immersion is acquiescence, a giving in. It occupies the senses completely and offers instead the prospect of a blissful dissolve. It's the solution to end all limits and all lines. To be immersed is to become completely involved.

This section has a soundtrack: Merzbow's 'Agni Hotra Loops' from *Loop Panic Limited* – ⊙ **CD[29]**. Please press play. Listening is entirely optional. But why not take a dip in a sea of noise?

The relationship between the noise performer and the listener also seems to be informed by the rituals of sadomasochistic sex, as the audience agrees to submit itself to the sonic pain of white noise inflicted by the performers. (Heinritzi, 2001, p. 31) Everyone has felt (at least in fantasy) *the erotic glamour of physical cruelty and an erotic lure in things that are vile and repulsive.* (Sontag, 1982, p. 222) The antinomy of gaze and view is lost in pornography — why? Because pornography is inherently perverse . . . . Instead of being on the side of the viewed object, the gaze falls into ourselves (Zizek, 1992, p. 110) . . . it would be better to speak of sonic pornography in a literal sense: *the naked mechanisms of our fetishistic relationship with the instruments of cultural domination are (over)exposed by this music.* (Heinritzi, 2001, p. 32) . . . this spectacularly cramped form of the human imagination has, nevertheless, its peculiar access to some truth. This truth — about sensibility, about sex, about individual personality, about despair, about limits — can be shared when it projects itself into art. (Sontag, 1982, p. 232) Listening to you, I get the music. Gazing at you, I get the heat. It is only we who gaze stupidly at the image that 'reveals all.' . . . we, the spectators, are reduced to a paralysed object-gaze. (Zizek, 1992, p. 110) The need of human beings to transcend 'the personal' is no less profound than the need to be a person (Sontag, 1982, p. 231) *Noise music is about losing control over oneself, about losing one's*

*relationship to the world, a music of catharsis and hysteria
... this is more a question of the pleasure provided by this
music   than   political   violence   or   a   critical   discourse.*
(Heinritzi, 2001, p. 32) (my italics)

Beyond self
(a significant touch)

Immersed meaning: We consume and subsume material and keep on with our
demands for more information. We take it for granted that we will continue to boldly
go, forever extending our reach (which is not the same thing as attaining a goal). In
seeking to extend our own behaviour, we recognize that we are *wanting* (this means we
both need and desire), and if we want something, that thing holds meaning for us. In
striving to go beyond our limitations, we must surely yearn to be immersed in all the
meaning in the world. But where does noise fit in to this? On the surface, it appears that
there is no place for desiring noise, since noise is 'unwanted or meaningless data'. This
brusque antinomy assumes that the flotsam and jetsam of 'unwanted' and 'meaningless' must always wash up on shore together.

If the whirring of bytes and behemoths is an exhilaration that springs from the
'beyondness' of human behaviour, then any noise that comes out of the attempt is the
Russolo rustle of our own making; it springs from a desire to approach the limit and
move the line. But whereas Luigi Russolo's 1913 Futurist manifesto asked for an ironic
orchestration of the noise of industrial society, now we can't evade the catchy capitalist
tune that keeps re-emerging inside our head. The noise we encounter is our fault, and
the irony is lost: I may feel acute discomfort at Kylie's tra-la-la shrink-wrapped
sexuality but commercial music's proliferation was just part of the digital knowledge
transaction. Now I just can't get her out of my head, without getting out of my head. It's
just too much! But although I don't want Kylie (insert your own aural bugbear here)
inhabiting my head, I know that her presence *means* something – worse, she represents
a cacophony of meanings. The 'too-much-ness' of the rising tide of information is
overwhelming (and I am drowning in crass liquid metaphors!).

But perhaps we can also want to immerse meaning for a while, and so to gain some
relief from all this all-ness. So, how to drown out the noise of meaning? Immerse it.
Push meaning under the surface. Yet immersion is not destruction. Once underwater,
things and people do not disappear so much as digress from their normal appearance.
Stones that were dull and unappealing now gleam with new lustre, clothes float and
billow uncontrollably, and ordinary movement is reinvented as an incongruous slow
ballet. Meaning shifts along a notch or two, and that's some kind of extension.

Much of the base material of Merzbow's *Loop Panic Limited* is derived from
recordings or pre-generated sounds – white noise, other music, field recordings and
performances. What the matter is doesn't really matter, because it is reinvented as
detritus that ostensibly lacks any function other than to be subject to new meaning. So,

in this recycling process, meaning suffers a sea change. Materials become fetishistic: now they are objects that have lost their originally intended purpose and instead serve to initiate arousal. Perversely, meaning is re-created for them through aurally noisy procedures – the 'meaningless and unwanted data' of feedback, repetitions, overloads, cutups, and decomposition. So there are, at once, all the discomforting cues that indicate noise (the too much-ness of distortion and saturation), alongside some vestige of the material's previous or supposed 'purpose'. Listening is stuck in a noisy loop: the sound of noise music is a sound we do not 'want', but the 'noise' is meaningful. (Right now, as I write this, I'm being plagued by the incessant noise of a distant, barking dog. But I'm also troubled by visions of a distressed animal, outside in this cold weather. I just can't stop thinking about what the sound might mean.) This interesting conflict buzzes away between our subjective interpretation of sound and the stories that we attach to it. We even attach stories to unwanted and meaningless data – white, pink, brown, grey – these colours serve as analogies for different flavours of aural noise. To get beyond that compulsive naming of things (which is largely to give them signification as different from one another) we have to get beyond making distinctions, and beyond associative meanings for sound.

---

as the audience agrees to submit itself to the sonic pain of white noise inflicted by the performers. (Heinritzi, 2001, p. 31) Everyone has felt (at least in fantasy)

(Sontag, 1982, p. 222) The antinomy of gaze and view is lost in pornography — *why? Because pornography is inherently perverse ... . Instead of being on the side of the viewed object,* the gaze falls into ourselves (Zizek, 1992, p. 110) ... *it would be better to speak of sonic pornography in a literal sense:*

(Heinritzi, 2001, p. 32) ... *this spectacularly cramped form of the human imagination has, nevertheless, its peculiar access to some truth. This truth* — about sensibility, about sex, about individual personality, about despair, about limits — can be shared when it projects itself into art. (Sontag, 1982, p. 232) If you want to follow me, you've got to play pinball. And put in your earplugs, put on your eyeshades. *It is only we who gaze stupidly at the image that 'reveals all.' ... we, the spectators, are reduced to a paralysed object-gaze.* (Zizek, 1992, p. 110) The need of human beings to transcend 'the personal' is no less profound than the need to be a person

(Sontag, 1982, p. 231)

(Heinritzi, 2001, p. 32) (my italics)

Immersed object: The materials of *Loop Panic Limited* are immersed objects. Noise soaks into these sounds whose identities are obliterated and wrought anonymous as a result. Sampling is not, in this particular work, the means to a camp aural nostalgia of recontextualized pop, neither is it a clever juxtaposition of diverse non-sequiturs. Instead there is – in the majority of tracks – a jagged, jumbled 'mass' of activity that, while chaotically noisy, appears inexorable: differentiation is apparently random and irregular, but almost immediately the sound is revealed as both predictable and static, since the initial noisy seconds are looped and repeated. So noise is controlled, within restraints. In general, after a minute or so the loop changes marginally, moving into the next track without breaking stride. Timbres shift slightly as aural noise is redistributed over the spectrum, but tempo and intensity remain largely the same. And this looped repetition creates its own noise because there is nothing more infuriating than being put on indefinite hold.

[PAUSE: This infuriation perhaps springs from a multi-level objectification. To be put 'on hold', and left to listen to music against our will, is to be left with a machine in 'pause': we are aggravated by the impossibility of interaction, in a situation where we specifically *required* interaction. And when we complain about not being able to get through to a human operator, we are acknowledging that we, too, are being treated as machines, placed against our will in a state of waiting – we are objectified. And music itself is also objectified, or rather the object of music is demeaned to functioning merely (only) as a means of audibly filling time, as a 'proxy' for human presence.]

To get back to it: are we also caught in another loop? An immersed listening hints at a passive acceptance of all sound. Cage repeatedly bobs to the surface with his maxim to 'let sounds be themselves'. But, in truth, his listening philosophy asks for an enormously active commitment to all listening, and one that intends to be truly life-changing. And in any case, 'all sound' is a fairly neutral classification while 'noise', as is becoming resoundingly clear, is a definition for 'all sound' that is open to subjective interpretation. Conversely, listening attentively to organized sound (in which category I include composed music) demands some kind of engagement in which critical and intellectual judgements gang up with individual emotional and sensory responses. Some kind of neutral objectivity informs personal response, and vice versa. Whatever the conjunction of these various responses to sound – organized or not – and to whatever extent they are consciously implemented, the process is at root an active one. We hang on in there, trying to make sense.

How to let go? In submitting to the noise of *Loop Panic Limited*, perhaps you agree to become both immersed and objectified. While noise can obliterate the indirect discourse of our more troubling thoughts, its loud, insistent and continuous presence also invades the room we made for personal reflection or reverie. Either way, we're objectified (we're 'out of it') – we have put in our earplugs and put on our eyeshades when it comes to critical perception. If you choose to listen (because you can still choose to keep your heads above water if you prefer) you are obliged to surrender to sensation and just feel. It is hardly an accident that many artists in the 'school' of Japanese Psychedelic Music – Merzbow is often cited as an erstwhile member – pay homage to the psychedelic heavy rock and punk that is the ugly twin of new age sensibilities.

(Heinritzi, 2001, p. 31) *Everyone has felt (at least in fantasy)*

(Sontag, 1982, p. 222) *The antinomy of gaze and view is lost in pornography*

(Zizek, 1992, p.110)

(Heinritzi, 2001, p. 32)

— about sensibility, about sex, about individual personality, about despair, about limits — can be shared when it projects itself into art. (Sontag, 1982, p. 232) <u>Now you can't hear me, your ears are truly sealed. You can't speak either, your mouth is filled</u>.

(Zizek, 1992, p. 110) *The need of human beings to transcend 'the personal' is no less profound than the need to be a person (Sontag, 1982, p. 231)*

(Heinritzi, 1992 p. 32) (my italics)

Immersed in extremes: Noise music can yank us from one extreme to the other: first we are objectified (and our individuality thus 'concealed') by surrendering to the sensation, then we are exposed by our own raw discomfort. The gaze falls back on us, as dissociated 'objects', but it also reveals our arousal, since the endurance of discomfort is certainly some kind of stimulation. And endurance is itself an extremity, in which we try and 'stay' the course (through choice or not). If extremity is our choice we are like the roller-coaster fanatic who wants to break the record for staying on the ride; we regard the length of our exhilarating discomfort as some kind of goal in itself.

To Freud, as Anthony Storr points out, 'all forms of art and literature are sublimations of unsatisfied libido' (Storr, 1993, p. 91). (But Freud was also – to his sorrow – immune to the pleasure of music.) Do we go to sonic extremes in some kind of explicit enactment of a Freudian pleasure principle? For even in the case of relentless noise, there's always the possibility of being released by a sudden system panic induced by endless demands. In sonic terms, extremes are most often sought in intensity of amplitude or frequency, measured in relation to the limits of human perception (significantly, the limits of conscious perception since the extreme that goes beyond this is ultrasonic). Roughly translated to more overtly musical vocabulary this means extremes of loudness and pitch, and also extremes of timbre, rhythm and tempo (thumping techno meets Glenn Gould's race through Bach). And Merzbow's music is extremely loud. In performance – when I heard him at least – it can be very loud indeed. Painfully loud. Sensationally loud. But listening to a CD, you can set the knob where you will and the noise will still immerse you. I read one listener's description of playing Merzbow at low volume to 'clear his mind'. So there must be other extremes at work.

Sometimes we don't want to make ourselves too comfortable. I've got another extreme here, let's try it on for size: too still, too quiet, too uneventful, too loud, too long, too short ... it's the 'too' that's extreme here. Although 'too' is different for each of us, surely there comes an extreme point where most of us would agree to 'too' as indicating the approach towards an *unwanted*, and therefore noisy, line. And if 'too' looks back to some kind of normality which has been transgressed, to enjoy 'too' is to indulge in the illicit and go too far. Merzbow's *Loop Panic Limited* is 'too' long – it occupies an entire CD – and his works are 'too' much – he recently brought out a 50-CD boxset.

Extremities can enforce stillness. This can be the blissful stillness of having no time at all, or it can be something less savoury. Drones, loops and other sonic invitations to stillness crop up in everything from La Monte Young to techno, Arabic improvisation to trance. Douglas Kahn documents how 'during a highly amplified La Monte Young concert ... it was not people talking in the audience that disturbed him but people moving. He stopped the performance to berate two people who had begun to move with the music and explained later that he needed to set an example to instruct people on the discipline needed for listening' (Kahn, 1999, p. 233). Noise music has a slightly different (but not unrelated) approach to discipline. It fixates us by exerting control while promising ecstatic release. But the stillness that can arise from being immersed in noise is not, for instance, the ecstatic listening to Arabic music improvisation, which arises from deep knowledge and appreciation of creative 'finesse' on the part of both the listener and the performer. 'Japanese Noise relishes the ecstacy of sound itself'

(Merzbow, 'The Beauty of Noise', web interview). Certainly the repetitions of *Loop Panic Limited* are perceptible, and enduring enough to encourage a trance listening. But, just as it's getting 'too comfortable', another, more brutal loop begins. Listening is held in bondage.

                                                          (Heinritzi, 2001,
p. 31)

                              (Sontag, 1982, p. 222)

(Zizek, 1992, p. 110)

                                                          (Heinritzi, 2001,
p. 32)

                                          (Sontag, 1982, p. 232)

You can't see nothing

                  (Zizek, 1992, p. 110)

            (Sontag, 1982, p. 231)

                                          (Heinritzi, 2001, p. 32) (my
italics)

Immersed in intensity: If we are immersed listeners, made 'impersonal' and still by Merzbow's relentless noise, perhaps also we are re-energized by the intensity of the sonic 'liquid' that surrounds us. Intensity is a measure of energy; in sonic terms it is a subjectively perceived quality, felt as an increase in perceived loudness. The intensity of sound is measured by the SPL (Sound Pressure Level) which also takes account of timbre, duration and other factors (Gordon, 1999, p. 1055). Noise is, or can be, in very real psychological and physiological terms, an intense feeling that borders on pain. To be both immersed and aroused by this feeling has its own allure. If 'everyone has felt (at least in fantasy) the erotic glamour of physical cruelty and an erotic lure in things that are vile and repulsive' (Sontag, 1982, p. 222) we have to own up to enjoying how it feels.

(

)

(

)

(

)

(

)

(

)

(

)

(

)

(

)

(   ) (

)

Noise fills up the gaps: it erases divisions gradually until there's only everything to choose from and no room at all to think (first 5 lines, then 4, then 3...). Noise obliterates the senses: it overwrites them gradually until there is only whiteness and empty parentheses (a feeling that something was there but has gone). Give in? Where there is everything, there is no point in talking of a distinction between music and noise, and there is certainly no mileage in patterns, bars and beats: 'There is no difference between noise and music in my work. If "Noise" means uncomfortable sound, then pop music is noise to me' (Masami Akita (aka Merzbow), liner note to

Immersion, Starkland CD S-2010). And there is no noise to be had in pinning down different types of noise. Noise obliterates the question 'Is this human or machine?'. There is no longer room for making a decision. Noise obliterates the relevance of the question, 'Is this me or is this not me?'. There is no longer a limit or a line.[23]

Chapter 8

(1) THE ENDNOTES

(Just what is it that makes yesterday's songs so different, so appealing?)

Records and recording as electronic music. (Featuring some popular appropriations)

/NB: 5 blank lines between text here (what comes around goes around)/

---

(2)
MAKE YOURSELF
COMFORTABLE

Lyrics Bob Merrill, Rylan Music Corp. (ASCAP).
Track 3 on *Sarah Vaughan's Golden Hits*
Duration 2:38
Prepared for Compact Disc by Richard Seidel and
Paul Ramey
Digitally Remastered by Dennis Drake
824-891-2 Mercury
(CD copyright 1990 PolyGram Records Inc)
First entered the Cash Box Top 50 Week ending
November 20th, 1954.

The perfect choice to be playing in the background
of Richard Hamilton's Pop Art photomontage, *Just*

*what is it that makes today's homes so different, so
appealing?* (1956). His notorious collage
appropriates images from contemporary advertising
as a parody of the post-war obsession with gadgets
and household appliances, symptomatic of the new
enthusiasm for technology and material objects.
Everyone's sitting comfortably now.

INTRO (it's a cover version)

---

(3)

If you keep to the left, Chapter 8 becomes the
endnotes for Chapter 7. But then *again*, Chapter 8's
opening is also a parody of Chapter 7's introduction.
So you've heard it all before. But still you're going to
have to decide which of those trajectories to follow,
or whether to flip from one to the other. It's just a
matter of context.

Of course, I hope you'll recognize something
familiar in all this reconstruction (otherwise it hasn't
worked). I'm relying on you to turn the pages
between now and then.

                              So here's the deal for
                                        Chapter 8:

                          Several things are going to
                            reappear. There are three
                            'takes' on three familiar
                        examples. These clues lead to
                            three other places (see
                                          below).

                        (Stay with me. I try to be what
                            I'm about, in a roundabout
                                          manner)

Eventually you'll come across three short essays that talk about some examples of appropriation. There are a couple of mainstream pop hits and one popular operatic diva. My three hit selections are neither an academic survey of the plunderphonic aesthetic, nor an enthusiast's record collection. If anything, I've just nicked some favourite examples, to show just how idiosyncratic the reasons for appropriating a recording can be. On a personal level, I'm interested in thinking about pieces that — in their different ways — keep me hanging on. Listening to them, I get the music — and locate new meaning in things I thought I knew.

The endnotes between these essays may have been 'previously enjoyed' by the preceding chapter but now that they're second-hand, I see no reason why they can't also be used to think about recording, sampling, and models for musical composition that might have started life elsewhere.

But first, here's something I prepared earlier.

(Ooh, oooh. Make yourself comfortable)

Ooh, oooh ... oooh. **Make yourself
comfortable**
Ooh, oooh ... oooh etc **repeated by
Richard scale to put yourself
comfortable**
**I feel romantic and the dance
Left before to put yourself
comfortable baby**
*(brass wah, swooping strings, slow
brushed cymbal beat)*

AGAIN Take ONE. (See definition
below.)
There's a pleasure in spotting
a secret steal. It makes us
feel so darned ... well,
clever to have spotted the
clips from the favourite songs,
or the cheesy rock opera lyrics
embedded in some worthy
academic prose (I hope you
scored full points for
Chapter 7). We appreciate the
familiarity, we appreciate the
difference, we appreciate the
appropriation and we
appreciate our appreciation of
all this. In some of the more
esoteric sampling repertoire,
there's a hell of a lot of
mutual appreciation to digest.
(Re-evaluation of this kind can
be a rather smug
regurgitation).

And, then again, sometimes our
enjoyment is far more earthy
and juvenile: we can be reduced
to laughing hysterics by the
wrong playback speed. In the

groove between 'Is this Dolly
Parton?' and 'Is that really
how it's meant to go?!' there's
some room for having a giggle.
**(see ESSAY: On 'again' —
TAKE 1)**

*(Ooh, oooh ooh make yourself
comfortable
I've got some time for size)*
**The phone is off the hook so no
one can intrude**
ooh. Make Yourself comfortable
baby
ooh. Make yourself comfortable
Ooh, oooh ooh etc repeated by
Richard

(4)

YOU'RE THE ONE THAT I WANT

By John Farrar.
A number 1 hit in 1978 for by Olivia Newton John
and John Travolta.
Soundtrack to the film, *Grease* (a musical set in the
1950s)
Two 12" LPs (USA: RSO 4002) (July 1978)
Two 12" LPs (UK: RSO RSD 2001) (1991)
CD (USA: Polydor 825 095-2) (March 1998)
Digitally Remastered CD (USA Polydor 825 095-2)

'You're The One That I Want'
Cover version sung by Arthur Mullard and Hylda
Baker, two veteran UK TV comics in their seventies.
Reached number 8 in the charts before flopping
spectacularly. Now chiefly remembered – if at all –
for their humiliatingly bad performance on the UK
TV pop show, *Top of the Pops*.

AGAIN Take TWO. (See below.)
While spotting the
straightforward steal is one
thing, enjoying the mangled
travesty is also fun.

Those comfortable Golden Hits
come round again. If you read
the last chapter, you'll have
seen it all before, but have
you noticed the way things have
changed? Sarah Vaughan now
duets with Travesty, a program
by Bertil Homberg that analyses
and then reassembles text. The
reconstruction attempts some
grammatical rules and lets the
user define how random things
are going to get. Of course,
I've also had a directorial
role in deciding what bits I
offer you to read. I'm the
composer here. You want to make
something out of that?

(If you do, at the time of
writing you can download
Travesty and some other textual
goodies, *gratis*, at
www.burningpress.org/
toolbox/)

In the groove between 'Is this
familiar?' and 'Has there been
a change?' there's some room
for trying to figure out the
difference. And because it
takes a length of time to do
that, this attempt could be
music of one kind or another.

**(see ESSAY: On 'again' —
TAKE 2)**

**I feel romantic and through the
dance**
Left before to put yourself
comfortable baby
*(brass wah, swooping strings,
slow brushed cymbal beat)*
Ooh, oooh make yourself comfortable
**The phone is off the verself
comfortable**

(5)
I'VE GROWN ACCUSTOMED
TO HER FACE
(From *My Fair Lady*) Lerner/Loewe original
recording: 1956 Original Broadway cast with Rex
Harrison (almost) singing. There are numerous cover
versions of this song, many of them by female
singers who generally – but not always – change the
words to conform to heterosexual expectations ('to
his face').
But not all.

'I've Grown Accustomed to Her Face'
Marlene Dietrich in Rio. Musical Supervision by
Burt Bacharach (Bras.CBS 1959) 15910.

AGAIN Take THREE. (See below.)
And then again, poking gentle
fun at popular icons has some
rewards worth recording. The
revered celebrity with the
inescapable voice and the

enduring following can be quite unstoppable. Her picture's on all the records, and even now she's lurking in the charts. Her voice is in the cultural background as the definitive diva. Perhaps there's some mileage in getting her to sing again, simultaneously knocking that reverence on the head.

In the groove between 'Is this homage?' and 'Is this ridicule?' there's some room for comparison. It takes a moment to decide, 'This is'. During that length of time (a familiar refrain) there's room to start a record collection. **(see ESSAY: On 'again' — TAKE 3)**

(duet)
Hurry through the dance
Ooh, oooh make your dinner
(first two lines doubling strings, slow brushed cymbal beat)
Ooh, oooh. Make yourself comfortable
Ooh, oooh make off the phone is off the records here to **put yourself comfortable**

(6)
IT TAKES **TWO**
(S. Moy, W. Stevenson)

The original version, recorded by Marvin Gaye and Kim Weston in 1967, reached number 14 in the Billboard Hot 100.

There are numerous cover versions, one of the most apparently incongruous couplings being Tina Turner's duet with Rod Stewart, produced by Rod Stewart and Kim Weston and recorded on Tina Turner's *Simply The Best* (1991). (Marvin was no doubt turning in his grave.)

You have to play it again. The success of a parody is dependent on our familiarity with the source. Mainstream music — in particular those golden oldies or classical music hits — provides a glut of recognizable material to play about with through the medium of recorded sound. Those old sounds are always easy prey for taking a pop at mass media culture or for making a knowing nod (we're talking nostalgia not remix virtuosity here). And there's a strange attraction too (a knock-on effect). After all, you've got to admire something just that little bit if you want to take the cultural icon and expose it to ironic recontextualization.

Ooh, oooh make you in the hook so no one is off the records herself comfortable

**I feel romantic and
kissakissakiss wah, oooh**
oooh ... oooh .. oooh etc repeat)
Ooh, oooh make Yourself
comfortable
I've got soothing string string
cadence)

AGAIN (some definitions)

(see Take 1, above) 'in addition
to a previously mentioned
quality'
(as in John Oswald? Essay 1)
(see Take 2, above) 'on the
other hand'
(as in Terre Thaemlitz? Essay 2)
(see Take 3, above) 'in return
or response(archaic)'
(as in Robert LePage and Martin
Tétreault? Essay 3)

(repeats) keep going!(as a
character yells in Berio's
Sinfonia)

---

(7)

GOOD LOOKIN' (Say, hey good lookin',

what you got cookin'?)

Hank Williams. Recorded on *Hank Williams* (MGM
10961, 1951)

'Good Lookin''
on *Hank Williams, Jr. Sings Hank Williams, Sr.* as
featured in the film: *Your Cheatin' Heart* (a biopic of
Hank Williams) recorded 1964, reissued on CD,
Rhino Records, 1998. Hank Williams's grandson has
also recently rebranded himself as Hank Williams III
(previous connections are worth cashing in on)

Listen . . .
You want to try that again?

Behind the joshing
familiarity, the silly word
games, the pretence,
pretension and the textual
fragmentation, I'm trying for
some kind of understanding.
This writing is an experiment,
and it's a very personal one
that inevitably goes up some
blind alleys.
We can always double back.

(8)

AIN'T **MISBEHAVIN'**

(by Andy Razaf and Thomas 'Fats' Waller) Featured
in a Broadway musical called *Connie's Hot
Chocolates*, 1929, where it was sung by 'Satchmo'.
Waller recorded the song with his orchestra in 1929
and 1938, and with the All Stars in 1947 and 1955.

'Ain't misbehavin'
on *Songs I Wish I Had Sung the First Time Around*
(Decca) recorded 1956. Bing Crosby with the Jack
Pleis Orchestra. A whiter shade of chocolate ....

Ooh, oooh. Make yourself comfortabled through the verself comfortable baby
(brass wah, oooh make yourself comfortable baby
ooh etc records herself comfore to put yourself comfore *to put you in the phone cadence)*

Maybe, to misquote John Cage, this is indeed an experiment because 'I don't know exactly what I'm doing'. I don't particularly mind, and hope you won't either (this is a personal address). It's a risk, but, after all, we're nearly at an end. And it's customary to look back at that point, before making sage projections for the future. So I thought I'd steal that idea, since this whole book is about looking back and forth through music.

(9)
AT THE HOP

Danny and the Juniors, 1957 (written by Danny and the Juniors, recorded on Singular). One of the all-time hits of rock and roll, buoyantly capturing the atmosphere of youthful verve and exuberance that characterized the optimism of the post-war years.

As of 2002, Danny and the Juniors are still performing '**At the Hop**' and other hits, and you can hire them for corporate events and retirement dinners. They are a little less junior now, perhaps even a travesty of their former selves.

'Thank you for making our tournament fun,
enjoyable and successful.'
Al Carmosino – Rocky Mountain Italian Golf
Association
(from www.dannyandthejuniors.com)

I doubt their current audience can hop.

/These cover versions turn a few pages
between serious and pop
(a flippantly kitsch connection ...)/

Comfortable?

Or

---

(10)
ALL SHOOK UP
originally recorded by Elvis Presley. Released 1957.
Music and lyrics by Otis Blackwell and Elvis Presley.
Produced by Steve Sholes on RCA.

There's a shaken but not stirred cover version on
Elvis goes Baroque performed by Peter Breiner and
his Orchestra (in Bratislava) 1995 (Naxos): *Concerto
grosso I* featuring trumpet: All shook up, Can't help

falling in love, Help me make it through the night, If
I can dream, Don't be cruel.

Be cruel, bare your listening! Dare to be
uncomfortable, distracted, confused, even if
you think you've heard it all before.
Something may change, beyond all
recognition.

Ooh make
(cre yough ooh, one Youghts hur
swoooping shed ing st sin **for**
stried comfords Goldence
I've dan ford comfords
.....oooh..ood
oooh, ooh, ooh sooothe put
bable
Ooh.......ooh.
Make brushe Yourself cat)
I'some
od   mak   y   s   conte   y
Le k aketoono... ooursse you
hef ow mery
Hictah... lffefosth   **(t** *sh 38*
Wh w
I've bles
ooomar?)
Tonoryooman've
Tough   *(c)*

---

(11)

'Can't Get You Out of My Head' (written
by Cathy Dennis/Rob Davis) was a

worldwide hit for Kylie Minogue in late 2001, staying in the charts for over four months – a length of time more usual in the 1950s, when hits hung around and popstars were vinyl, rather than visual, personalities. The video of this song is a paean to an uncomfortably voyeuristic approach to representing a sexuality that prioritizes sight – revealing clothes, retro-futuristic dance group and the obligatory shots of her famously pert behind. The release of the song coincided with the aftermath of the events of 11 September 2001, and Kylie was swiftly adopted as a rather more salacious reappropriation of the 'force's sweetheart', visiting troops and bucking morale like some parody of Vera Lynn. Nevertheless, Kylie's appeal as a heterosexual cover girl doesn't mute her pink power as a gay icon. Her familiar image is different things to different people.

Without the pop video, Kylie would not be where she is today. In the 1980s, at the start of the digital revolution, she made an unusually successful move from soapstar to international popstar. Yet really she made a well-timed transition from one visual medium to another. Sound had very little to do with it.

/that's enough foolery.
(can we return to the original text?)/

(12)
'In my mind and in my car,
we can't rewind we've gone too far.'

'Video Killed the Radio Star' by The Buggles,
from the album *The Age of Plastic*, 1979, written by
Geoff Downes, Trevor Horn and Bruce Wolley.

This was the first music video to be played on MTV.

ESSAY: On 'again' — TAKE 1
There's noise at the end of the track
(I feel romantic and the record changes automatically)

(digital vinyl)

'Crackle', the last track of John Oswald's *Plunderphonic* CD,
might seem an odd place to start because it comes at the end.
    This short recording consists of a six-second sample of
'record noise' which includes three 'bips' as the needle
audibly encounters the vinyl. The duration, the number of bips
and their regularity is precisely enough listening information
to define 33 revolutions a minute, the appropriate speed for
an LP record. 'Crackle' is a compact essay in retrospection
that speaks all the louder for its context. In this essay —
embedded in its own context — I'd like to dwell on this sample
                of noise at the end of the track.

This is a sound that digital technology snatched away. Now,
after the last CD track, there is nothing but an abrupt return
        to normality. Listening to vinyl, for those of us who
remember, there was always some kind of finishing up: we heard
the sound of the record going round, the stylus traversing the

groove, and finally the lift and clunk of the returning arm. The record needle sounds the nick of time while the end of the CD is a silent jolt, back into the void of everyday listening. And unless we shuffle the playback (and perhaps even then) the last track of the CD will always be a finale — the sound that precedes the moment when listening returns to clock time. But the last track of a record doesn't labour under the same responsibility; it will always be followed by that familiar noise at the end of the track, providing not so much a barrier as a border crossing from one state to another. This small mechanical performance gently moves us to and fro — here we are, we are arrived at the end of the journey of listening to the recording. Get ready to disembark, you have been given some time to prepare.

Of course, this is to romanticize the allure of the analogue, when too often such noise is obtrusive (why else would we have embraced digital sound with such relieved enthusiasm?). But this kind of romantic nostalgia is at present a familiar groove, expressed by many who cut their listening teeth on CD technology. Perhaps the current cult amongst (overwhelmingly male) electronica performers for using 'antique' analogue equipment, and the reverence they show towards electronic music that dates from that era (early Schaeffer, Henry, Stockhausen and so on) has something in common with the concurrent 'camp' enthusiasm for the popular music and fashion of the 1950s. Timothy Taylor sees the latter as a 'way of voicing our own era's disillusionment with the promises of technology' and also, more disturbingly, 'about the male anxiety over what has happened to authority of the male in the late twentieth century ... intimately connected to questions about domestic space and technology in the 1950s' (Taylor, 2001, p. 104).

So the noise at the end of the record is a long-range comforter in sociological terms — something for little boys to hold on to? But it also comforts our ears. This remembered sound that some do not even remember reminds us that all that preceded was but a recording. We knew this, but this technological riff lures us into an indulgent appreciation of knowing it. It warms us to the nostalgia of listening to the past. Listening may have been a transport of delight but we're now reminded that it was also enabled by a transport of cogs, drives, wires, rotations and electrical impulses. And while the turntable may have been resituated in a public forum — 'DJs resocialized the turntable: music sounded by turntables at parties brings people together'(Taylor, 2001, p. 204). The intimate 'crackle' of vinyl is still the antithesis to the performance of the 'scratch'.

That crackle can be a nifty little theatrical trick to borrow. That sound of the record going around, and in particular the sound of its ending, is regularly appropriated to make reference to listening to music and, more specifically, to time. The record player arm that thumps unheard against the spindle is a thriller cliché. For some unfortunate victim — no doubt lying bloody on the floor beside it — time had stopped in its tracks. A less frequent appropriation, the sound of the tape machine and the tape being rewound and stopped, has a more functional connotation.

One can own a load of tapes, but a record 'collection' is something that carries more weight. The vinyl's crackle has an association with old or 'archive' recordings and by extension, with a disappeared but, we presume, valued experience. But it also alludes more generally to the intimate familiarity of 'domestic' or personal listening — at home, in comfort — alone, or with friends. Aggravating the distance between these two associations — archive and personal — can be a powerful way of exploiting our close relationship with the recorded past. George Katzer's 'Aide Mémoire', originally released in 1983 on vinyl, and now on CD, is a collage made from archive recordings of Nazi speeches and fascist songs. The crackle of the documentary recording here revives an horrific remembering of sound, brought right into the comfort of your home.

The domestic consumption of recorded music is more commonly a CD listening experience at present. But in comparison to the record player, the CD machine itself doesn't offer such poetically resonant mechanics — it is largely silent. (And this silence extends to visual associations: a film close-up of a CD player's numerical display is never going to have the affective power of the record arm moving across the LP.) Moreover, the CD is not tactile in the same sense as vinyl: its medium is physically hidden while it plays, and to make the machine's mechanics audible — hot-wiring the laser or reprogramming the shuffle — requires a more self-conscious invasion than spinning a disc. Whereas scratching subverts the record-deck's original function, hot-wiring just breaks the machine. Nic Collins' *Broken Light* (1991) for string quartet and hot-wired CD player allows the players to interact with

looped playback of Baroque string music CDs. The aural effect
is definitely one of 'looped digital sound', but is not
particularly indicative of any particular technology (it could
be looped from sampler or hard disk).

Oswald's brief crackle — which is the last track on a *CD* —
alludes to all these analogue to digital conversions. But it
also summarizes a more stratified series of familiarities.
This particular crackle is more than a plundered reference to
the last sound on a record; it is itself the last in a series
of sonic quotes and tropes.

The CD *Plunderphonic* was never sold or intended for sale. The packaging included
detailed credits of the sampled sources which constitute nearly 100% of the sounds
from which *Plunderphonic* was made. Copies were distributed to radio stations,
libraries and reviewers. A *shareright* notice in an accompanying booklet permitted
listeners to make a free copy of the disc (*shareright* is borrowed from the not-for-profit
distribution of computer software).
(Information listed on http://.www.plunderphonics.com/xhtml/xnegation.html)

Appearing in around 1989, *Plunderphonic* became notorious as
the CD that provoked the threat of a lawsuit from Michael
Jackson (hardly surprising, even though a cover image grafting
Jackson's head on to a naked woman's body might seem somewhat
less disconcerting than his subsequent forays into plastic
surgery). To summarize its history: Oswald blithely raided
numerous well-known pop and some classical works, and
subjected these recognizable icons to amusing, and
deliberately irreverent, processes. Many of the processes were
themselves ironic 'appropriations' of recording techniques
(for instance, 'Don't' takes an Elvis track and adds separate
overdubbed instrumental parts in the manner of a multitrack
studio recording, but here the individual instrumentalists did
not hear the other tracks while they recorded and are
consequently somewhat out of sync).

Though Oswald distributed the CD for free (ostensibly in an
attempt to evade copyright issues) the flack was inevitable,
and no doubt sought (see Oswald, 1985). Threatened with
litigation, he agreed to withdraw all remaining copies of the
'original' (the defining of what is the 'original' of a
digital work engendered a new dilemma), but digital copies
remain freely downloadable from various online sources. In its
cacophonous journey *Plunderphonic* has intentionally rattled a
great many cages, assaulted and challenged the ethics of
copyright, appropriation and artistic ownership and has

brutally illuminated the limitations on artistic freedom posed
by the economic weight of the commercial recording industry.
(For a lengthier discussion see, for example, Cutler, 1994;
Polansky, 1998, web reference.)

But *Plunderphonic*, and the aesthetic of 'plunderphonics' that
takes this CD as its eponymous figurehead, differs in intent
from numerous other works that appropriate sampled music.

> The definition I'd set up for plunderphonic was music that was recognisable in
> some way, and the transformation of that music. I think the most successful
> examples use music that is the most recognisable. It's more delightful to me to
> have these pop figures, and by pop I also include Beethoven, as the working
> materials.
> (Oswald, online interview with Brian Duguid, 1994)

Every track on Oswald's *Plunderphonic* CD relies on your input
— name that tune, and laugh at its new incarnation. You don't
have to go out of your esoteric way to spot the difference.
These sources are not only familiar, but have a familiar role
(to anyone exposed to pop culture) as 'hit records' — all are
'classics' and none are contemporary releases. Before you've
even started, you're dealing with the past — with *your* past,
our past.

⊙ CD[31] 'White', by John Oswald

> Bing Crosby sounds a little pink on our version of the best-selling single of all
> time. We've separated him from the chorus and let his tendency to wallow in
> melisma (melodic elaboration on a syllable) run amok. The 2nd half of this
> cut features an unprecedented collaboration between African Pygmies and a
> tango orchestra.
> (liner notes to *Plunderphonic*, www.plunderphonics.com/xhtml/xunavailable.html)

> Bing Crosby on varispeed, his croon proliferating into a
> wavering wail that is sickening rather than seductive.
> A chorus similarly prone to nausea and eventually all the
> voices transposed to inhuman, or at least pygmy, heights. It's
> a playful, albeit juvenile, bit of experimentation that refers
> to the mechanics of the record-player (its rotation speed) and
> the transpositions made facile by 'new' sampling technology.
> Rather than erasure, Oswald's romp through pop's 'blasts from
> the past' provides a pop-art amplification. It turns the
> volume up on both the pop hit's surface appeal and the
> different lengths to which our familiarity with pop, and with
> recording, can be taken.

The cultural and political significance of Oswald's work is such that discussion of what he actually does with sound is hard to isolate: to quote Polansky, 'Plunderphonics is not aesthetic piracy, but piracy as an aesthetic'. But Oswald has affectionate respect for his stolen cargo.

In general he admires and likes his sources, and doesn't seek their obliteration. Each of the tracks is an amused caricature rather than a character assassination. Oswald picks up on the essential sonic features of those hits — the things we 'know' — Bing's croon, James Brown's whooping machismo, the saturated string utopia of 'Somewhere Over the Rainbow', or the pointillistic non-sequiturs of Webern's op. 10. He appropriates performance too — Glenn Gould's performance of the *Goldberg Variations* is taken on a new line of flight by a computer-created reperformance that meanders into a random walk where pitches are in the right place at the wrong time.

While Merzbow 'pirates' the sounds and techniques of hardcore academic electracoustic music in his *Batzoui with Material Gadgets (De-Composed Works 1985-86)* and describes the result, with noisy irony, as 'Fake Electro Acoustic Music Dedicated to GRM/INA, WERGO, DEUTSCHE GRAMMOPHON, PHILIIPS&ERATO RECORDING ARTISTS', Oswald's gentle subversion aims at bigger prey.

> Listening to pop music isn't a matter of choice.
> Asked for or not, we're bombarded by it.
> (Oswald, 1985, web reference)

There's no getting away from it, so you might as well use it rather than be used by it. Every appropriation steals a little power.

And that crackle?

Oswald's crackle is a stolen moment with a specific agenda; it is the ending to end all endings, the quote to contextualize all quotes. As a musical joke it has the last laugh.

(13)

> It did not need photography to show people what they looked like – the image itself might surprise them, but not the fact of a visual representation … But Edison, speaking of hearing the first recording he ever made, remarked 'I was never so taken aback in my life.' For no one before this moment could know what their voice sounded like. (Chanan, 1995, p. 137)

But – one has to be careful when interpreting quotations of any kind: in his haste to make a particular allusion, Chanan neglects to quote Edison in full. Here's the original:

> 'I was never so taken aback in my life – *I was always afraid of things that worked the first time.*' (Thomas A. Edison on hearing his voice played back to him from his first tin foil phonograph. From http://memory.loc.gov/ammem/edhtml/edsndhm.html)

(14)

Philip Jeck's *Off the Record*, featured at *Sonic Boom – the Art of Sound* (27 April–18 June 2000), Hayward Gallery, London, consisted of an installation for 72 old dansette and beaten-up record-players, set on timers to play records intermittently. Chalked inscriptions inside the lid of each record-player provided individual slogans for life, time and memories of music.

They're playing our song. And so we do seem to feel we can 'rewind' time, beyond experiencing 'memory' and onwards to the past – our past – itself. (But, happiness is just an illusion.)

ESSAY: On 'again' — TAKE 2
It doesn't sound quite right
(somewhat nostalgic)

(don't go changing)

Sound recordings entice varying degrees of associative retrospection, whether it's the locating of effect and cause ('that's the sound of a door'), the identification of a place ('that's a street market'), or the frisson of a Carpenters' hit ('that's so seventies'). Some of our associations with sound are individual to us and some are going to be more generally to one or other cultural grouping.

If you know the melody, feel free to hum along (hey, I haven't heard this one for a while) and off we'll go together, wallowing in the feelings of nostalgia; happiness and sadness, regret and perhaps a trace of longing. It's yesterday once more (sha-la-la, la-la ...).

Probably, our nostalgic response to mainstream pop hits is one of our least individual, and most ordinary, responses to sound. Besides specific personal associations (essentially memories stirred up by listening) there is the simple 'gratification' of recognizing something familiar. We might not like — or have ever liked — that darned song, but we recognize its appeal. And its appeal is the fact that we know it. Nostalgia is a pleasurable sensation, one that softens us up and encourages us to wallow in a self-indulgent immersion. Our willingness to do so is easily exploited — recently, on UK TV, by a glut of cheap compilation programmes and recordings — *I love the 70s*, *I love the 80s* and even (in 2001 for goodness' sake!), *I love the 90s*.

But 'love' is not really the issue, although it can be a useful four-letter word to keep emotion at a tongue-in-cheek remove (don't you just *love* that kind of insincerity?). We love to love, but perhaps we no longer love to dance to those golden oldies — we're happy listening in from the sidelines, a little more leery this time around. Thankfully, I no longer encounter Donny Osmond's hits with the same squealing mindset as my pre-pubescent self, but if I inadvertently come across his adolescent tones my listening is in some part a remembered cover version of a previous response. Unfortunately. Nostalgia requires distance.

Now, don't go underestimating the lure of the past. The thing with nostalgia is that part of us wants to go back (we don't

feel nostalgic for bad times). But going back is bound to
disappoint — hey, they've pulled down the cinema! Nostalgia
has to be an unfulfilled desire because the desire is for the
pleasurable pang of distance. Even if there's no getting away
from its schmaltzy appeal, you can use that desire to
advantage.

> In nostalgia ... we have the illusion of 'seeing ourselves
> seeing', of seeing the gaze itself.
> (Zizek, 1992 p. 114)

The 'gaze' is a construct appropriated from Lacanian
psychoanalysis by film theory, which then pursued the gaze as
a gendered dynamic. The gendered film 'gaze' makes the
implicit assumption of a film spectator's identification with
the male protagonist of traditional film. This voyeuristic
'male gaze' views the passive female 'object'. This is to make
a cursory summary of a large area. In any case the 'male gaze'
is certainly not the only way to look at it (see Paglia, 1998
for a vociferously alternative view). Nostalgia lets us take a
good look at ourselves; we catch ourselves having another
peek. It can show us just how far we've travelled on life's
long journey (it feeds off greeting-card sentiments like this
— but, of course, you know those sepia snapshots are faked?).
Maybe that tantalizing 'illusion of "seeing ourselves
seeing" ' that Zizek describes can extend to listening too? So
I'll just borrow it for a while.

Or should I? The language of visual culture doesn't
necessarily throw much light on sound — a sonic gesture
described in visual terms appropriates a voice that may be
struck dumb in the process. Too often the vocabulary of one
discourse doesn't travel well when applied to another, or
unhelpfully becomes a different thing altogether. Perhaps
it even *restricts* our understanding of sound to speak — and
think — of pink, white and grey noise. Since when did
digital sound processing come with a kiddies' paint palette,
and who chose that decor? On a grander scale, when one
ideology tries to speak through the methods of another
there's always the danger that neither side will understand
a word of it. Worse, both may *think*, wrongly, that they know
what the other is saying. At its very worst this lazy
intertextuality is a useless appropriation of someone
else's toys. Academic writing on electroacoustic music
regularly borrows terminology from phenomenology and

information science. Sometimes this fashionable
predilection seems to spring from a desire to slap on
'scientific' credence, rather than an urge to hack out new
and wider routes. But on a clear day, the cross-disciplinary
sharing can be illuminating; it can really sing (as a light
goes on with an audible 'ping').

In landing these sidelong glances at golden oldies, nostalgia
and cross-synthesized ideas I'm meandering towards an
encounter with a song.

Polemic over? Oh no, polemic just beginning — but in other
words:

Statistical: Edit, filter and resynthesize a 'politically regressive' pop
standard so that the end result presents a restructuring of the
original sound source while triggering an overtly nostalgic desire for
that source.

Rationale: 'I Love You Just the Way You Are' by Billy Joel, was
chosen for its general ability to evoke a pleasant sense of nostalgia,
as well as for its historical lack of appeal as an 'anti-Feminist'
anthem against concepts of change. A resistance to social change
may be fuelled more by a fear of unfamiliarity than any
conspiratorial malice of cultural consensus that things are 'fine as
they are.' Similarly, direct action groups must typically develop
discourses primarily in response to their oppositions' fears of
cultural loss (the threat of lower material and/or ethical qualities of
life) rather than simply engaging 'positive' desires for social and/or
personal betterment. In order for resistance to resign itself to
change, resistors must find some semblance of their current
objectives within new communal initiatives. Therefore, the long
term impact of social change seems to involve transformations
which engage nostalgia, rather than radical historical breaches of
context which may result in repressed desires that erupt in
conservative backlashes. The difficulty lies in adapting decon-
structive discourses which evoke a sense of nostalgia sufficient to
establish familiarity without overwhelming the resulting scenario
with a desire for the past.
(Terre Thaemlitz, liner notes for *Resistance to Change*)

⊛ CD[32] CD[33] 'Resistance' and 'Transformative nostalgia' – excerpts: movements 2 and 4 of *Resistance to Change*, by Terre Thaemlitz

If 'don't' is the negative rallying cry of the arch-
conservative — keeping the status quo — 'change' is the

positive shift from one state to another. And nostalgia is
one way to rub those two up against each other. Terre
Thaemlitz is someone who has chosen to try to make that
friction sound. The text above is the written component of
his work, *Resistance to Change*. These words *are* the
explanation of both how and why, and the sonic component of
Resistance to Change is created by the means he describes (in
four short sections, each using Joel's hit as one of their
source materials).

The sonic element is the result of the interaction of a
computer-spoken activist text and a popular song (as an
'anti-Feminist' anthem in Thaemlitz' interpretation, the
song is the polar opposite of any desire for change). The
four short sections to the work present the results of the
cross-synthesis of these two sources in different ways —
most explicitly in the vocal resynthesis of the first
section, 'Commentary', and the presentation of the residual
sounds that are generally discarded in vocal resynthesis, in
the second, 'Resistance'. The written notes for each section
refer elliptically to both the techniques used to create the
sound and the ideas that these sounds become representative
of. Because this is a piece where sound manipulation
techniques, and specifically digital ones, enable the
realization of Thaemlitz' intent: the *processes* that create
the music themselves become allegorical of the call for
social change (and the way to achieve it) expressed by a
Marxist text.

To speak of 'colouring' a sound by filtering it is to employ an
analogy to explain the way we perceive the audible result,
whereas filtering considered as restructuring refers more
directly to the means of achieving a formal change.
Morphological descriptions serve analysis of electroacoustic
music quite well (for example, Smalley, 1986), perhaps since
these ideas centre on form and structure rather than specific
properties picked up by sensory perception, such as colour or
texture. Cross-synthesis — when the shape of one sound is used
to filter the profile of another — provides a result where the
way in which form has changed can be deduced: the appeal of
hearing the sound of speech cross-synthesized with the sound
of water is that we comprehend the nature of the restructuring
through some kind of 'before' and 'after' comparison. The
nature of the change that has taken place is audible (it can be
conjectured from aural clues). Our appreciation of the change

relies on the fact that there is something familiar about this strange new object.

I want to labour this point because I think Thaemlitz achieves something that is still quite extraordinary, and that is to create a truly digital work (as distinct from a work merely realized through digital media). The techniques of digital signal processing become allegorical symbols. And because these symbols are dynamic (both the process and perception of cross-synthesis occupy time) they can participate in an aurally realized allegory that is itself temporal. And that is a very interesting kind of music.

> The difficulty, or I guess I should say challenge, is to reconcile the literalness of written text with what might typically be ambiguously-defined abstract electroacoustic audio. I never want my texts or graphics to be simply reiterations of the audio ... I want each component ... to contribute somewhat different discourses around a common theme.
> (Thaemlitz, online interview with Christopher Strunz)

The appropriation of a MOR hit is only the most overt of his borrowings. Other borrowings — or rather redirectings — are appropriated from our listening: the nostalgia we feel towards the familiar song, the active deciphering to explain the dynamics of sonic processes and the way we'll always listen out for some sense of development. The last section's fragmentary remixing of a significant phrase from the song, with words continually cut off mid-flow, frozen harmony and no sense of going anywhere leaves you almost crying out for change.

Resistance to Change as a purely sonic experience is incomplete — the first thing to do on listening is to look at the liner notes to see what it's 'about' — but it is not merely a sonic illustration of a written text or a setting of a spoken one. The sound does not depict; its role is richer than that, because it pulls us towards a different relationship with the words. We go back and forth between abstract sonic processes and linear text. But this is not an electroacoustic work that plays with the sonic content of the voice as an appealing, abstracted source, because the meaning of the words (not the voice) is hugely significant. Yet neither is it a setting of a text — since the written text is not *interpreted* by sound. Sound is just one stratum in this discourse's delivery.

Perhaps Thaemlitz's work makes a covert change in its
definition of music. Music here is an exposition of ideas, a
composed, sequential 'out loud' exploration of thinking that
has an opinion to communicate. Perhaps this is music as
listenable prose. It sounds like a good read.

(15)

'... the medium is the message' (McLuhan, 1964, p. 9). The slogan
has a nice rhythmic lilt that perhaps has contributed to it ringing,
sometimes mindlessly, through the curricula of numerous Media Studies
courses.

(16)

... two typical slogans that pervade American advertising. The first, widely used by
Coca-Cola but also frequent as a hypolic formula in everyday speech, is 'the real
thing'; the second, found in print and heard on TV, is 'more' – in the sense of
'extra'. (Eco, 1990, p. 7)

Umberto Eco's virtuoso essay on his journeys around the USA, during
which he hunted out theme parks, waxwork museums, replicas of *The
Last Supper* and other surreal experiences of reproduced art, offers some
more reflection on going that bit further than the real thing. The tacky
reproductions that he visits and provides commentary on are bizarre
examples of a desire for 'owning' something 'even better' than the real
thing, and of making improvements on the original – with excesses of
one kind or another.

(17)

But temporarily inhabiting someone else's being – rather than merely
adopting their persona – is a state of 'becoming' we can pretend to reach,
in fantasy: *Being John Malkovich* (1999, Universal Pictures, dir. Spike
Jonze) had a surreal plot involving the ability to 'rent out' Malkovich's
head and thus allow paying punters to become him on a temporary basis.
The film sold itself with the promotional slogan: 'Ever wanted to be
someone else? Now you can.'

ESSAY: On 'again' — TAKE 3
And finally, a diva who won't stop singing
(I've got some records here to put you in the mood)

(for ensemble with worm)

Maria Callas is reputed to have followed a rather gruesome
1950s weight-loss fad, involving the ingestion of a live
tapeworm. It's hard to imagine how it would have felt to
inhale, tighten that formidable diaphragm to support the
production of that extraordinary, strong voice while all the
time, internally, that squiggling parasite was hoiking itself
about in the intestines, eating away. In 1954 (the same year
that Sarah Vaughan — 'The Divine One' — was making herself
comfortable) 'La Divina' apparently had to have the tapeworm's
head surgically removed from her body. What an alarming
ensemble.

But I digress, in a way. Actually, a diva doesn't need to take
such drastic action to accomplish a physical disappearing act.
All she needs to do is to do is sing into the microphone while
someone presses 'record'. And after that, the voice takes on a
disembodied, independent life. Not quite immortality, but
getting there. And the record is going to be divine, for those
who worship vinyl.

Callas: La diva et le vinyle is a collaboration between two
Montréal-based musicians — Martin Tétreault (on turntables),
Robert M. LePage (on clarinet) — and also features Maria
Callas (on disembodied voice). The tapeworm doesn't appear.
But there are quite a few other people who do, because in fact
this CD is quite a production. I feel bound to list the
additional members of the cast:

Original idea: Réal La Rochelle
Conception: Réal La Rochelle, Raymond Gervais, Robert M.
LePage, Martin Tétreault
Music: Robert M. LePage, Martin Tétreault (together or
individually)
Recording, mixing and montage: Robert Langlois, Studio 270.

Mastering: Jim Rabchuk
Photos: Bertrand Carrière
Text: Réal La Rochelle
Translation: Terry Knowles
Graphics: Nicole Morisset

I think that's everyone accounted for.

But the music is essentially a performance by LePage, Tétreault and . . . well, not Callas exactly. In sixteen short movements, the two performers play about with Callas recordings, variously transformed (ridiculed?) by Tétreault's turntable manipulation and imitated (mocked?) by LePage's clarinet riffs. Things go back and forth in an unpretentious fashion during which time the Diva's inimitable tones are made to swoop, speed up and slow down, now high, now in a farcical basso profundo. The introduction of an Italian-language class record, and applause and audible adulation (presumably taken off original 'live' recordings) provides a few extra laughs.

The clarinet improvisation is largely melodic and quite straightforward, and there is a real sense of a listening, improvising ensemble in action. To my ears, it comes across as slightly dysfunctional contemporary parlour music. There is, as with much improvisation I think, an element of hermetic exploration, but the result is both intimate and outgoing.

But there's also a little dissimulation going on here too. This CD has the air of being a recording of a performance (a performance that entails the appropriation of recordings of another performance). But in fact there has been quite a bit of mixing, montage and additional creative work outside the 'live' improvisation. Although all CDs of recorded instrumental music have post-production input, the CD is still a 'proxy' for a live performance. Here it isn't. *La diva et le vinyle* is a CD work that stands complete as it is, while playing with all those 'recorded music' associations.

It's not only the sound that is presented with a bit of fakery. The object itself is meticulous in design. The CD is charmingly decorated to look like a (rather small) LP, the CD liner notes include interesting archive photographs, and photographs of LePage and Tétreault in mid-performance, all reproduced in a similarly sombre and authoritative monochrome. On the CD cover, Callas looks on via a single, imperious and unmistakable eye.

There is a lot of detail: the archive photographs are carefully annotated — three relating to Emil Berliner and his Montréal gramophone business (he set up EMI, for whom Callas recorded), an image of Callas, resplendent on the cover of La Rochelle's book *Callas l'opéra du disque* and a photograph of the record cover of her final Montréal concert, 'the last concert by Callas in the West'. An interesting essay entitled 'Berliner, Callas, Montréal' is contributed by La Rochelle, in French and in English translation. The CD is — as the essay makes clear — a 'tribute to the Diva's role in recording history', and also to the Montréal connection. The title of the CD was also the title of the original edition of La Rochelle's book. The date of the CD's release, 1997, coincides with the 20th anniversary of Callas' death. This is truly a tribute to the disembodied diva.

So far so good — a piece of kitsch that promotes all kinds of Callas connections and has some fun in the meantime. You can either enjoy its witty pretensions or be aggravated by such apparent delusions of grandeur. Of the several interesting reviews of the CD around, one of the more searching appraisals picks up on an interesting ambiguity that, I agree, appears indicative of intent beyond mere parody:

> ... perhaps this conventional musicality is all part of another kind of joke, a sort of meta-joke about making a record of opera diva cutups with a straight face. This is a genuine ambiguity for a lot of this disk, the confusion between irony and sincerity, and that too is something of a strength in comparison with all those earnestly wry referential works which tend to dissolve into kitsch.
> (Richard Cochrane, *Earscape #3*)

La diva et le vinyle does seem to play a somewhat equivocal, dual role as both sincere celebration and ironic reinterpretation of the voice of Callas. But just how camp is this 'production'? And what exactly is the object of its appropriation? The appropriation of the recorded voice and the association of a popular, revered icon is a given, but the practical appropriation of bits of vinyl points towards another silent steal. Any appropriation of a recorded song is an appropriation of the historical and cultural paraphernalia surrounding the recording. But a turntable artist has this directly to hand.

Although *Callas: la diva et le vinyle* requires nothing more than listening to make completely satisfying aural sense, it is more than sound. That spiral worm trace that inhabits the record is the gouged-out remains of a distant collaboration between a sounding body (no doubt swathed in full evening dress) and the technology that captured it, and set it in vinyl for future listening. Make another copy of that vinyl, or even dub it to CD, and you're still holding that trace.

So I'm not especially concerned with the aura of the 'original artwork' here. Walter Benjamin's notion is hauled up fairly regularly in encounters with the kind of music that exists only in recorded form; it surfaces in intellectual skirmishes around the 'problem' of the 'perfect digital copy', and anguish as to whether our CD cabinets are all stocked up with an aura-free original. I'd prefer to leave that dilemma for Michael Jackson's lawyers. But, in his influential 1968 essay Benjamin proceeds from the 'original' as opposed to the reproducable artwork (essentially film and photography) towards a related reflection on the *audience*. The tools of mechanical reproduction also change artistic approach, and create a concomitant change in audience perception and desire.

I think Benjamin's thought has particular relevance for works for sound alone when he comes to consider film's ability to penetrate its subject (his metaphor being the cameraman going in close, as an invasive surgeon). His observations on how a mass audience exposure to the results of this shift of perspective changes expectations of art offers food for continuing thought, particularly with regard to our listening to works for sound alone. We are that mass audience, even when we are all sitting at home alone with only our CD player for company. To quote Benjamin: 'the desire of contemporary masses to bring things "closer" spatially and humanly ... is just as ardent as their bent towards overcoming the uniqueness of every reality by accepting its reproduction' (Benjamin, 1968, p. 223).

What exactly is made more immediate by Tétreault's real-time machinations and LePage's response? Does *La diva et le vinyle* bring Maria Callas 'spatially and humanly' closer to us? The turntable performer certainly dives in with the 'invasive' close-up hands of the aural 'surgeon'; Tétreault often cuts up, manipulates and otherwise distresses the vinyl itself. And the recorded voice of Callas is certainly made 'live' by this real-time manipulation. But it is the recorded voice, not Callas, that gets the treatment: the material transformation and its aural results, provide a performed commentary on 'recordings'. We hear 'the recording' — that fixed, historic relic — in the process of being brought back into the present.

You think this is going round and round in an ever-decreasing spiral? I fear you're right. It's hard to pin down just how Tétreault entices that parasitic behind-the-scenes addition from the vinyl. Perhaps this is because there are several distinct camera angles to consider (so any appearance of continuity will have to be a composite response).

Camera 1: Instrumental

Some guy outside my window has been hacking down a tree all day. He has provided me with a useful analogy. The whine of his chainsaw sounds almost human. Why? Because it's a continuous, almost vocal timbre and because the energy and rhythm of his effort is translated, directly, into sonic terms — via the response of the saw's machinery. When he has to put in more effort, the sound slides up in pitch; when he releases the pressure or meets resistance the sound slows and goes down. The shape and duration of these coloratura phrases is defined by the task in hand, and the performer's physical ability. The sonic gestures I hear seem to have a 'human' contour, to my mind (because I am trying to bring the sound humanly, if not spatially, closer).

As an instrument the turntable can be similarly responsive to nuances of pressure, texture, and touch that create their analogue in sculpted sound — it's an interface that a hard-pressed pianist might envy. And the relationship of the human performer — Tétreault — to his instrument — the turntable — is direct, generally tactile and expert. If he slows down a recording of Beethoven, or slows down a recording of a bus, both will make a sliding descent to a halt, both will sound like 'human' gestures in that respect. (You don't necessarily need to put anything on the platter: Otomo Yoshihide's 'Solo for turntable and guitar amp' is a searingly aggressive example of performing the turntable itself.)

Camera 2: Following the shot

Of course, Tétreault is using his physical gesture to extract
a particular sound from his instrument — his Callas 'voice'-
just as LePage is controlling the timbre of his clarinet. But
while LePage moulds a sound that's under the control of a
particular fingering, Tétreault sculpts a material that was
already fixed in its own time. Now, set in motion by the
stylus, that activated tapeworm vinyl groove acts out that
time again. Controlling that involves a bit of a chase.

Because, for the most part, the recorded diva is not slotted
into place as a object of sampled curiosity (though granted,
on a couple of occasions she does get reduced to piping up
fragments on the beat). No, the recording brings its own time,
and Tétreault improvises with that past. That's quite an
appropriation.

Camera 3: Hidden ritual

Early on in his essay, Walter Benjamin gives the example of a
cave-painting as an 'instrument of magic'. He sees it an
authentic artwork that retains the aura of ritual because
although it can be viewed, it was not created to be viewed. The
record of an 'historic archive recording' also has some aspect
of that magic, I think. Of course, it *was* made to be listened
to, but was also made — or has subsequently become — an object
to be collected and revered for its place in history. Like the
footage of Monroe singing, or Kennedy being shot, the
'historic recording' has significance for its collector as a
ritual talisman that allows some kind of time travel, or at
least some kind of ownership of 'fixated' past time.

The 'recording of Callas singing' is elevated beyond the
actual sound of her disembodied voice to a position as a vinyl
relic. The vinyl LP, and even its cover and packaging, is
important (even though this is itself a mass-produced object,
it is one that is of a time, and time cannot be mass-produced).
All this documentation, what it represents and what it
preserves acquires its own aura. (The digital 'improvement' of
old 'original recordings' is certainly an issue with regard to
what is being removed along with hiss and pop.)

These angles perhaps suggest some of the appropriations that

come along for the ride when the voice of a disembodied diva
sings. In *La diva et le vinyle* the divinity of Callas and the
'divinity' of the record are both debunked with humour. As we
get further from the technology that made it, the LP is
perhaps in danger of becoming even more revered — the object
of a cult (whether the cult of DJ-ing or the cult of 'antique'
collecting). It seems odd to hear a record of an Italian-
language course now — reminding us that there was a time when
vinyl was just the normal, functional way of recording and
then playing back sound, rather than being constantly
concerned with keeping it 'for the record'.

Edison may have reacted to the sound of the recorded voice
with astonishment; this CD work lets us react with a little
more levity, but still it similarly directs us towards being
'astonished' by what technology can perform. It is not just
Callas that becomes newly sounded, but the past as a subject
for audible virtuosity.

⏵ **CD[34] 'Callaérobique' – track 13 of *Callas: La diva et le vinyle***

---

(18)

Otomo Yoshihide's 'sampling virus' project, realized in one incarnation on his CD *The
Night Before the Death of the Sampling Virus* amasses a collection of 77 short sound
samples (the shortest being one-second long) taken from Japanese commercials, TV,
movies and other technological sources. Yoshihide states that 'The original objective of
developing this virus was for examining the condition of prejudice in Japan. However,
end results will not always agree with the intents of the artist. This virus is known to
ignore the artist's intention and attempt to behave according to its own will.' The 'viral'
analogy he adopts extends to instructions to play the tracks in random order, to set
tracks on repeat and to play copies of the CD on multiple machines. Lists of machines
and technology employed take the role of conventional liner note explanation. A
proliferation of mass media 'dross' is captured by sampling, and subjected to a creative
destruction – both in structural terms and in terms of how one 'should' listen.
Yoshihide's project perhaps encourages us to think about how we are listening to
recontextualised sound, but the viral analogy remains primarily a metaphor referring to
an individual artist's attitude to assembling material. The self-conscious reiteration
'The purpose ... not to create a musical work ... may sound like words, or appear to be
music' is perhaps a gentle challenge concerning definitions. Unlike many of
Yoshihide's projects, this CD is not itself an overt collaboration with a specific
performer or performers, although the listener's collaboration – following instructions,
or not – is invited from the start.

(19)

When high-powered number crunching emerged from the confines of mainframe computing and landed on the laptop, a whole candy-shop of 'generative music' software became explicitly available to a wider community of musicians and composers. Proliferating, rule-based processes can be a useful broad-brush way of generating material that is textural, ambient or has ateleological stasis. It can result in inspired confluences of means and intent. The response to the tools of generative music can be naive, but perhaps hints at the way a current *Zeitgeist* – where the 'third culture', science, in particular biology and genetics, is the 'new intellectual thinking' – has perhaps rubbed of on the popular growth of these compositional tools. Or perhaps generative software citing has become the new techy trainspotting – now that it's no longer impressive to merely flash your hard-drive specs. It's easy to make a generative noise.

(20)

> We have assigned clever pseudonyms to prevent recognition. Why have we kept our own names? Out of habit, purely out of habit. To make ourselves unrecognisable in turn. To render imperceptible, not ourselves, but what makes us act, feel and think. . . . We are no longer ourselves. Each will know his own. We have been aided, inspired, multiplied. (Deleuze and Guattari, 1987, p. 3)

(21)

Musicians give themselves names which are unspecific as to number or gender (though they are in reality almost exclusively male) – Autechre, Matmos, Squarepusher, Oval, Pole . . . and the make-up of groups is thus disguised, or flexible. And then individual musicians move from one collaboration to another, in a flexible performing community that has, in this respect, a great deal in common with jazz performers, and where a musician's 'sound' is also talked about in similar terms. Of course, now the performers in an 'ensemble' do not need, necessarily, to meet, if the result is a recorded CD project.

> Subject: cascone / chartier / dupree
> Just wanted to recommend this . . . I was really surprised at how well the three performers work together on the 20 min track. Comes off being highly musical, and enjoyable to listen to, . . . with the inclusion of kim cascone adding some more noisy elements to the overall project, personally I find that there is a noisy side to microsound out there, and I would love to see 12k maybe do something more in that direction, . . . I just think it would be very interesting to see how taylor or richard might handle such a project as label leaders.
> (A fan writing on the microsound email list)

(22)

> Viral tropes . . . have proven as pervasive and contagious within culture as actual viruses among their host populations, no doubt because they can choose among any number of hospitable cultures . . . the

telematic contagion of computer viruses, reproductive technologies, and genetic algorithms; genetic engineering and the genome project; the memetics of a mutating Darwinism .... (Kahn, 1999, p. 294)

Language is a virus from outer space. (Laurie Anderson, under the influence of William Burroughs)

---

(23)

These words were just a suggestion.

Appendices, Bibliography and Recordings

Texts for *Sous le regard d'un soleil noir,* by Francis Dhomont
(Reprinted from CD liner notes, by kind permission of empreintes DIGITALES)

Movement 1 (beginning) CD[28]

Pareil à un voyageur perdu (Like a lost traveller)

Figure-toi…Figure-toi des hommes qui vivent dans une sorte de demeure souterraine en forme de caverne possédant une entrée qui s'ouvre largement du côte du jour. A l'intérieur de cette demeure, ils sont, depuis leur enfance, enchaînés par les jambes et par le cou, en sorte qu'ils restent à la même place, ne voient que ce qui est en avant d'eux, incapables de tourner la tête en raison de la chaîne qui la retient.

[Picture … Picture men living in a cairn-like underground dwelling, with an entrance opening widely unto the daylight. Inside this dwelling, they are chained at the legs and neck, since childhood, in such a way they remain in the same place and see only what is in front of them, incapable as they are of turning their heads, restrained by the chains.]

Movement 6 (complete) CD[29]

Citadelle intérieure

Inner citadel

Voix de femme (imperceptible):
'intérieur […] rien […] à l'extérieur […] vide'[1]

Woman's voice *(unperceptible)*
'inside […] nothing […] outside […] empty'

Voix d'homme 2 et de femmes:
'peur'[2]

Man's voice 2 and women's voices:
'frightened'

Voix d'homme 2:
'J'ai organisé mon terrier et il m'a l'air […] mais […] bien réussi. De dehors […] qui ne mène […] on voit un grand […] nulle part […] trou. La véritable entrée […] à quelque mille pas […] cachée […] de mon habitation […] se trouve […] de là; elle est aussi bien défendue […] puisse l'être […] qu'une chose […] en ce monde.'[3]

Man's voice 2:
'I have organized my burrow and it seems to me […] well done. From outside […] that leads […] one sees a large […] nowhere […] hole. The actual entrance […] about one thousand steps […] hidden […] from my dwelling […] is found […] there, it is as protected as […] something […] can […] in this world.'

Voix d'homme 1 et/ou de femme:
'On est à l'intérieur
puis à l'extérieur ce qu'on a été à l'intérieur
On se sent vide […]
    manger et être mangé
pour que l'extérieur devienne l'intérieur
et pour être
    à l'intérieur de l'extérieur
Mais cela ne suffit pas […]
et à l'intérieur de soi il n'y a toujours rien.'[4]

Man's voice 1 and/or woman's voice:
'One is inside
then outside what one has been inside
One feels empty […]
    to eat and to be eaten
to have the outside inside and to be
    inside the outside
But this is not enough […]
and inside oneself there is still nothing.'

1 R. D. Laing, *Noeuds.*
2 R. D. Laing, *Le moi divisé.*

3 F. Kafka, Le terrier (The burrow).
4 R. D. Laing, *Noeuds.*

Track listing and acknowledgements for the accompanying CD

All are short excerpts from longer works unless stated otherwise.

Track number	Artist
1. *Concret PH*	Iannis Xenakis
2. *Petit Jardin*	Magali Babin
3. *Presque Rien avec Filles*	Luc Ferrari
4. *Birds*	Luigi Ceccarelli
5. *Bhakti (movement IX)*	Jonathan Harvey
6. *China*	Phill Niblock
7. Field-recording	made by KN
8. Field-recording	made by KN
9. Field-recording	made by KN
10. Excerpt from 'The Changing Soundscape'	from *The Vancouver Soundscape CD*
11. 'Canalside atmosphere'	sound recording by Peter Cusack
12. *Pendlerdrøm*	Barry Truax
13. *Night Traffic*	Paul Lansky
14. *untitled #90*	Francisco Lopez
15. Interview with Hildegard Westerkamp	made by KN
16. Interview with Hildegard Westerkamp	made by KN
17. *Talking Rain*	Hildegard Westerkamp
18. Interview with Hildegard Westerkamp	made by KN
19. Interview with Hildegard Westerkamp	made by KN
20. *Talking Rain*	Hildegard Westerkamp
21. Field-recording	made by KN
22. *Talking Rain*	Hildegard Westerkamp
23. *Frantic Mid-Atlantic*	Evelyn Ficarra
24. *Hidden Lives*	Cathy Lane
25. *Geekspeak*	Pamela Z
26. *Pareil à un voyageur perdu* (opening of movement 1, *Sous le regard d'un soleil noir*)	Francis Dhomont
27. *Citadelle intérieure* (movement 6 complete, *Sous le regard d'un soleil noir*)	Francis Dhomont
28. 'Make Yourself Comfortable'	from Sarah Vaughan's *Golden Hits*
29. 'Agni hotra loops'	from Merzbow's *Loop Panic Limited*
30. 'bine'	from *Confield* by Autechre
31. 'White'	*Gibbons Cry* (John Oswald)

Continued

Track number	**Artist**
32. 'Resistance' (movement 2 of *Resistance to Change)*	Terre Thaemlitz
33. 'Transformative nostalgia' (excerpt: movement 4 of *Resistance to Change)*	Terre Thaemlitz
34. *Callaérobique*	Martin Tétreault

All excerpts are reproduced by kind permission of the composers or labels concerned, except track 1 which is by kind permission of Bernard Bruges-Renard of GRM. CDs are listed in full in the Bibliography under 'Recordings'.

Bibliography

Books and articles

Anderson, Laurie (1994), *Stories from the Nerve Bible*, New York: HarperCollins.

Bachelard, Gaston (1988), *Air and Dreams*, tr. Edith Farrell and C. Frederick Farrell, Dallas: The Dallas Institute Translations. Originally published 1943 as *L'Air et les songes, essai sur l'imagination du mouvement,* Paris: Librairie José Corti.

Bachelard, Gaston (1994), *The Poetics of Space*, tr. Maria Jolas, Boston: Beacon Press. Originally published 1958 as *La poétique de l'espace*, Paris: Presses Universitaires de France.

Barthes, Roland (1977), *Image-Music-Text*, New York: Noonday Press.

Barthes, Roland (1993), *Camera Lucida*, London: Vintage Books. First published 1980.

Benjamin, Walter (1968), 'The Work of Art in the Age of Mechanical Reproduction' in Harry Zohn, (tr.) (1969), *Illuminations*, New York: Shocken.

Bergson, Henri (1910), *Time and Free Will: An Essay on the Immediate Data of Consciousness*, tr. F.L. Pogson, London: George Allen and Unwin. Also available online through the Mead Project: http://spartan.ac.brocku.ca/%7Elward/Bergson/Bergson_1910/Bergson_1910_toc.html

Bois, Mario (1967), *Iannis Xenakis. The Man and his Music*, London: Boosey & Hawkes Music Publishers Ltd.

Borges, Jorge Luis (1998), *Collected Fictions*, trans. Andrew Hurley, New York: Viking Penguin.

Cage, John (1966), *Silence*, Cambridge, MA: MIT Press.

Cavell, Stanley (1979), *The World Viewed*, Cambridge, MA: Harvard University Press.

Chadabe, Joel (1997), *Electric Sound: The Past and Promise of Electronic Music*, Englewood Cliffs, NJ: Prentice Hall.

Chanan, Michael (1995), *Repeated Takes. A Short History of Recording and its Effects on Music*. London/ New York: Verso.

Chion, Michel (1994), *Audio-vision. Sound on Screen*, New York: Columbia University Press.

Clark, Kenneth (1998), *Leonardo da Vinci*, London: Penguin. First published in 1939.

Clarke, E. and Davidson, J. (1998), 'The Body in Performance' in Wyndham Thomas (ed.), *Composition-Performance-Reception*, Aldershot, UK: Ashgate.

Cook, Perry R. (ed.) (1999), *Music, Cognition, and Computerized Sound: An Introduction to Psychoacoustics*, Boston, MA: MIT Press.

Cutler, Chris (1994), 'Plunderphonics', revised version of 'Plunderphonia', *Musicworks*, 60 Toronto; republished in Simon Emmerson (ed.) (2000), *Music, Electronic Media and Culture*, Aldershot: Ashgate.

Cros, Charles (1960), *Oeuvres Complètes*, ed. Jean-Jacques Pauvert, Paris: Pauvert.

Cros, Charles (1992), *Inédits et Documents*, collected and presented by Pierre E. Richard, Paris: Éditions Jacques Brémond.

Crystal, David (1987), *The Cambridge Encyclopedia of Language*, Cambridge: Cambridge University Press.

Deleuze, Gilles and Guattari, Félix (1987), *A Thousand Plateaus – Capitalism and Schizophrenia*, London: Athlone Press.

Derrida, Jacques (1973), 'Différance' in Kearney and Rainwater (eds) (1996), *The Continental Philosopher Reader*, London: Routledge.

Derrida, Jacques (1991), 'Tympan' in *A Derrida Reader: Between the Blinds*, ed., intro. and notes Peggy Kamuf, Hemel Hempstead: Harvester Wheatsheaf.

Draaisma, Douwe (2000), *Metaphors of Memory: A History of Ideas About the Mind*, Cambridge: Cambridge University Press.

Dyson, Frances (1974), 'The Genealogy of the Radio Voice' in Diana Augaitis and Dan Lander (eds), *Radio Rethink: Art, Sound and Transmission*, The Banff Centre for the Arts: Walter Phillips Gallery, pp. 167–86.

Eco, Umberto (1990), *Travels in Hyper Reality*, New York: Harvest.

Edgerton, S.Y. jr (1975), *The Renaissance Rediscovery of Linear Perspective*, New York: Basic Books.

Emmerson, Simon (ed.) (2000), *Music, Electronic Media and Culture*, Aldershot: Ashgate.

Forestier, Louis (1969), *Charles Cros – l'homme et l'oeuvre,* Paris: Minard.

Foucault, Michel (1988), *Aesthetics, Method and Epistemology* in James D. Faubion (ed.), *Essential Works by Foucault 1954–1984, Volume Two*, London: Allen Lane, The Penguin Press.

Freud, Sigmund (1990), 'The Uncanny' in *Art and Literature*, vol.14, The Penguin Freud Library, London: Penguin.

Gelatt, Roland (1955), *The Fabulous Phonograph: From Tin Foil to High Fidelity.* Philadelphia: J. B. Lippincott.

Godfrey, Donald G. and Leigh, Frederic A. (1998), *Historical Dictionary of American Radio*, Westport, CT: Greenwood Press.

Gombrich, E. H. (1960), *Art and Illusion. A Study in the Psychology of Pictorial Representation*, Princeton, NJ: Princeton University Press.

Gordon, John W. (1999), 'Psychoaccoustics' in Curtis Roads (ed.), *The Computer Music Tutorial*, Boston: MIT Press.

Gould, Glenn (1987), *The Glenn Gould Reader*, ed. Tim Page, London: Faber and Faber.

Harvey, Jonathan (1999), *In Quest of Spirit. Thoughts on Music*, Berkeley and Los Angeles: University of California Press.

Heinritzi, Michel (2001) 'Extreme Contemporary – Japanese Music as Radical Exoticism' in Franck Stofer (coordination), *Japanese Independent Music*, France: Sonore (www.sonore.com).

Hull, John M. (1990), *Touching the Rock: An Experience of Blindness*, New York: Pantheon.

Kahn, Douglas (1999), *Noise, Water, Meat: A History of Sound in the Arts*, Cambridge, MA: MIT Press.

Koenigsberg, Allen (1969), *Edison Cylinder Records, 1889–1912.* New York: Stellar Productions.

Kress, Gunther (1997), *Before Writing. Rethinking the Paths to Literacy,* London: Routledge.

Kubovy, Michael (1986), *The Psychology of Perspective and Renaissance Art*, New York: Cambridge University Press.

Laing, R.D. (1970), *Knots*, Harmondsworth: Penguin Books.

Le Corbusier (1958), *Le Poème Electronique*, Paris: Les Editions de Minuit.

Lee, David (1992), 'Improvisation' in *MusicWorks*, 54, Toronto.

Lodge, David (2002), 'Consciousness and the Novel', in *Consciousness and the Novel. Connected Essays*, London: Seckery & Warburg.

McLuhan, Marshall (1964), *Understanding Media: The Extensions of Man*, New York: McGraw-Hill.

Marco, Guy A. (ed.) (1993), *Encyclopedia of Recorded Sound in the United States*, New York: Garland Publishing, Inc.

Marsden, Alan (2000), 'Music, Intelligence and Artificiality' in Eduardo Reck Miranda (ed.), *Readings in Music and Artificial Intelligence*, Amsterdam: Harwood Academic Publishers.

Masotti, Franco (2000), 'Die Resurrectionis, conversazione con Luigi Ceccarelli', *Catalogo Generale de Ravenna Festival 2000.*

Matossian, Nouritza (1990). *Xenakis*, London: Kahn and Averill.

Millard, Andre (1995) *America on Record: A History of Recorded Sound*, Cambridge: Cambridge University Press.

Pierce, John (1999), 'Hearing in Time and Space' in Perry R. Cook (ed.), *Music, Cognition, and Computerized Sound: An Introduction to Psychoacoustics*, Boston, MA: MIT Press, pp. 89–103.

Read, Oliver and Welch, Walter L. (1959), *From Tin Foil to Stereo: Evolution of the Phonograph*, Indianapolis: Howard W. Sams & Co., Inc.

Roads, Curtis, (1996), *The Computer Music Tutorial*, Cambridge, MA: MIT Press.

Roads, Curtis, (2001), *Microsound*, Cambridge, MA: MIT Press.

Russell, Bertrand (1946), *History of Western Philosophy*, London: Routledge.

Russolo, Luigi (1986), *The Art of Noises*, tr. Barclay Brown, New York: Pendragon Press. First published 1913 as *L'Arte dei Rumori*.

Schaeffer, Pierre (1952), *A la Recherche d'une Musique Concrète*, Paris: Editions du Seuil.

Schaeffer, Pierre (1966), *Traité des Objets Musicaux*, Paris: Editions du Seuil.

Schaeffer, Pierre (1967), *La Musique Concrète*, Paris: Presses Universitaires de France.

Schafer, R. Murray (1994), *The Soundscape: Our Sonic Environment and the Tuning of the World*, Rochester, VT: Destiny Books. Originally published 1977 as *The Tuning of the World*, New York: Knopf.

Secor, Winfield (1920). 'The Versatile Audion' in *Electrical Experimenter*, February, pp. 1000–1001, 1080–83. Reproduced online at http://earlyradiohistory.us/1920au.htm

Smalley, Denis (1986), 'Spectro-morphology and Structuring Processes' in Simon Emmerson (ed.), *The Language of Electroacoustic Music*, London: Macmillan.

Sontag, Susan (1982), *A Susan Sontag Reader*, London: Penguin.

Steiner, George (1975), *After Babel. Aspects of Language and Translation*, New York and London: Oxford University Press.

Storr, Anthony (1993), *Music and the Mind*, New York: Ballantine.

Taylor, Timothy D. (2001), *Strange Sounds: Music Technology and Culture*, London: Routledge.

Varga, Bálint A. (1996), *Conversations with Iannis Xenakis*, London: Faber.

Watts, Alan W. (1990), *The Way of Zen*, Harmondsworth: Penguin. First published 1962.

Westerkamp, Hildegard (2002), 'Linking Soundscape Composition and Acoustic Technology', *Organised Sound: An International Journal of Music and Technology*, 7(1).

Woolf, Virginia (1977), *Orlando*, London: Granada, Panther Books. First published 1928.

Xenakis, Iannis (1985), *Arts/Sciences: Alloys*, tr. Sharon Kanach, New York: Pendragon Press.

Zizek, Slavoj (1992), *Looking Awry. An Introduction to Jacques Lacan through Popular Culture*, Cambridge, MA: MIT Press.

Additional web references

Note: All other web references are cited within the text. The author maintains an up-to-date list of all web pages referred to at soundingart.novamara.com

Cochrane, Richard, review of *Callas: La Diva et Le Vinyle* (Tétreault/M. LePage), *Earscape 3* at http://www.actuellecd.com/press.f/1045000.html

Oswald, John (1985) 'Plunderphonics, or Audio Piracy as a Compositional Prerogative' presented by John Oswald to the Wired Society Electro-Acoustic Conference in Toronto in 1985. Available at www.plunderphonics.com/xhtml/xplunder.html Also published in *MusicWorks*, 34, Toronto.

Paglia, Camille (1998), 'Enough with the Male "gaze"', Salon online journal at http://archive.salon.com/it/col/pagl/1998/10/07pagl.html (Find through http://archive.salon.com/archives/date.html)

Polansky, Larry (1998), 'Singing Together, Hacking Together, Plundering Together: Sonic Intellectual Property in Cybertimes', written for presentation at the Dartmouth College Humanities Institute, 'The Tangled Web: Ethical Dilemmas of the Internet', Summer 1998 at http://www.the-open-space.org/osonline/polansky/singing.html

Online interviews

John Oswald: 'John Oswald', Interview by Brian Duguid, September 1994 at http://media.hyperreal.org/zines/est/intervs/oswald.html

Masami Akita (Merzbow): 'The Beauty of Noise', an interview with Masami Akita of Merzbow by Chad Hensley at http://www.esoterra.org/merzbow.htm.

Sean Booth (of Autechre): 'The Ultimate Folk Music – A Little Interview with Sean from Autechre 1st of May 2001 in Berlin at the WMF' by Sascha Kösch (bleed@de-bug.de) at http://www.autechre.nu/reading.shtml (click on relevant interview).

Terre Thaemlitz: 'The Go Between – E-mail Interview with Terre Thaemlitz by Christopher Strunz' at http://www.comatonse.com/reviews/spex0101.html

Recordings

Anderson, Laurie (1995), 'The Salesman', on *The Ugly One with the Jewels and Other Stories*, Warner Brothers 9362-45847-2.

Autechre (2001), 'bine', on *Confield*, Warp CD 128.

Babin, Magali (2002), 'Petit jardin', on *The Freest of Radicals*, No Type IMNT 0201/02

Bach, J.S., *Goldberg Variations*. See under Gould.

Barron, Louis and Bebbe, *Forbidden Planet Original MGM Soundtrack*, GNP Crescendo D001.

Ceccarelli, Luigi (1996), *Birds* for bass clarinet and clarinet and bird sounds, David Keberle bass clarinet, Cultures Electroniques n.9 - Bourges 96, LDC 278060/61 GMEB/UNESCO/CIME.

Cusack, Peter (2000), 'Canalside atmosphere', track 6 on *The Horse was Alive, the Cow was Dead*, sound recordings by Peter Cusack, LMC, RES WOSM1.

Dhomont, Francis (1979–81), *Cycle des profondeurs, 1 – Sous le regard d'un soleil noir*, empreintes DIGITALes IMED 9633.

Erickson, Lotta (1997), 'Please, Mr. Coldstream', on *Resonance Radio Issue*, London Musicians' Collective Ltd.

Ferrari, Luc (1989), 'Presque Rien avec Filles', on *Acousmatrix*, INA/GRM BV HAAST CD 9009.

Ficarra, Evelyn (1995), 'Frantic Mid-Atlantic', on *Frantic Mid-Atlantic*, Sargasso SCD 28026.

Gould, Glenn (1955), *Goldberg Variations*, BWV 988, Aria with 30 Variations, J.S. Bach, CBS.

Gould, Glenn (1992), *Solitude Trilogy*, PSCD 2003-3 CBC.

Harvey, Jonathan (1982, recorded 1984), *Bhakti*, NMC D001.

Katzer, George (1989). 'Aide Mémoire' on ReR CMCD (ReR Records).

Lane, Cathy (1999), *Hidden Lives* unreleased recording (c.lane@lcp.linst.ac.uk).

Lansky, Paul (1992), 'Night Traffic', on *Homebrew*, Bridge 9035.

Lopez, Francisco (1991), *untitled #90*, Ohm Records.

Merzbow (Masimi Akita) 'Loop Panic Limited' on *Batzoutai with Material Gadgets. De-composed Works 1985–6*. RRRecords, USA.

Minogue, Kylie (2001), 'Can't Get You Out of My Head', track 3 on *Fever*, EMI/Capitol.

Niblock, Phill, 'China' on *China and Sunsets*, (video) Oodiscs, CT, USA.

Oswald, John (1989), 'White', on *Plunderphonic*. At the time of writing a reissue is available on the Seeland label (www.negativland.com). The entire work can be freely downloaded at www.plunderphonics.com (click on 'u' for 'unavailable and follow instructions).

Otomo, Yoshihide (1993) *The Night Before the Death of the Sampling Virus*, Extreme XCD 024.

Otomo, Yoshihide (1998) 'Solo for turntable and guitar amp', *Turntable Solos*, Valve/Amoebic AMO-VA-O1.

Tétreault, Martin and LePage, Robert M. (1997), 'Callaérobique', on *Callas: La Diva et Le Vinyle*, Ambiances Magnétiques, DAME – AM 059 CD.

Thaemlitz, Terre (1998), 'Resistance to change' on *Means to an End*, Mille Plateaux MP CD 44.

Truax, Barry, Westerkamp, Hildegard *et al.* (1996), 'The Changing Soundscape' on *The Vancouver Soundscape 1973 / Soundscape Vancouver 1996*, Cambridge Street Records CSR-2CD.

Truax, Barry (1996), 'Pendlerdrøm' on *Islands*, Cambridge Street Records CSRCD 0101.

Vaughan, Sarah (1954, rereleased on CD 1990), 'Make Yourself Comfortable', on *Sarah Vaughan's Golden Hits*, Mercury 824-891-2.

Westerkamp, Hildegard (1998), 'Talking Rain' on *Harangue I*, Earsay ES98001 (in case of difficulty obtaining the CD visit http://www.sfu.ca/~westerka)

Xenakis, Iannis (1958) 'Concret PH', on *Xenakis. Electronic Music*, EMF/INAGRM 1997 EMF CD 003.

Z, Pamela (1995), 'Geekspeak', on *Sonic Circuits IV*, American Composers Forum: Innova 113.

Index